PHOBIA

A Comprehensive Summary of Modern Treatments

Edited by
Robert L. DuPont, M.D.

BRUNNER/MAZEL, *Publishers* • New York

Library of Congress Cataloging in Publication Data
Main entry under title:

Phobia, a comprehensive summary of modern treatments.

Includes bibliographical references and index.
1. Phobias—Treatment. 2. Phobias. I. DuPont, Robert L., 1936- . [DNLM: 1. Phobic disorders —Therapy. WM 178 P573]
RC535.P47 616.85'22506 82-9
ISBN 0-87630-274-6 AACR2

Published by
BRUNNER/MAZEL, INC.
19 Union Square West
New York, N.Y. 10003

MANUFACTURED IN THE UNITED STATES OF AMERICA

Contents

Contributors ix
Introduction xiii

1. Faith and Fear 3
by Robert G. Allen

I. THE SUPPORTED EXPOSURE TREATMENT 9
2. A Method to Study and Conceptualize Changes in Phobic Behavior 11
by Manuel D. Zane
3. The Initial Contact with the Phobic Patient 27
by Doreen Powell
4. The Role of the Family Member in the Supported Exposure Approach to the Treatment of Phobias 35
by Jerilyn Ross
5. An Integrative Approach to Agoraphobia: Centrum—A Model Program 44
by Marvin R. Cohen

II. ALTERNATIVE TREATMENT APPROACHES 55

6. Combined Psychological and Pharmacological Approach to the Treatment of Phobias 57
by Charlotte Marker Zitrin

7. Phobics of Branford 77
by Jane Miller

III. THEORETICAL ISSUES 91

8. Phobic Thinking: The Cognitive Influences on the Behavior and Effective Treatment of the Agoraphobic ... 93
by Arthur B. Hardy

9. Going Solo: From External Support to Self-support 99
by Martin N. Seif

10. The Modern Syndrome of Phobophobia and Its Management 107
by Harley C. Shands and Natalie Schor

11. Psychobiology of Exposure In Vivo 117
by George Curtis, Randolph Nesse, Oliver Cameron, Bruce Thyer, and Michael Liepman

12. The Correlation Between Quantity of Fears and the Ability to Discriminate Among Similar Items 121
by Nancy Jane Flaxman

13. Depression and Agoraphobia—Chicken or the Egg? 126
by David L. Charney

14. Phobias, Death, and Depression 133
by Bella H. Selan

15. Changing Marriage Patterns of Agoraphobics as a Result of Treatment 140
by Gerald T. O'Brien, David H. Barlow, and Cynthia G. Last

16. Women's Issues in the Assessment and Treatment of Phobias 153
by Robert Ackerman

17. A Behavioral/Perceptual Model: A Teaching Strategy for Phobic Symptom Reduction 161
by Maralyn L. Teare

IV. SPECIFIC PHOBIC GROUPS 171

18. Up, Up, and Away 173
By T.W. Cummings

19. A New Technique for Treating Obsessions: Paradoxical Practice with Cassette Recorder 178
By Jonathan O. Crook and David L. Charney
20. Day Treatment: Rethinking School Phobia 182
By Blanche Goodwin and Eleanor Craig
21. The Psychology of Phobic Fear of Nuclear Energy 193
By Robert L. DuPont

V. DESCRIPTIVE STUDIES 201
22. Major Results of a Large-scale Pretreatment Survey of Agoraphobics 203
By Ronald M. Doctor
23. Profile of a Phobia Treatment Program: Two-year Follow-up 215
By Robert L. DuPont
24. Case Study of an Agoraphobic 231
By Robert L. DuPont

Index 247

Contributors

ROBERT ACKERMAN, M.S.W.
Consultant, St. Luke's Roosevelt Hospital Phobia Clinic, New York City; private practice, Brooklyn,

ROBERT G. ALLEN
Formerly phobic radio announcer

DAVID H. BARLOW, Ph.D.
Department of Psychology, State University of New York at Albany

OLIVER CAMERON, M.D.
Assistant Professor of Psychiatry, University of Michigan

DAVID L. CHARNEY, M.D.
Medical Director, Phobia Treatment Center, Alexandria, Virginia

MARVIN R. COHEN, M.A.
Coordinator, Centrum Phobia Clinic, Oak Park, Illinois

ELEANOR CRAIG, M.S., Counseling
Co-director, Day Treatment Program, Mid-Fairfield Child Guidance Center, Norwalk, CT

JONATHAN O. CROOK, M.Ed.
Chief Phobia Therapist, Phobia Treatment Center, Alexandria, Virginia

CAPTAIN T.W. CUMMINGS
Director, Freedom from Fear of Flying, Inc., Coral Gables, Florida

GEORGE CURTIS, M.D.
Professor of Psychiatry, University of Michigan

RONALD M. DOCTOR, Ph.D.
Professor of Psychology, California State University, Northridge, California

ROBERT L DUPONT, M.D.
Director, Phobia Program of Washington, Rockville, Maryland; Clinical Professor of Psychiatry, Georgetown University Medical School; President, Phobia Society of America

NANCY JANE FLAXMAN
Administrator, TERRAP, Menlo Park, California

BLANCHE GOODWIN, M.S.W., A.C.S.W.
Co-director, Day Treatment Program, Mid-Fairfield Child Guidance Center, Norwalk, Connecticut

ARTHUR B. HARDY, M.D.
Founder, TERRAP; private practice, Menlo Park, California

CYNTHIA G. LAST, B.A.
Department of Psychology, State University of New York at Albany, New York

MICHAEL LIEPMAN, M.D.
Instructor of Psychiatry and Family Practice, University of Michigan

RANDOLPH NESSE, M.D.
Assistant Professor of Psychiatry, University of Michigan

JANE MILLER, M.A., M.S.
Branford Counseling Center, Branford, Connecticut

GERALD T. O'BRIEN, Ph.D.
Department of Psychology, State University of New York at Albany, New York

DOREEN POWELL
Director of Programs, Phobia Clinic, White Plains Hospital Medical Center, White Plains, New York

JERILYN ROSS, M.A.
Director, Clinical Services, Phobia Program of Washington, Rockville, Maryland

NATALIE SCHOR
Director, St. Luke's Roosevelt Hospital Phobia Clinic, New York City; Director, Phobia Resource Center, New York City

MARTIN N. SEIF, Ph.D.
Director, Phobia Resource Center, New York City; Director, St. Luke's Roosevelt Hospital Phobia Clinic, New York City

BELLA H. SELAN, M.S.
Coordinator, Psychiatry Clinic, Mount Sinai Medical Center, Milwaukee, Wisconsin; Instructor, University of Wisconsin Medical School, Department of Psychiatry

HARLEY C. SHANDS, M.D.*
Director, St. Luke's Roosevelt Hospital Phobia Clinic, New York City; Clinical Professor of Psychiatry, Columbia College of Physicians and Surgeons, New York City

MARALYN L. TEARE, M.S.
Private practice, Beverly Hills, California

BRUCE THYER, M.S.W.
Department of Psychology, University of Michigan

MANUEL D. ZANE, M.D.
Director, Phobia Clinic, and Attending Psychiatrist, White Plains Hospital Medical Center, White Plains, New York

CHARLOTTE MARKER ZITRIN, M.D.
Director, Phobia Clinic, Long Island Jewish-Hillside Medical Center, Glen Oaks, New York

*Dr. Shands died during the production of this book.

Dedicated to Harley Shands, M. D.

In the phobia field, several pioneers have led the way to dramatically more effective, new treatments in the last two decades. One of these pioneers, probably the most intellectual and modest, was Harley Shands, M.D. In his quiet, often shy, fashion he built solid intellectual bridges between psychoanalysis and the new phobia treatment field. The richness of his thought and writings set a high standard for all followers. After the Second Annual Phobia Conference and after the founding of the Phobia Society of America (of which he was a charter member of the Board of Directors), on Friday, December 4, 1981, our colleague and teacher, Harley Shands, died. We all—therapists and phobic people—will sorely miss him. His work and his ideals live on. To honor his memory, and to express in a small way our indebtedness, we dedicate this book to our gentle friend, Harley Shands.

Introduction

Phobias were one of the first human disorders to be described. This is hardly surprising since they are so distinctive and so dramatic. Imagine the founders of Greek medicine, who were among the first to describe the disorder, seeing people in otherwise perfect health, unable to leave their homes to travel to the marketplace. It was this observation that led to the term "agoraphobia," literally, fear of the marketplace. Equally dramatic and, in some cases, equally debilitating are the specific phobias, such as fear of closed-in places (claustrophobia) and phobias of animals, such as snakes, insects, or mice.

Phobias were known in ancient cultures and they are evident today in all parts of the world. As a medical student in 1960, I traveled to Africa and was struck by the occurrence of leopard phobia in West Africa, even though leopards were, even then, quite unusual in that part of Africa, particularly in the settled areas. Many people had developed a distinct leopard phobia that kept them severely restricted. Although nobody in West Africa particularly wanted to meet a leopard on a lonely bush trail, most people were able to get around without any restriction because of fear of leopards. When someone was restricted to the village or even to certain parts of the village because of the fear of leopards, it was noticeable.

In the United States, of course, we rarely see leopard phobia and phobias of animals are not quite so obvious, although they definitely exist (usually as fears of snakes, spiders, dogs, cats, or birds). In the modern industrial world, and certainly in the United States, phobic stimuli are usually associated with new technologies which confront us with experiences for which we were not biologically prepared. Fears of elevators, escalators, air travel, super highways, bridges, and that most striking modern phobic situation, the shopping center, produce far more disabilities than do phobias of snakes or insects.

Without intending any disrespect for people suffering from phobias, it should also be noted that the human species is not the only one subject to phobic disorders. Phobias are well recognized in animal species as well. Fears of traveling by car and fears of thunderstorms are frequent among domestic animals. A year or so ago, the United Press International carried a story that was widely reported of an elephant in London who had developed a phobia of leaving her indoor cage to walk into a recreation yard immediately adjacent. No amount of coaxing or putting the food out in the outer areas or even tranquilizing drugs would convince this elephant to leave her familiar surroundings for the obviously "terrifying" exercise yard that had been so generously constructed for her.

While phobias are widespread among all cultures and have been widely recognized in all periods of history, there is something dramatically new happening that affects the lives of phobic people. Literally, for generations in medicine and later in psychiatry (the specialty area to which phobias have been assigned in modern medicine), the hallmark of the professional's attitude towards the phobic person was not only curiosity, but also therapeutic pessimism. It was taken as a matter of common knowledge among professionals that phobias were resistant to change and to therapeutic efforts. Looking back into the history of the treatment of phobias, we can see the dramatic developments at the beginning of the 20th century when Sigmund Freud hypothesized the meaning of the phobic symptom. The Freudian view of the phobic symptom, in an oversimplified presentation, was that the phobic person had displaced his fear from a stimulus which he felt uncomfortable fearing onto a more emotionally acceptable stimulus. The classic case was Freud's analysis of the phobia of little Hans (1), a preschool child who was unable to venture out of the house because of his fear of the horses in the streets of Vienna. Freud suggested that little Hans was not really afraid of horses but that his original fear was of his father. Although little Hans said he was afraid that the horses would bite him, what he really feared was that his father would punish him and in this case, castrate him, because of little Hans' amorous attentions towards his mother and his rivalrous feelings towards his father, which Freud called the Oedipal complex. Once this understanding was revealed to Hans' father and he was able to help Hans over this anxious emotional experience, Hans lost his fear of horses and was able to go into the street.

While the psychoanalytic view remains dominant in much of modern psychiatry's thinking about phobias, the therapeutic results of analytic treatment of phobias have often been disappointing to both therapists and phobic people. In contrast to little Hans, most phobic people have not been relieved of their symptoms when they were able to understand the displacement of their fears. In fact, psychotherapy, as well as psychoanalysis, have often produced good results with phobic people in every way except that the phobic symptom has tended to persist despite the insight and, in many cases, character change that successful intervention has encouraged.

The next great development in the treatment of phobias came in the 1950s with the development of modern behavioral psychology. The idea popularized by Joseph Wolpe was to help the phobic person *imagine* exposure to the phobic situation and through this process of imaginary exposure become gradually desensitized to the phobic stimulus (2). While this approach seemed to work well with relatively trivial phobias such as are often uncovered in college students subject to initial psychological studies, it quickly became obvious to most clinicians that people with more disabling phobias, an essentially clinical population as opposed to a research population, did not fare as well using this technique.

Later, during the 1970s, two new developments literally revolutionized the treatment of phobias and created, for the first time, a sense of therapeutic optimism. The first and, in my view, more limited development was the recognition that the use of antidepressant medications such as imipramine was associated with reductions in phobic symptoms even if the patient was not depressed (3). This concept has received general acceptance within the medical community, particularly among the more pharmacologically oriented medical and psychiatric practitioners. It is interesting to note, however, that even among the most zealous proponents of this approach, there is common agreement that most phobic people do not require antidepressants to overcome their phobias. There is also widespread agreement that pharmacological treatment in the absence of exposure treatment is unlikely to produce a reduction of phobic symptoms. It also should be noted that although in the 1950s and '60s there was some enthusiasm for the use of antianxiety drugs, such as diazepam (Valium), in the treatment of phobic anxiety, this enthusiasm quietly waned and today there is little support for the use of these drugs in the treatment of phobic individuals, even though millions of phobics find themselves dependent on antianxiety drugs as a result of the widespread use of these medications. It is unusual to find a phobic person who feels that these antianxiety drugs have produced more than minor symptomatic improvement.

The most important and widely applicable treatment development has been what I call the *supported exposure* treatment. Others have called this the "in vivo" or "in life" desensitization technique. These developments, on a more psychological basis, have sprung up relatively independently in a number of settings, both in the United States and elsewhere around the world. The hallmark of the new programs has been an education of the phobic person about the nature of the phobic disorder coupled with specific directions and, usually, direct support as the phobic person repeatedly enters phobic situations.

These treatments involve a variety of approaches, ranging from reading books such as the outstanding books by Dr. Claire Weekes (4) and Isaac Marks (5) to participation in self-help correspondence networks or self-help group programs based on essentially an Alcoholics Anonymous-type model to more structured treatment programs (6), such as those developed by Manuel Zane at the White Plains Hospital in New York and Arthur Hardy at the TERRAP Program in Menlo Park, California. These programs began in the late 1960s and early 1970s and remained relatively limited in their impact until 1977, when a remarkable explosion of media interest swept the country with information about the new treatment techniques and the dramatic successes they were achieving. Since 1977 most national media, including both the electronic and print media, have produced many useful and educational reviews of the modern treatment of phobias. Most phobic people have been recruited into the new treatment programs through their exposure to the media. Even many of the therapists, psychiatrists, psychologists, social workers and others now working with phobic people have been recruited into the new phobia field through direct media exposure or, more commonly, through the education that is brought to them from the media by their own phobic patients.

This media catalyst has created a chain reaction, exponential growth of phobia treatment in the United States with programs literally springing up in all the major cities and many smaller communities since 1977. These efforts are often small. A big step in this field was taken in 1979 when the pioneering White Plains Program held the first national conference on phobias. This one-day conference brought together experts from the New York and Washington areas and attracted interested professionals and phobic people primarily from these two cities and those directly around them. This new movement took another step forward in 1980, when the Second Annual Phobia Conference was held in Washington, D.C. This two-day conference brought together experts from all over the United States and Canada and from a wider variety of disciplines and points of view. It established for the first time a true national network of people interested in treating phobic people, using the most modern techniques.

Throughout these developments, it should be emphasized that phobic people themselves have played a central role not only in identifying and labeling the problem from which they suffer, but also in understanding the new treatments, educating the treatment providers to the new treatments and, in many cases, literally providing the services themselves, through self-help programs and through working with more traditional mental health professionals. In addition, the new phobia field has attracted a number of research experts and health professionals interested in related, but distinctly different, treatment approaches to phobias, ranging from hypnosis to dietary alteration.

This book, *Phobia: A Comprehensive Study of Modern Treatments,* contains the major papers presented at the Washington Phobia Conference. It is the first time that the general public and the interested health professionals have had access to the new information about the treatment of phobias written by the pioneers in this field. It is my hope that this book will prove useful to professionals interested in more effective treatment of phobic people, and to phobic people themselves who are interested in learning about the disorder and about treatments for phobias. Included in this is the expectation that these phobic people will find this document useful in promoting education of professionals in their local communities so that not only they can receive help, but other phobic people can receive more effective treatment. The volume is also intended to provide an introduction for researchers interested in phobias to help them understand developments in the rapidly growing phobia field.

One of the more exciting developments at the Washington Phobia Conference was the decision to form a non-profit organization called the Phobia Society of America, to promote public awareness of the problems of phobic people and to promote more effective treatments of all kinds. This organization will provide national leadership in the field in the future.

This book provides the reader with a broad overview of the problems of phobias and also a range of papers reflecting the rich diversity that now characterizes phobia treatment in the United States. No attempt has been made to define which of the new approaches is "the best," since I am convinced that they all have contributions to offer. My hope is that phobic people in the future will find available in their local communities a broad range of treatment alternatives. For the first time in history, phobic people will be able to break out of the shame, the isolation, and the futility that has handicapped them for thousands of years to find effective treatment, overcome their phobias, and in so doing not only find more satisfaction in their own lives, but also play a more effective role in their families, in their communities, and in helping other phobic people overcome their own problems.

Phobic people are special people. They are uniquely able not only to understand their needs and to get treatment and make it work, but also to contribute enormously to meeting the needs of other phobic people. This book can, in some way, repay the debt I owe the hundreds of phobic people I have met and worked with in the Washington Phobia Program and in other programs around the country and contribute, with them, to reaching the unmet needs of the literally millions of other phobic people who are yet to have access to effective treatment.

After knowing and working with hundreds of phobic people in the Washington Program and elsewhere around the country, there are certain common features that have become striking to me. Not everyone can become phobic! Only some are chosen. Phobias can be broadly catagorized into four groups. *Agoraphobia* is by far the most common phobia of people coming into treatment, although agoraphobics constitute a minority of phobic people in the general population. Overall, between 60% and 75% of people coming into phobia treatment programs are agoraphobic, with their primary phobic problem having two characteristics. First, the phobic symptoms are associated with being away from a safe person or a safe place. This I call "adult separation anxiety." It is common and often humiliating. The agoraphobic individual, even though he or she is a fully functioning, mature, intelligent adult, experiences the panicky feelings of a two-year-old separated from his or her mother in the supermarket, suddenly feeling helpless and alone. As many agoraphobic people have explained to me, this is a terrible and a humiliating feeling. The second characteristic of agoraphobics is that they tend to have multiple phobic stimuli, often literally dozens.

The second broad group of phobias are the *specific phobias.* Usually there are only one or two phobic stimuli, often such things as claustrophobia, fears of freeway driving, fears of public speaking, fears of flying. This group constitutes, perhaps, 15-25% of the phobic people coming into a typical phobia treatment program.

The third group of phobics are the *social phobics*. These are individuals whose phobic stimuli relate to being around other people. They essentially fear that they will make a fool of themselves. The prototype for this type of phobia is stage fright, which is so common as to be almost universal. The social phobic individual, however, experiences similar feelings, sometimes in public speaking situations, but at other times when eating with other people or even, in severe cases, just being around other people.

The fourth and final group are the *animal phobics*. These people are phobic usually of one species of animal, although occasionally of several. Typical phobic animals are dogs, cats, birds, insects and snakes. In some instances these phobias are fairly trivial, in which case these people rarely seek treatment, but in other cases they can be as incapacitating as the more frequently disabling agoraphobia. For example, one woman in the Washington Phobia Program was phobic of crickets to such an extent, that, for much of the year, she was not only unable to walk on grass but also often literally unable to walk out of her front door for fear she would run into a cricket.

There are some notable characteristics about these broad groups of phobias. About 60-80% of the people coming into treatment for agoraphobia, specific phobias and animal phobias are women. Among the social phobics, the percentage is closer to 50% female and 50% male. There are several hypotheses for the sex differences, but all of them remain hypotheses. Agoraphobia, specific phobias, and social phobias typically have their onset in young adulthood, primarily between the ages of about 17 and 30 years of age. By contrast, animal phobias almost invariably begin in childhood, and when seen in a treatment program have usually persisted since childhood.

More than two-thirds of the people coming to phobia programs remember their first panic attack—their first phobic experience—vividly and can describe in exquisite detail the onset of their phobia. Prior to the phobia, some phobic people were shy and dependent but many were quite extroverted and independent. Whether shy or extroverted, once the phobia began, it typically assumed an increasingly dominant role in the phobic person's life, leading to characteristic avoidance of important activities or situations. Most of the disability associated with the phobia is secondary to the avoidance. The mental suffering the phobic person endures is compounded by the avoidance and the handicap this presents, as well as by the pain of the phobic experience itself and the humiliation of having a handicap which cannot be seen or understood by most other people. Therefore, it is hard to accept and hard to bear. Occasionally, we have seen phobic people who do not avoid their phobic stimulus but continue to experience it, each time suffering agonizing anxiety symptoms prior to coming into a treatment program. Although this pattern of non-avoidance does occur, it is unusual. Similarly, we have seen the onset of phobias at a younger age than 17 and older ages than 30, although, again, this is an unusual pattern.

There are a number of personality characteristics associated with people who become phobic. By and large, they have since childhood been emotionally hyper-reactive to a variety of stimuli, having often been told by their parents that they laughed, cried, wiggled, and in other ways expressed emotions to an excessive degree. Also, from early ages, they have been perfectionistic and obsessional, generally finding only two ways to do anything, either perfectly or horribly. It was hard for them typically to see a middle ground. Also, from early ages, phobic people have usually had difficulty coping with unpleasant aspects of life, such as the sight of blood or pain, suffering, and the death of an animal. These are universally unpleasant stimuli but for phobic people these are often acutely and severely painful experiences. By and large, phobic people are intelligent, which is not surprising when one realizes that the essence of the phobic experience is "what if" or future thinking. Phobic people are rarely overcome by what is happening to them in the present tense, but they are dominated by fears of what will happen to them in the future. Future thinking is also the sine qua non of intelligence.

Phobic people are acutely sensitive not only to their own feelings, but also to the feelings of others, and they often exaggerate the awareness other people have of the phobic person's own feelings and behaviors. Phobic people characteristically feel that they are making fools of themselves or demonstrating their anxiety in some outrageous fashion, even when other people in their lives either do not notice the unusual behaviors at all or treat them as trivial. Phobic people are overwhelmingly concerned with trying to avoid embarrassment or humiliation. Related to this is their strong desire to please others, particularly important other people in their lives.

In terms of work performance, it is interesting that most phobic people make excellent employees, because of their desire to please, their intelligence, and their perfectionism. Although many have left jobs or even given them up and even more have limited their ambition because of phobic symptoms, they are almost universally perceived by their employers as excellent employees. Many observers have been surprised by the loyalty of family members to a phobic spouse, even when the phobia has severely handicapped the entire family. There are many potential explanations for this, but one obvious one that has struck me is that phobic people often make good parents and good spouses, for the same constellation of reasons they make good friends and good employees.

While people who come into phobia treatment programs have typically been phobic for many years, I have also spoken in nonclinical settings with a number of people who have recovered from phobias, either spontaneously or as a result of a variety of treatments, ranging from psychotherapy and hypnotism to dietary changes. From a clinical setting, what is more impressive is the failure of all other treatment approaches, but of course the only people who would come in for treatment are people who have failed at other forms of treatment!

There are many unfinished agendas in the phobia field. In terms of understanding, we still do not know why one person becomes phobic and another does not, or why a stimulus that produces a phobia for one person produces merely an uncomfortable feeling for another. Although we have much to celebrate in the development of new treatments, particularly the supported exposure treatment and, to a lesser extent, the development of antidepressant medications, our understanding of the treatment of phobias is still in a primitive state. Finally, and perhaps most importantly, we have hardly begun to think about the question of preventing phobias before they begin. This certainly is the most important of all the items in the unfinished agendas facing those concerned with phobic people and their needs.

One final word about the chapters in this book. With the exception of my chapters, "Understanding Fear of Nuclear Power" and "Case Study of an Agoraphobic," and the chapter, "The Role of the Family Member in the Supported Exposure Approach to the Treatment of Phobias" by Jerilyn Ross, each chapter was an original presentation at the Second Annual Phobia Conference. Unfortunately, the large number of excellent presentations at the Conference and the limits of space in this book made it necessary for us to eliminate many contributions.

Robert L. DuPont

REFERENCES

1. Freud, S. Analysis of a phobia in a 5-year-old boy (1909). Reprinted in: *Collected Papers (Volume 3).* New York: Basic Books, 1959.

2. Wolpe, J. *Psychotherapy by Reciprocal Inhibition*. Stanford, CA: Stanford University Press, 1958.
3. Zitrin, C.M., Klein, D.F., and Woerner, M.G. Behavior therapy, supportive psychotherapy, imipramine, and phobias. *Archives of General Psychiatry*, 35(3): 307-16, 1978.
4. Weekes, C. *Simple Effective Treatment of Agoraphobia*. New York: Hawthorn Books, 1976.
5. Marks, I.M. *Living With Fear*. New York: McGraw-Hill, 1978.
6. Esterbrook, J. *Glad Tidings*, Vol. 1, No. 12, May 1980.

PHOBIA

A Comprehensive Summary of Modern Treatments

1

Faith and Fear

Robert G. Allen

When Dr. DuPont first asked me to make this presentation, frankly I didn't know where to begin. Then it slowly dawned on me that a good way to discuss any problem, initially, is to define it. So one day when I was sitting in my office between work projects, I picked up my trusty copy of Webster's New World College Edition Dictionary and found this definition of the word "phobia": "an irrational, excessive and persistent fear of some particular thing or situation." Well, that definition may be okay for the layperson, but it struck me as a bit shallow and off the mark. As a person with a public speaking phobia who has had numerous contacts with other phobic individuals through Dr. DuPont's program, I knew that Webster had come up short.

Actually, it was Franklin D. Roosevelt who supplied the most on-target definition of a phobia when he said, "The only thing we have to fear is fear itself!" If we remove just two words from F.D.R.'s statement we reach the crux of the problem: The only thing we fear *is* fear itself! It's the mirror image of fear that causes all the tension and heartache—the reflection not the reflector. It's the fear of the fear.

Fear implies so many negatives, so many destructive forces at work. But the antithesis of fear is faith. So the question naturally arises: How do we banish fear and supplant it with faith? Well, the remarkable thing about these two characteristics is how they can both spring from the same soil—but never simultaneously! Fear and faith cannot coexist. Try it sometime. You can't have a faith thought and a fear thought all at once. They cannot occupy the same psychic space at the same point in time.

The presence of fear in the garden of your mind causes faith to wither and die. You see, the soil, the growing medium that produces both, is really your life, that is, the situations that develop, the happenstance of living, the events over which we have no control. Fear grows quite readily at the start, like weeds or dandelions; *it crowds out space for anything else.* The longer you let it be, the deeper and stronger grow its roots, the harder to remove. But finally the fear reaches a maximum point of growth and sort of sits there like a satiated octopus, content with the stranglehold it has on your life.

Faith, on the other hand, doesn't grow of its own accord, at least initially. It must be planted, seeded, cultivated, encouraged. The weeds of fear must be pulled out, quite violently at times. It takes a bit of strength. Room must be cleared in your garden for the faith seeds to be planted and grow. And, you know, the good thing about faith is that once you've planted it, it never reaches a maximum growth point. There is no limitation. It can grow and grow—to infinity.

In 1966, I took my first job as a radio announcer at a station in upstate New York. It was a summer job between semesters at college. Radio was the passion of my young life. I loved the job and it loved me.

In 1968, I got my second radio job at a suburban New York City station. Everything was gangbusters until one day in April. I'd read a number of commercials during the course of the afternoon for a local sponsor. He didn't like the way I'd read them and called the station to vigorously "chew me out." Well, I didn't know it then, but that was a very significant day in my life, because that was the day my phobia was born.

The next time I read the fellow's commercials, after he called, I became very tense and concerned about my performance. I became tight-throated, a natural fear reaction. Then (I'm not sure if it happened that day or later on in the weeks and months ahead), I developed a fear of this tight-throatedness—a fear of the fear. I was afraid I would choke up and be unable to speak over the air.

This fear carried over into other areas of my life. As a drama major in college, I feared long speaking roles. I ran disco dances, but prerecorded the announcements between records.

Years went by. There were no more radio jobs. College graduation came in 1969. Then, I went into the service in '70 and out in '72—back to my first radio job in four years.

That first day on the air was a nightmare. After all that avoidance, the phobia wasn't going to let me off that easy. The tightness in my throat was like a vice grip by now. I lived in mortal fear of choking up on the air, but I stayed with it. On top of that my boss was a hypercritical sort of chap.

Then it was on to my next radio job in a bit larger market. The tightness was a constant factor, my dread of it spiraling ever higher.

A year later I came to the Washington, D.C. area to work at a suburban station. I grew to detest any live air work and would go to absurd extremes to prerecord more and more of it. It was then that I became convinced that I had a physiological problem with my throat. So I sought out the services of a speech pathologist. His diagnosis further mystified me. He told me there was no problem. But there was a problem! I knew that, but no one else did!

Meanwhile, a dream job offer came from a major Washington, D.C. station. Should I take it? Wouldn't I make a fool of myself? Lose control in front of 100,000 people?

I took it, still not having the slightest idea what was wrong with me or what a phobia is. I started on a Monday, knowing I'd be doing street reporting from outside the studio during the week, which I could prerecord, but also aware that on Friday I was scheduled to do live studio newscasts. Monday afternoon, the very first day on the job, I learned the station was being sold and that as the last hired in the newsroom, I'd be the first fired. Of course, I was just aching for an excuse to avoid facing those Friday newscasts. In any event, I switched jobs that same day, intending to fight this thing in my throat by going to an all-news station where I'd be on the air 30 minutes at a time rather than just five. Well, I can't really describe what the terror of facing the mike was like. But I did—white-knuckling it all the way. (Quite literally, I'd hold the mike switch with one hand so tightly that my knuckles turned white.) Things gradually settled down to a dull phobic roar. I was starting to loosen up.

Then, four months later I was called into the General Manager's office one day and was told that I could no longer occupy the prime morning position which I'd been covering since the day I'd been hired. I was further informed that the reason for this was that the owner of the station did not like the sound of my voice. That's all I needed to hear. The long final slide to oblivion then began.

Although I was offered the mid-day time slot, I asked instead for the all-night shift to avoid the larger audience. I wanted to banish myself to Siberia. And the atmosphere I created for myself was climactically very much like that frozen wasteland. I adjusted the studio thermostat so as to keep the room as cold as a meat closet in an attempt to dry up the sweat that poured forth from all over my body. The terror became so acute that my hands and feet began losing circulation though my heart was pounding so hard I sometimes thought it might leap out of my chest.

After each shift, I'd return home and run long distances in sheer frustration as the sun came up, trying to ease the mental anguish. One day, I stumbled and fell, ripping my knee cartilage to shreds. Finally, with my leg in a brace, no other job in sight, and burdened with an unbearable panic which grew worse each day, I resigned in defeat. A few weeks later I was in the hospital undergoing a three-and-a-half-hour operation on my leg.

When fear has been growing in the garden for a long time—the longer you let it be the deeper and stronger grow the roots—the harder to remove. The weeds of fear must be pulled out, quite violently at times. It takes a bit of strength.

There's a man in Chicago who does a talk show you might have heard about. He invites all kinds of unusual guests to talk about a variety of interesting topics. One day, two years ago, Phil Donohue was talking with a doctor named Arthur Hardy from Menlo Park, California. The doctor was relating about how he'd had a public speaking phobia at one time and how he had come to be interested in offering professional treatment and support for phobic people. My wife saw the Donohue show and something in it rang a bell.

She told me about it and I set out to write a 15-page typewritten medical history which was sent to Dr. Hardy. As busy a man as I'm sure he is, he took the time to read it and answer it. It was through him that I learned of Dr. DuPont. It was another year, though, before I actually went to see him.

In the meantime, I enrolled in a very popular public speaking training course in my area. This helped a lot, but it still didn't identify or treat the phobia which was at the heart of the problem. There was something missing.

So, in the spring of 1979, 11 years after it had taken up residence with me, I took my phobia to Dr. DuPont and the Phobia Program of Washington.

Dr. DuPont and Jerilyn Ross helped me to pull up the weeds and make room for the planting of those faith seeds. The phrase which had echoed through my mind for so long—"What if this or that happens?"—became a new motto—"So *what* if this or that happens!"

Knowing the nature of the beast made all the difference in the world. Armed with the power which is knowledge, I went back into the thick of confrontation, placing myself before live audiences five or six times a week—as a church lector, a group leader in my public speaking class, as a TV telethon host, as a member of Dr. DuPont's phobic support group, testifying at public hearings, and on, and on. . . .

As the fear weeds were being uprooted, more space was being cleared to plant that faith. Faith is not self-limiting. It never reaches a point of maximum growth. It can grow and grow—*to infinity!*

For the past three years I've been stuck in a hollow job with no future. A disc jockey turned desk jockey. In two weeks I'll be leaving it.

In August, I'll be joining a University teaching staff as an Assistant Professor. I'm very excited about this position, for among other things I'll be teaching people how to overcome their fears to speak in public.

I thank God. And I thank Jerilyn Ross, Dr. DuPont, and Dr. Hardy for teaching me about the nature of the problem I was fighting blindfolded for so many years. Without all of you, it would not be possible for me now to drink as fully from this precious cup of life.

For those of you who aspire to proudly wear the label "former phobic"—and what a beautiful sound that is—I urge you to light the lamp of knowledge and banish the darkness forever. Learn what a phobic is. Learn and practice without ceasing the techniques for dealing with it. Don't run from it, run *with* it! Be a little more patient and kind with yourself. Clear some space in your garden for faith. Then watch it grow!

I began this presentation by taking some generous liberties with one of Franklin Roosevelt's best remembered quotations. So perhaps then it is all the more appropriate that we call on that great family again for a closing thought. These words, spoken in 1899 by Theodore Roosevelt, have a special meaning for phobics and phobia clinicians:

> Far better it is to dare mighty things,
>   to win glorious triumph
>   even though checkered by failure,
> Than to rank with those poor spirits
>   who neither enjoy much
>   nor suffer much,
> Because they live in the great twilight
>   that knows neither
>   victory nor defeat.

PART I

The Supported Exposure Treatment

The four chapters in this section comprise an overview of the dominant treatment technique used in the United States for phobic people. It has been called by several names, including "contextual therapy" by Dr. Manuel Zane and "TERRAP" by Dr. Arthur Hardy. More behaviorally oriented researchers have called it the in vivo (or in real life) exposure technique. The first chapter, by Dr. Manuel Zane, entitled "A Method to Study and Conceptualize Changes in Phobic Behavior," outlines the basic conceptual framework for the contextual therapy as developed by Dr. Zane and practiced at the White Plains Program and the many derivative programs in the United States. This chapter by Dr. Zane is central to the new clinical approach to the treatment of phobias, as expressed by one of the predominant leaders of clinical practice in phobia treatment.

In this section, we also have the chapter by Doreen Powell, entitled "The Initial Contact with the Phobic Patient," which forms a clear and empathic guideline for clinicians seeking to establish rapport with a phobic person entering treatment. Jerilyn Ross' chapter, "The Role of the Family Member in the Supported Exposure Approach to the Treatment of Phobias," outlines the central role of the family, not only in understanding the genesis and continuation of the phobia but more importantly in terms of reinforcing the new treatment approach. Finally, the chapter by Marvin R. Cohen, entitled "An Integrative Approach to Agoraphobia: Centrum—A Model Program," is a description of an eclectic approach to the treatment of phobias, including psychodynamic, behavioral and psychopharmacologic approaches.

In its totality this section presents a wide-ranging statement of the current clinical approach to the treatment of phobias in the United States.

2

A Method to Study and Conceptualize Changes in Phobic Behavior

Manuel D. Zane

In the phobias, as in other forms of mental illness, we see people reacting unrealistically and adhering to unrealistic beliefs and expectations. During exposure treatment of phobias, our common objective is to create the individualized conditions under which phobic people can gain access to corrective information that enables them to behave and think more realistically (1). There are many forms of exposure treatment (2-8); however, we do not yet have an adequate and accepted theory to explain our successes (9) nor, I wish to add, our failures. A replicable method to study what happens during an individual's treatment could contribute to the development of such a theory.

THE PROBLEM

In the phobias we observe something remarkable. In a few moments a person's phobic behavior can get better and worse many times in the same phobic situation. What causes these observable changes in phobic behavior? Why, repeatedly, does a person who may behave so realistically at one moment become so unrealistic the next? These questions necessitate direct observations of the changing phenomena. They cannot be answered from observations made in the office alone or by statistical averaging or by some preconceived theory. We must observe directly what happens at the many moments of change. This becomes possible during any form of exposure treatment.

A CONTEXTUAL APPROACH TO THE STUDY OF CHANGES IN PHOBIC BEHAVIOR

I call my work "contextual analysis and treatment" or "contextual therapy" for short because I choose to study behavior as it changes in its natural contexts during treatment. Phobic behavior, arising in commonplace situations, consists of 1) automatic feelings of fear and distress and 2) acts of avoidance. Therefore, both the internal and external aspects of phobic behavior must be studied. The therapist observes what is happening externally while, complementarily, the patient is encouraged to introspect and to report what is happening internally. Only patients, of course, have access to information about their thoughts, imagery, feelings and expectations. Therefore, treatment conditions must be designed to facilitate introspection and reporting by the patient of internal events.

From such studies I believe that in the phobic situation people become more or less phobic as their response to the realistic context shrinks or grows. Contextual therapy seeks, therefore, to create the conditions that will restore and build responsiveness to realistic elements in the phobic situation. For example, a person who is phobic about snakes may look at a picture of a snake in a book and become highly disturbed and panicky. Inquiry reveals that for the person the snake began to "move" and was experienced as being "alive." At that moment the realistic context, including my presence, was almost completely obliterated. The therapist sought to reorient the person to the realistic context by having the individual touch the page and say aloud, "Picture on paper, picture on paper." These actions immediately lowered the fear and the snake stopped "moving" and again became a static, harmless picture.

A METHOD TO STUDY CHANGES IN PHOBIC BEHAVIOR

By focusing precisely on the points where behavior changes, the variables, relationships and processes causing observable changes can be identified, studied, and conceptualized. While emphasizing the importance of understanding the processes of behavior change, Agras, Kazdin and Wilson state that such process-oriented studies of change "have barely begun" (10).

The ideas behind contextual therapy are concerned with process because they seek to understand what causes phobic behavior to get better and worse during treatment. They have been developed from both systematic and clinical single case studies of phobic behavior as it changes.

1) Systematic Studies of Changing Phobic Behavior

For the systematic studies I use audiotape recordings. First, I record phobic behavior as it occurs during contextual therapy. Next, I select and, by a simple editing process (11), isolate and splice together the sections in which sequential changes in phobic behavior and their immediate contexts occur. Then, on a scale from #0-#10 patients estimate changes in their feelings of distress, as heard in the recording. A #10 means that distress is almost unbearable while a #0 means that distress is absent. Except at the absolute levels of #0 and #10, patients exhibit simultaneously both phobic and realistic behavior. In other words, a patient responds *both* phobically to unfamiliar elements in his phobic situation which to him are unmanageable and realistically to familiar, manageable factors. For example, at an estimated level of #4, we can assume about 40% of a patient's responses are phobic, while 60% are realistic. The relative strength of these opposing responses at any time depends on the information being received from the existing conditions. As information changes, perceptions and behavior change.

Next, for each change noted, patients are asked to describe their thoughts, feelings, imagery and expectations while I note what is happening externally. Thus, for each sequential change we have complementary observations from the inside and the outside. Such detailed systematic studies of recorded sequential changes and their contexts give rise to concepts of change that can be publicly validated.

2) Clinical Studies of Changing Phobic Behavior

Ideas, derived from a few systematic studies, then guide and influence the clinical studies and in turn are shaped and given broader meanings by the innumerable and constantly changing clinical observations. No ideas are allowed to stand unaltered that conflict with the systematically derived ones.

Clinical studies include any observations of changes in phobic behavior that arise in the office and patients' reports about changes observed elsewhere and in the past. The #0-#10 scale may again be used by both patient and therapist to study in their contexts observed or reported changes in phobic behavior. Over and over again information from such clinical studies is linked to the systematically derived concepts. Thereby, we learn the specifics of what makes phobic behavior better and worse and develop ever more broadly based, validatable concepts about the causes of change in phobic behavior.

A CONCEPTUALIZATION OF PROCESSES CAUSING CHANGES IN PHOBIC BEHAVIOR

Phobic people have become conditioned or sensitized by their past experiences in phobic situations. Therefore, they automatically react with fear and distress to such situations *and to thoughts and images of them.* From past experiences, they also anticipate that if they remain in the phobic situation their initial disturbed state will involuntarily increase, becoming unbearably painful, and they will lose control physically and mentally. Therefore, they avoid the phobic situation. They are bewildered (12) by what is happening to them. They may by themselves develop, believe in, and react to the most unrealistic explanations.

Studies of changes in phobic behavior disclose that, once it emerges, the initial fear may rise as the person focuses on and reacts to *new* anticipated dangers. Involuntarily, fear intensifies further and there is progressive loss of bodily and mental control as people think about, imagine and react to increasing and accelerating numbers of expected dangers. I have called this fear-generating, spiraling process, in which disturbed feelings breed frightening thoughts, more disturbed fearful feelings, more frightening thoughts, more fear and so on, "the phobogenic process." As bodily and mental disturbance grows, concentration on the disturbed feelings and expected dangers intensifies. Simultaneously, the person is involuntarily removed from what is known, familiar and comforting and sucked into a terrifying, cognitively created world full of insurmountable dangers. Sherrington states that when there is a sense of bodily injury it "captures the mind's attention even to the exclusion for the time being of all else" (13). Understanding the intensification of panic as a product of identifiable, understandable, current processes instead of as a recapitulation of an infantile, instinctual fear (14) or a reproduction of a learned fear (15) focuses attention on the current context as perceived by the individual and its ceaseless flow and change—another area of investigation that has been neglected (16).

These studies also establish that phobic behavior gets better when the person is responding to realities that are perceived by the individual as known, familiar and manageable. Treatment, therefore, seeks to affect the person's focus of attention so as to decrease responsiveness in the phobic situation to frightening thoughts and imagery and to increase involvement with comforting realities.

TAPE-RECORDED STUDIES OF CHANGES IN PHOBIC BEHAVIOR

Brief edited tape recordings from a phobic person that span a ten-year period of treatment will be presented to illustrate systematic and clinical methods of studying changes in phobic behavior and the concepts derived from such empirical data about immediate and long-term change.

Roy began treatment in 1967 at the age of 25. He was recommended by his internist because of an intractable spastic colon. He had seen other psychiatrists. He was phobic since early childhood and was now severely agoraphobic. He was afraid to stay at home alone or go into department stores or supermarkets alone. He could not drive alone or ride elevators or trains. He was markedly handicapped and depended heavily on his wife and parents. At times he was violent and at times suicidal.

Tape 1 (Systematic Study)

Roy was also afraid of the dark. In 1969, to systematically study his changing behavior in a phobic situation, I suggested we go into a dark closet together and tape-record his reactions. The following is a transcript of his comments (my comments are in italics):

> You're just talking about going in there and I'm scared. (CHANGE 1) My stomach's starting to get butterflies. . . . *(What do you feel will happen?)* Well, I feel that I'm going to start suffocating and really make a fool of myself. You know, I'll start clawing at the door and start screaming. (sound of door closing) *(How do you feel in here now?)* I'm scared. *(Do you see any light at all?)* No. *(Nothing happens when you're in the dark?)* Not right now. (CHANGE 2) *(Can you make it happen?)* Oh, yes . . . very easy. *(Let me see you do it. Try to make yourself get scared a little.)* Make myself get scared? *(Yeah. Try to make the thing come on.)* I can't. . . . (CHANGE 3) It's happening involuntarily now. It's coming . . . it's completely black . . . I see the blackness, I feel like it's pushing me up against the wall. (CHANGE 4) *(All right. Now you just try to stay with it.)* (breathes heavily) You know, I'm losing myself. I don't know where I am. (CHANGE 5) I'm trying to. . . .*(Here, I'm going to touch you. Okay?)* Yeah.

> (CHANGE 6) *(What do you mean by losing yourself?)* I'm losing where I am. I start to feel *(Uh, huh.)* that . . . I'm not in a closet. I'm some place else, you know. I'm . . . I'm some place where I can't get to the closet door. *(Mhm, huh.)* And I can't open it and I can't get to that light and I'm (sighs) just lost. *(Mhm, hmh.)* And I'm stuck like I'm . . . I'm in a coffin. *(Mhm.)* I feel like I'm nailed in and I can't get out. *(Mhm, huh. Now, can you orient yourself to anything here?)* Oh, I know where I am. *(So what's happened? How did you get back to . . . you know, reality?)* You're here. *(I was here before.)* Uh, well, I . . . I don't know. *(Mhm, huh.)* But I . . . now I'm starting to see light. (CHANGE 7) *(Starting to see light?)* Yeah. *(Where?)* Cracks in the door. *(Oh yeah, there is light . . . very faint.)* You know, I never stayed in the dark long enough that I . . . could get used to the dark like this. I never let myself get . . . get this far *(Mhm.)* . . . into it where I could see anything. When it was that black, I'd run. (CHANGE 8)

Later in that session, reviewing his moment of panic, he said: "Even though you were there with me, I felt I was in a place where there was no beginning and no end. I could hear your voice but I was alone."

Comments

In the following, (+) means that his fear level got better; (−) means that it got worse; (±) means that it was unchanged in a changed situation. (See also Figure 1.)

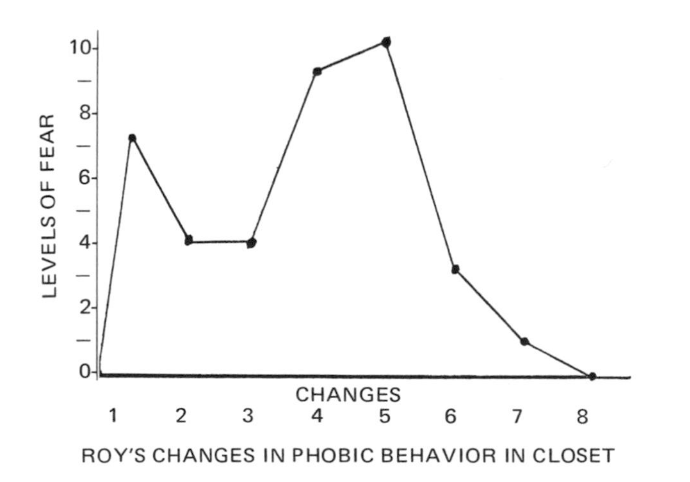

ROY'S CHANGES IN PHOBIC BEHAVIOR IN CLOSET

CHANGE 1 (−) His fear level rose to #7 with thoughts and imagery of anticipated dangers.

CHANGE 2 (+) Dropped to #4. Involved with realities in the actual closet, he was less distressed than with his thoughts about the closet during anticipation.

CHANGE 3 (±) Neither my suggestion nor his effort could make his level rise voluntarily in that setting.

CHANGE 4 (−) Rose swiftly to #9 as involuntarily he focused on and reacted to the "blackness"—perceived as a danger by him.

CHANGE 5 (−) Rose to #10 as he began to imagine he was nailed into a coffin and could not get out. As this happened he lost contact with where he was.

CHANGE 6 (+) Dropped abruptly to #3. When he reacted automatically to the known and familiar touch, he immediately became reoriented and responsive to the realities of the closet.

CHANGE 7 (+) Dropped further to #1 as he focused on and reacted realistically to the familiar, known, and comforting streak of light.

CHANGE 8 (+) Dropped further to #0 as he began to think actively and reasoned realistically about the adverse effect of previously having always run from the dark.

This tape illustrates how at first my positive influence allowed him to enter and stay in the closet despite his negative automatic expectations and feelings. But once he focused on and became involved with the dark involuntarily and with astonishing rapidity, suggestive of the swift operations of the "phobogenic process," he became deeply involved with privately imagined dangers and simultaneously lost his responsiveness to me and to the comforting realities of the closet. I feared he might do something wild as he had predicted. Intuitively I reached out and touched him, which immediately reoriented him to reality and dropped his fear. Apparently at that moment the more primitive and familiar tactile mode of sensory contact was more effective than my presence and voice.

I continued to see him weekly. We drove on highways, rode elevators, talked over a two-way radio as he walked out into a wide open field, spoke on the telephone when he became panicked, and held joint sessions with family members. There was little apparent progress.

Tape 2 (Clinical Study in the Office)

About seven months later, at my suggestion, he entered and stayed in the same dark closet alone. As he emerged he said:

> When I first went in there . . . as that black mask started to come in on me . . . like . . . I remember . . . I went . . . (makes loud snorting noise) I took a deep breath like that and at the same time my mind was going, "You're in the closet. (speaks loudly) You know where you are. All you got to do is touch the goddamned door and open it." . . . It's something new to me. I just kept pounding at myself, so to speak, and saying to myself where I am.

Comments

Clearly he was beginning to get the idea of learning to talk to himself in order to stay oriented and responsive to reality instead of allowing himself to get completely lost in his imagery and thoughts. Yet his phobic behavior did not change significantly. This was a puzzle. But it was obvious that the many realistic behaviors and ideas that were manifest in my office were not being carried out elsewhere. He continued to come for treatment. Each week he had an individual session plus a group session with other phobic people. In addition, he attended the first eight-week program at White Plains Hospital in 1971 for people phobic about elevators. He made progress there but soon lost it even though he seemed to understand the theory better than most. His progress outside was hardly noticeable. Then suddenly, in 1977, he began to make great strides. For almost a year he drove alone on highways, rode elevators, went into stores, and even stayed at home alone. He also began to stop taking sleeping medication which he had insisted on because of his fear of being alone at night. I was amazed but welcomed the remarkable change. I assumed he was now putting into practice ideas that he had learned.

Then one day, as he happily left his family and walked alone along a river bank to fish, he was suddenly gripped with the old fear which quickly rose to terror. All at once his confidence was shattered. His gains vanished. Thereafter he felt and looked like a beaten and helpless man. He clung to his family. In a flat, weak voice he expressed a deep hopelessness of ever getting better. He said, "I was pretending that I was like other people and that the principles would also work for me. For the year they did. Now I don't feel like I belong on this earth. I hate myself for being so meek and cowardly and dependent."

He began, for the first time, to express doubts about the value of my treatment for him. He explored other psychiatrists and medications without much gain. He could no longer drive to my office or to work alone. He made several suicidal attempts but fortunately, mainly because of the watchfulness of his wife, none got too far. Once, he was hospitalized overnight by his family because of an episode of panic in which he began to run wildly from his house. Though he was set back in his functioning elsewhere, his work with me seemed more open and honest. He expressed dissatisfactions and hopelessness more specifically. His despair seemed more real during a session. He also exposed many bizarre ideas. For example, during a panic he often felt and believed that he was from another planet, that all his folks had died, and that he was all alone in the world. Other people were experienced then as mechanical robots or "androids" whom he could not influence.

His wife worked hard to keep him oriented to their realities while exhibiting unusual understanding for his misery. Socially he made new friends with neighbors and began to admit that he was phobic, which had always been most difficult and embarrassing for him. Some people, including family members, began to seek his help and advice because he had a good understanding of what they were going through and had good suggestions. For himself, he seemed to still be looking for a miracle drug or advice that would transform him. He felt hopeless. His father died in February 1980. This sent him into another tailspin and again he attempted suicide on several occasions. He was saved largely because people came to his rescue. Somehow, despite these horrendous negatives, I felt more hopeful about him if he would only survive and I told him so and asked him to now make "survival" his main goal. I think my hope came from the fact that I felt he was divulging more meaningful information to me about his inner turmoil. At times he drove alone to my office and to work but this was sporadic. More often he came with his little boy and his wife.

Tape 3

In March 1980, to objectively study what had changed over the years, I suggested he listen to the closet tape made in 1969 and give me his current reaction. I played the tape which ended with "I'm losing myself. I don't know where I am. I'm trying to. . . . *(Here, I'm going to touch you. Okay?)* Yeah." He listened and said:

> That's exactly what happens. *(What?)* That's exactly what happens. You just lose where you are at the time. Okay? *(Yeah.)* You sort of get lost in the world where you're imagining. And that scares the hell out of you because it's a nightmarish type world. *(How about the second part where you said, "I never stayed in the dark*

long enough to get used to it. When it was that black I'd run"? How about that?) Right now I tend to be a runner too. It's very difficult not to be a runner when you have to face this type of fear. It's just hard, you know. It's hard. You're pushing against like a stone wall. You're pushing against something that's very strong. The thing says, "Run, run, run, run, run, run." And you're going, "No, I'm not going to run. I'm not going to run. *(What kept you from learning from what you said that many years ago?)* Mainly because I'm petrified to try it out and to go into the situation. I think that knowing what you have to do and doing it are two different things, you know. What you have to understand is that I don't have the control I need. *(Of what don't you have control?)* Of these thoughts taking over and they'll run wild and there's no way that I can control them. You can help me with the controls but I can't do it. *(Yet.)* Right. I feel that I can't pilot this, this brain. I felt like I told you before . . . I was floating out into space and there was nobody else to help me and I couldn't help myself. I needed somebody else to grab me and pull me back. *(I believe that.)* Because I couldn't control that. And . . . and I still feel that same feeling. *(I know.)*

Comments

In this tape Roy showed a much increased awareness of the power and the nature of the forces controlling his behavior in the closet tape and of their relationships. He recognized his rigid pattern of running from a phobic situation as his way of avoiding the petrifying power of his fearful thoughts to propel him helplessly into space. He also acknowledged feelings of total dependence upon another's help to restore him to reality. Apparently, just thinking about the subject as he spoke evoked some of that same feeling of powerlessness and dread.

Later in that same session he described the development of an episode of panic in his own house as his mind focused on a recent feared situation.

Tape 4 (Clinical Study of a Reported Episode of Changing Behavior)

All of a sudden I'll be driving and I'll be on the road and the car will break down. *(You mean mentally now?)* Yeah . . . I get into a panic and I'll say, "But I'm in the house. Why am I having the reaction?" That makes it even more . . . realizing that I had drifted off . . . *(Right.)* . . . and taken this little trip. And when I'm having all these feelings, I'm saying, "I'd better call Dr. Zane. I'm having it for nothing. It's coming out of nowhere." *(Right.)* And actually I'm going into the future but I forget about it. When the feelings come in, then I concentrate on the feelings. I say, "My God, my intestines are going. My hands are sweating. I'm getting these cold feelings through my veins. I'm starting to hyperventilate. Where did that come from? You know, it's happening to me and it's coming from nowhere!"

Comments

This tape shows how, at home, he expected to be safe from fear and how he panicked when fear suddenly erupted with its scary bodily disturbances. Immediately he thought of contacting me for help. Until he was able to see and accept the connections of his panic to thoughts of a possible future danger he was terrified by regarding it as coming from nowhere. It is probable that, previously, his habitual efforts to escape his feared feelings with their dreaded potentialities always failed because endangering thoughts cannot be quarantined. Such repeated failures must have contributed to his deep, unrealistic belief in being inescapably hopeless, and helpless about himself and his problem.

The indissoluble links between thoughts and feelings and his automatic efforts to escape his distressing feelings are again revealed in this next tape. In May 1980, as he was speaking to me in my office, he suddenly became upset.

Tape 5 (Clinical Study of Changes Occurring in the Office)

I'm getting that right now. *(What are you getting?)* I was just thinking that I'm gonna go home. I wonder if I'm going to be frightened when I'm home. I have to go someplace this afternoon where I'm going to be frightened when I go to that place and all of a sudden I got that funny feeling—cold in my legs. And it just came over me and I says, "Oh, I hate that feeling! I wish it goes away." *(Where did it come from?)* Just thinking about. . . .*(Just thinking, but you can't stop it. You've been trying to stop it, I think.)* Yeah. I just tried to stop it then. *(What do you mean?)* Oh, I was trying to push it away and get it away because I hate that feeling, you know. Because it's sooo-ooh. . . . It's such a disgusting feeling, you know. It's just . . . uh . . . I can't describe it. It's so . . . really . . . it's a horrendous type of thing. You just . . . ooh. I think I'd rather feel

> pain rather than that. *(How is it right now?)* It's gone. *(What do you think of that? Did you make it go?)* I don't know. *(You didn't. It was just there and then it went away as you got talking as an observer . . . reality.)* Uhh. *(But if you thought about it from another angle, that "I can't handle it; I can't stop it," it would have gone up again.)* I think I'm also afraid, afraid of the feeling that I won't be able to stay with reality and that it'll automatically suck me in.

Comments

When fear suddenly emerged in my office, Roy linked it to his perception of a future danger. He acknowledged his profound fear of the feeling and its horrendous quality. As he described, realistically, his disagreeable feelings, his fear disappeared. Then he again expressed his abiding expectation that it would involuntarily disconnect him from reality and pull him into his nightmarish world. This, of course, had been first observed in the closet tape in 1969 and was what he dreaded each time in the phobic situation.

The deleterious effects of these unrealistic and ominous cognitions are amazingly enduring in this man. Apparently, when alone his old beliefs still dominate his behavior, and his growing new insights, expressed in my office, are not yet operative. He has still to learn and believe, when alone and panicky, that his feelings of fear do come from thoughts and that there is no realistic danger despite his feelings. For this to develop he requires many successful experiences of reconnecting to reality *after* he becomes panicky and thus controlling his phobogenic thinking and its dreaded consequences. I am confident that conditions will allow this to happen.

Let us now contrast Roy's 13-year-long and still uncompleted treatment with the relatively brief time required by another patient for successful change. The same contextual approach was used.

Len was a 43-year-old, uneducated construction worker. He had been phobic since the age of 20. He could not walk a block away from his car, avoided trains, and was afraid of theaters and restaurants. During an attack he felt dizzy, his hands became numb with feelings of pins and needles, and he was afraid of fainting and of being embarrassed. He began treatment in 1976. He came for individual therapy on eight occasions, during which we often went out, walked away from his car, separated, and then discussed possible causes of observed changes in his phobic behavior. He also came five times to one-and-a-half-hour group sessions with other phobic people.

Total treatment lasted for ten weeks. He improved rapidly. At his last session in December 1976, I asked him what he had learned. He said:

> Well, I learned that I can be in a place now and if I get the feeling, I'm not afraid 'cause I know what the feeling is. If I get the feeling it's just a nervous feeling that everybody gets and I got to learn to cope with it . . . don't let it run away with my imagination. *(Uhm.)* Before I wanted a cure. I wanted to take a medicine that would cure me, put a hole in my head and say, "Well, I'm cured . . .I won't get that feeling." Everybody gets the feeling. It's just a feeling of fear, some fright . . . like if you see somebody run over with a car, you're going to get the feeling. You're gonna say, "Ooh," and you're gonna get scared and you're just not gonna let it run away with you. It's not gonna happen to you. You see, before, I'd put the radio on and they used to talk about different things that I didn't like. So I just closed it off 'cause I didn't want to hear it. But you gotta hear it. You got to listen and say, "Well, look, that's part of life and you got to accept that if these things happen, they're going to happen and you can't be afraid of it. And if it's gonna come (laughs), that's it." *(Uh.)* So you can't push it away. Before, if I don't like it, I just push it away. I don't want to think about it.

He had no further treatment and I did not see or speak to him again until *I* phoned him in June, 1980:

> *(You were here in 1976?)* Right. *(And what's happened to you since?)* Well, I tell you, it's like a complete opposite. When I went to you, I would be afraid to walk down the block. Now, I can handle most of my life. And a lot of things that I wasn't able to do before I saw you, now I am able to do. I don't think . . . I'll never be 100%. But I'd say I'm about 95%.

Unlike Roy, with very little help Len was quickly able to regard his fear as understandable from his own experiences and those of other people. Very soon, therefore, he was able to accept his responding with feelings of fear and distress, to stop trying to push the feelings away, to stay related to realities, and to improve progressively in the phobic situation by himself. For many years Roy's feelings of fear remained utterly inexplicable to him, absorbed his attention, involuntarily removed him from reality, led to the development of isolating and intimidating beliefs, and heralded horrendous feelings of panic and utter loss of control.

These differences in responses of their phobic behavior to treatment, therefore, were related to their differences as people—to differences in their private views, goals, expectations, and evaluations in the phobic situation. While most phobic people respond relatively quickly to contextual therapy, some, like Roy, may require years of help to get the individual experiences that they need to change their unrealistic private beliefs, expectations, and behavior in phobic situations.

DISCUSSION

Studies of sections where phobic behavior changes observably during treatment seem to have many promising practical and theoretical consequences.

1) Clinicians become investigators and indispensable contributors to the study of what causes phobic behavior to change in the single case. By linking their innumerable, private clinical observations and studies of changing behavior to even a few, public systematic ones, as was attempted in this presentation, therapists can develop sound and testable ideas about the causes and processes of change.

2) Since phobic behavior changes over and over again under highly varied conditions, these changes can be sampled at random and searched for their common determinants. Theories developed from such data should be capable of experimental as well as public validation.

3) Current phobic behavior results from automatic reactions to frightening situations that are observed in the present, recalled from the past, and anticipated in the future. Instead of looking to the past to illuminate the present, the study of phobic behavior changing in the present provides a firm validatable basis for theorizing about how it probably changed elsewhere and in the past.

4) By digging out internal information about observed changes to communicate to the therapist, patients become aware themselves of the many causes of change. Thereby, they begin to notice and to understand how the body and mind interact, and to recognize their own role and that of other people in causing and also in correcting their disturbed behavior. They begin to forumulate more realistic ideas from their new experiences about themselves and their world.

5) As we learn about the processes that make behavior better and

worse, more effective therapies become possible. Contextual therapy has been applied since 1971 at White Plains Hospital Medical Center's Phobia Clinic to eight-week group programs for phobic people, most of whom were long-standing agoraphobic patients. This treatment program has resulted in improvement, as determined by questionnaires, in 84% of 191 participants after six months (in 97% of 165 respondents) and in 85% of 49 participants questioned four years after completion of the program (in 95% of 43 respondents). In most, improvement continued even after the program was completed. Obviously, these impressive results pertain only to the population of phobic people that came to our clinic. Understanding causes and processes of change also enable us to understand more of how all therapies may help phobic people and what interferes with treatment.

6) When alone, the problem confronting the phobic person seems almost insoluble. Feeling threatened, the person involuntarily focuses on and reacts increasingly to rapidly expanding numbers of anticipated dangers, making the fear worse and worse. Therapy, therefore, seeks to create conditions that enable the person in the phobic situation to focus on and react more and more to what is familiar and known in the realistic context and less and less to imagined, expected dangers.

CONCLUSION

The direct study of changes in phobic behavior seems essential to our comprehension of their causes, opens new realms of cognitive and contextual data relevant to the observed changes, and allows for the development of validatable concepts about immediate and possibly long-term changes. If others, as in this presentation, would also focus on and study observable changes in phobic behavior, vast amounts of relevant information could be rapidly accumulated from which scientifically sound theories could be developed. Psychoanalytic and behavioral therapies have developed their theories about phobic behavior from historical or animal-based data. Both have largely ignored the question of what causes observable changes in phobic behavior. It seems necessary now to shift attention to the phenomena of observable changes in their contexts to open new and more promising directions for the study and treatment of phobic people. In addition, the study of changes in observable behavior is probably important for all mental illness (17).

REFERENCES

1. Beck, A.T. *Cognitive Therapy and the Emotional Disorders.* New York: International Universities Press, 1976.

2. Weekes, C. *Simple Effective Treatment of Agoraphobia.* New York: Hawthorn Books, 1976.
3. Hardy, A.B. *Agoraphobia: Symptoms, Causes, Treatment.* Menlo Park, CA: Terrap, 1976.
4. DuPont, R.L. *Profile of a phobic treatment program: First year's results.* Presented at the 132nd Annual Meeting of the American Psychiatric Association, Chicago, IL, May 18, 1979.
5. Ross, J. The use of former phobics in the treatment of phobias. *Am. J. Psychiatry,* 137: 715-717, 1980.
6. Marks, I.M. Exposure therapy for phobias and obsessive-compulsive disorders. *Hospital Practice,* 14: 101-108, Feb. 1979.
7. Marks, I.M. *Living With Fear.* New York: McGraw-Hill, 1978.
8. Zane, M.D. Contextual analysis and treatment of phobic behavior as it changes. *Am. J. Psychotherapy,* 32: 338-356, 1978.
9. Marks, I.M. The current status of behavioral psychotherapy: Theory and practice. *Am. J. Psychiatry,* 133: 253-261, 1976.
10. Agras, W.S., Kazdin, A.E., and Wilson, G.T. *Behavior Therapy—Toward An Applied Clinical Science.* San Francisco: W.H. Freeman, 1979, pp. 145-146.
11. Zane, M.D. How one psychiatrist utilizes his tape recorder with patients. Roche Report, *Frontiers of Psychiatry,* 6: 1, 1969.
12. Weekes, C. *Peace From Nervous Suffering.* New York: Hawthorn Books, 1972, p. 5.
13. Sherrington, C. *Man On His Nature.* New York: Doubleday Anchor Books, 1953, p. 231.
14. Freud, S. Analysis of a phobia in a five year old boy. In: *Collected Papers,* vol 3. Translated by A. and J. Strachey. London: Hogarth Press, 1949, pp. 149-289 (original printing 1909).
15. Wolpe, J. *The Practice of Behavior Therapy.* New York: Pergamon Press, 1969.
16. Mancuso, J.C. Current motivational models in the elaboration of personal construct theory. In: *Nebraska Symposium on Motivation,* vol 24. Lincoln, Nebraska: University of Nebraska Press, 1977, pp. 43-97.
17. Committee on Research. Psychiatric research and the assessment of change. *Group for Advancement of Psychiatry,* vol 6, report 63, Nov. 1966.

3

The Initial Contact with the Phobic Patient

Doreen Powell

As with other mental health patients, the initial contact with the phobic person is most important. It provides an opportunity to convey information, not only about the treatment which is available, but also to correct many misapprehensions and misconceptions which the phobic may have about his condition. It can inspire confidence in the patient that he can be helped. It can be the beginning of a rapport between the patient and the people who will be working with the phobic person.

Most of our patients become acquainted with the White Plains Hospital Phobia Clinic via the media. In the past nine years there have been numerous newspaper and magazine articles about our work, as well as a number of radio and television programs. These have not only resulted in hundreds of inquiries from all parts of the country, but also inspired additional media interest in our work. In the past couple of years we have had an increasing number of referrals from general practitioners, psychiatrists, psychologists, social workers, and mental health agencies. Some patients come to us on the recommendation of another phobic.

The initial inquiries about our program are usually by telephone. For participation in our various programs, we require a personal interview with two exceptions. One is for participation in our Outreach Program when the phobic cannot get to the hospital. The other is for the Intensive

Course, which is for people who live at a distance and plan to stay in White Plains for two or three weeks for daily treatment. These interviews are usually done by telephone or mail.

The initial telephone conversation we consider a most important step in the patient's welfare and should be therapeutic. The conversation should be as informative as possible. Usually I begin with the question, "May I ask what your phobia is?" After the inquirer has explained the symptoms, I am usually able to reassure the person that his condition is not unique or even rare and that his symptoms fit in with the pattern of most phobic sufferers.

Following a description of the programs available and the recording of the inquirer's name and address, an intake interview is scheduled, if the patient desires this. We make it a practice to mail free literature on our Clinic to all inquirers. Depending on the urgency of the inquiry, we may suggest that the phobic read our literature first and then call back for an appointment. I conclude the conversation with simple but detailed directions for reaching White Plains Hospital and my office. If a person has an elevator phobia, for example, I will arrange to meet him in the lobby.

Before discussion of the intake interview with the patient, it will be useful to outline some of the characteristics we have found phobic people have in common. This will be helpful to the therapist interviewing the patient since the interviewer should be aware of the phobic's sensitivities.

1) Phobic people usually tend to be very sensitive—overly aware of other people's reactions.
2) They are highly imaginative. Often thinking takes place in the form of pictures in the mind.
3) They are negative thinkers in their phobic situations, concerned about the worst that can possibly happen to them.
4) Many have a feeling of insecurity and have lost confidence in themselves.
5) They tend to give an outwardly calm appearance while churning inside.
6) They want to please. They tend to do what others want rather than please themselves.
7) They are self-conscious, easily embarrassed and overly concerned about what other people think of them.
8) They tend to be placid, to fit into their environment, thus avoiding conflicts and even hiding from them.

Bearing all these characteristics in mind, at the initial interview, as well as later on, the therapist should be a caring, understanding person who can give reassurance, hope and a sense of ease to the patient. You must always keep in mind that you are dealing with a very scared and frightened person even though he may not show it.

At the initial interview, my first questions are usually, "How do you feel?" and, "Did you find it difficult to get here?" This indicates to the patient that the interviewer is sympathetic to and understanding of his feelings. These opening questions assume that the patient may have had a hard time getting to the hospital. They allow the patient to feel "not alone" and indicate that others have similar problems. Hopefully they help the patient to accept his phobia, as he is usually ashamed of and embarrassed by his condition. It also opens a path for discussion of his specific phobia.

As the interview progresses, I explain the theory of contextual therapy—that the patient can help himself by changing the pattern of his negative thinking in the phobic situation—to try to remain related to the present rather than getting involved in the phobogenic process (1) which results in a spiraling of his thoughts and fears until the patient is so upset that he has to flee from the situation. Also, I explain to the patient that while the frightening feelings he is experiencing are frightening to him, he will learn that they are not dangerous. We talk about the anticipation which every phobic patient has to learn to deal with.

The Clinic has an intake form which I complete as the interview progresses. I find that I can get more information about the patient by filling out the form myself and this is often more acceptable to the patient. I have been asked several times during telephone inquiries, "Do I have to fill out any forms?" When I answer, "None," the inquirer expresses relief since he would be too nervous to do this. It is obvious that at this point the patient should be made as comfortable as possible, since he is probably having a hard time facing up to the prospect of treatment, which involves facing the problem instead of avoiding it. Later, as the patient becomes familiar with the theory of contextual therapy, he can begin to reenter his phobic situation.

Some of the questions on the intake form besides the usual name, address, age, etc. are:

- How long have you had your phobia?
- How did it develop?
- Describe your phobic reaction.
- To what extent does your phobia affect your life?

- Did you have your phobia in childhood?
- How do you currently function? Describe your daily activity.
- List any phobias in your family.

The second page of the intake form is devoted to a history of psychiatric problems, previous treatment (if any), hospitalizations, outpatient treatment, etc. We also record the patient's medical history, surgical history, current physical complaints, and medications being taken. These questions are asked for various reasons: 1) to gain knowledge of the patient's condition; 2) to gain information regarding previous and current therapy and the name of the therapist. We inquire of the patient if he has discussed our mode of treatment with his therapist. Occasionally the patient desires a contact between the therapist and us; and 3) to assist our own research and help in assigning an aide to work with the patient.

Lastly, we discuss how the patient feels about joining an eight-week clinic and how he anticipates he will react. There is also a discussion of charges and methods of payment.

If, during or after the initial interview, I have any doubt whether the patient's problem is a phobia or if I judge that the patient might not be appropriate for our programs, I refer the person for evaluation to Dr. Zane or one of the other psychiatrists who work in our clinic. The interviewing psychiatrist may decide the problem is phobic and agree to admit the patient to our clinic. Otherwise he is referred to another appropriate channel for treatment. I would add that this has happened in only about ten or 12 cases during the past seven years that I have been doing the initial interviews.

About 90% of our patients who join our eight-week program have had or are having some kind of psychiatric treatment when they come to us. I should point out that the two treatments are compatible and we have never detected any conflict or confusion in the patient who attends our clinic and at the same time may be having private psychiatric sessions.

When, during the course of the initial interview, I have established that the patient is phobic and could benefit from a course of treatment, I then discuss our several programs to ascertain which of them is best suited to the particular patient.

Our basic treatment is the eight-week program or clinic which we offer six or seven times a year, maybe more according to the number of applicants. The participants may have differing phobias since the approach to all of them is basically the same. The program involves a group session weekly of one-and-a-half hours duration and work sessions of one hour weekly with a trained phobia aide. This involves patients going out and entering phobic situations which they have hitherto been avoiding. We limit the size of each clinic to ten patients, since this is the maximum size to permit each individual to make a contribution. Each clinic is under the supervision of a qualified psychiatrist or psychologist.

A second aspect of our program is the self-help group, of which we currently have six. They meet on an ongoing basis and come together for one-and-a-half hours weekly. Each group consists of about eight phobics and is led by one of our trained phobia aides.

The self-help groups were originally designed for patients who had been through the eight-week clinic but felt that they needed further treatment. They needed the support of a group session, but felt that they would work on their phobic situations without the help of a trained therapist. More recently we have been admitting patients into our self-help groups without their first having been through the eight-week program. There are several reasons for this. Some patients contact us when a clinic has just commenced and they feel a need to start working on their problem immediately. Other patients feel that the eight-week clinic would initially be too structured for them. In fact, two of our recovered agoraphobic therapists started in the self-help group, transferring later to the eight-week clinic. Both of them have told me that if they had attempted to go immediately into the eight-week clinic, they would probably have had to drop out.

We put many people with flying phobias in the self-help groups so that they can learn the theory of contextual therapy. Then we recommend that they join a fear-of-flying group to get the practical experience as well. Obviously the work sessions with flying phobics would be impossible to handle in an eight-week mixed phobia program. Incidentally, in 1973 we did run a fear-of-flying eight-week phobia clinic out of LaGuardia, which was very successful.

A third facet of our program is the series of private work sessions with one of our 26 trained phobia aides. When they come to us some patients feel that they are not ready to talk in a group situation. They may feel that it will be too frightening to listen to other people's problems. They are not prepared to discuss their fears and feelings in a group or they are afraid that when they hear about other patient's problems they will acquire those phobias as well. More often than not, we find that after these people have worked with a therapist for a time, they become less embarrassed about their phobias and are prepared to join one of our group programs.

Our outreach program is used when we have patients who cannot go far from home and thus cannot get to the hospital for treatment. Sometimes we can arrange for trained therapists to go to the patients' homes and work with them there with the goal of getting them to the stage where they can come to the hospital and join one of our group programs.

We encourage patients to have family members or friends who they feel could be helpful to them to sit in on the meetings so that they can learn how to assist them. In some instances they may be able to replace the therapist after a time. Sitting in on the meetings will help family members understand what happens to phobics, that they are neither malingering nor directing their phobic behavior against the family or friends.

Family members or friends can help in the following ways:

1) Make themselves available to reorient the patient to reality.
2) Provide the patient with a way out. Phobics do not work well under pressure or commitment, but, if they feel it is possible to leave the situation, they are more likely to stay in it.
3) Should not expect that because the phobic was able to enter and cope with the phobic situation one day that he will be able to do so the next. Some regression often occurs and this should not be discouraging either to the family or to the patient.
4) Should be prepared to talk to the patient and help him to put his phobic experience into words.
5) Help to plan step by step the ways for the patient going into and staying in the situation.
6) Help the patient focus on the present in phobic situations to prevent his thinking from taking off into imaginary future situations.
7) Help the patient recover from unexpected episodes of panic and high levels of anxiety. Encourage the patient to try to remain in the phobic situation even when the fear level is very high.

During the course of the initial interview, there are a few questions which are invariably asked by the patient. To these I have developed standard replies.

1) Is there a cure for my phobia?

> Yes, I have known people to recover completely from their phobia. But the eight-week program is designed to help you understand how your phobia is affecting your body and your mind and to learn techniques for dealing with your thoughts, feelings, and fears.

2) How long will it take me to get better? (This is usually followed by the remark, "I know you can't tell me exactly.")

   It depends on the individual. By the end of the eight weeks you should have had some success reentering your phobic situation and thus have gained the confidence to go on and work on your phobia by yourself. You will have learned the theory and practice of contextual therapy. Each person progresses at his own rate depending on the patient's attitude, the amount of practice he is prepared to put in and the severity of the phobia.

3) Is it true that if I lose one phobia I will replace it with another?

   No. We have no evidence of this.

4) May my symptoms change? If I lose my heart palpitations or shaking will I then develop blurry eyes or experience hyperventilation?

   Not necessarily. I can only recall one or maybe two cases where this may have occurred. In one case, the patient was a driving phobic who reported that when she was starting to get better a new symptom appeared. Her right leg went stiff when she was driving and this occurred only on thruways. Whether this was actually a new symptom or whether she had only just become aware of it, no one can say. However, continuing the same treatment, this symptom also disappeared.

5) Does the treatment really work? What is your success rate?

   Yes, the treatment does work. We do follow-ups after six months and four years. We are greatly heartened at the results. Our four-year and six-month follow-ups show that out of 240 participants we received 208 replies—of those 201 were helped—six completely, 121 very much, 50 moderately, 24 slightly—and seven were not helped.

In conducting the initial interview, our purpose and hope are that at its conclusion the phobic person will be less fearful of his symptoms, and will realize that he is not "going crazy" and is not alone with his problem. Above all he should leave with a knowledge that there is treatment now for phobics and that something can be done to relieve their suffering.

REFERENCES

1. Zane, M.D. Contextual analysis and treatment of phobic behavior as it changes. *American Journal of Psychotherapy,* 32: 338-356, 1978.

4

The Role of the Family Member in the Supported Exposure Approach to the Treatment of Phobias

Jerilyn Ross

The supported exposure approach to the treatment of phobias combines short-term group counseling with individual therapy (1). The latter is administered by a phobia therapist, either a mental health worker or a former phobic who has been trained to guide phobics into real life anxiety-producing situations while teaching specific anxiety-reducing techniques. The phobia therapist helps phobics set achievable goals and take the necessary steps to be able to enter into and to remain in the phobic situation long enough to see that the feared reactions (i.e., going crazy, having a heart attack, fainting) will not occur and that intense anxiety levels will diminish (2).

During the group session the leader, generally a psychiatrist or some other mental health professional, spends the first 20 minutes of the 90-minute session focusing on one particular aspect of the phobic process, i.e., dealing with anticipatory anxiety, goal-setting, handling setbacks. During the remainder of the session phobics discuss their accomplishments and disappointments of the previous week, with emphasis placed on learning to feel good about achievements, no matter how small. Family members or other support people are encouraged to attend and to participate in the group session.

The degree of support phobics receive from family members affects

Reprinted with permission from *Learning Theory Approaches to Psychiatry*, edited by J.C. Boulougouris, New York: Wiley, 1982.

the outcome of treatment. In a recent study of 18 agoraphobic married women (3), it was found that overcoming phobias often causes severe marital problems because neurotic symptoms can cement a marriage; when the mental health of one spouse improves, the relationship between the partners sometimes deteriorates. Hardy, however, observed over 100 couples in his agoraphobic treatment program and concludes that, regardless of personality type, spouses who participate in treatment are less resistant and more willing to accept change in their mate and also to make changes in themselves (4).

The supported exposure approach emphasizes the seriousness of phobic fear, focusing on it as a real, severe experience which is not imagined by phobics and is not the same as the "fears" of non-phobics. This enables both phobics and family members to see the phobia as a real handicap rather than something to feel guilty or judgmental about. Thus, it becomes a shared problem which can be overcome by hard work and which can produce pride rather than shame. Prior to treatment, family members often try to cover up and excuse or to blame phobics for the disability and inconvenience. During treatment they are taught to encourage, support and celebrate. When neurotic patterns get in the way, these, too, are approached as practical problems to be overcome with the support of the group. Family members are not made to feel guilty for undermining the phobic's progress. Instead, they are made aware of their behavior and shown how to be supportive by changing it. By including non-phobic family members in the group sessions, the non-supportive family members learn how to become supportive and the supportive, but ineffective, family members learn how to become effective.

HELPING THE SUPPORT PERSON BECOME EFFECTIVE

Feelings of shame and embarrassment about asking for help and/or appearing foolish often lead phobics to hide their anxiety and, yet, at the same time, to expect others who are close to them to be "sensitive enough" to realize they are experiencing difficulties. Rarely does phobic anxiety manifest itself externally (5); therefore, phobics have to be taught to take responsibility for letting others know when they are having a problem. Rather than passively waiting for a family member to initiate support and then becoming angry and disappointed when it is not given, phobics are taught to say, "I am feeling phobic and would like your help." It is important for phobics to be able to tell the person who is helping them exactly what is helpful and what is not. At times phobics need to be held or talked to; at other times they want to do the holding or talking and sometimes they want to be left alone. The support person has to understand that these inconsistencies in needs have to do with the nature of the phobia and should not take them as a personal rejection.

Much of the anxiety phobics experience involves their fear of loss of control (6). To be able to enter into the phobic situation, phobics need to feel in control of themselves and of their environment, including everyone around them. The more control phobics feel they have over the situation, the less they feel trapped and thus less anxious. The nonphobic might ask, "What would you like me to do to help you feel more comfortable?" and not act offended or put out by the reply. Phobics are taught to tell the family member exactly what would be reassuring, even if the request is irrational. For example, a young woman who was afraid of going into high buildings for fear she would lose control and jump out of the window asked her boyfriend to reassure her that if she did lose control, he would knock her out so she would not be in any danger of hurting herself. They both knew how absurd this request really was, but having this reassurance enabled the woman to go up to the top floor and remain there long enough to see that her feared reactions would not happen.

Phobics always need an "out" and it is helpful to decide with the family member what this will be prior to entering the phobic situation. For example, if a person is hesitant to go into a crowded theater for fear of panicking and having to leave, the family member might suggest, "Let's get tickets and go with the understanding that if you wish to leave at any time you may, even if it is in the middle of the performance, and that I will leave with you." This is difficult to say because the support person is often afraid that this kind of leniency perpetuates the phobia. However, just knowing that a way out is an option enables phobics to enter phobic situations. Once they are confident that they are not trapped and trust that their family member would leave without being critical, it becomes easier to enter into the feared situation.

As phobics begin to get better, they experience concern about what will be expected of them now that they have demonstrated that they can do the things which they were previously unable to do (7). It is helpful for them to express this concern to the person helping them. For example, the phobic might ask the helper, "Since I did the shopping today, will you expect me to do it all the time?" or, "If I drive to the party tonight, will I have to drive home?" or, "If I go up in the elevator, can I walk down the steps if I want to?" The family member should assure the phobic that there are no additional expectations and should help the phobic to focus on the present. When phobics do not feel the pressure to perform, they are more likely to enter into and remain in feared situations.

Family members often cannot understand that phobics may be able to do something with a stranger, their phobia therapist, and yet not be able to do the same thing with them. This increases the family members' frustration and doubt regarding the intensity of the phobic's fear, which causes the phobic to become more defensive and withdrawn. The thought that there is an expectation to perform and that there will be judgment raises phobic's anxiety level, which perpetuates phobic thinking and decreases willingness to confront the phobic situation. It is common for phobics to do the same task several times with little or no discomfort and then suddenly feel paralyzed and unable to proceed. The phobia therapist understands this and explains it to the phobic. The family member, however, sees it as an indication of the phobic's inadequacy. In order to be helpful, the supportive family member must convince the phobic that support will be provided irrespective of whether the phobic completes the task.

THE ROLE OF THE FAMILY MEMBER DURING THE PRACTICE SESSION

The supported exposure approach involves encouraging phobics to take two steps forward while allowing them to take one step back. The family member often asks, "When am I being supportive and when am I being too pushy?" This fine line is illustrated in the following hypothetical conversation between a phobic person (PP) and an effective, supportive family member (FM). The phobic's goal in this practice session was to drive two blocks.

PP: I really don't think I can do it today.
FM: How about if we just get into the car and you turn on the ignition?
PP: Okay, but that's all I can do. I'm too scared.
(PP and FM enter car. PP turns on ignition.)
FM: How about just driving to the end of the block?
PP: No way.
FM: Can you just go to the end of the driveway?
PP: I don't know. I feel so silly. OK, I'll try.
(PP drives to end of driveway.)
FM: Good. Now, let's go to the end of the first house.
PP: I can't. What if I panic and lose control?

FM: Stay in the present. Are you panicking now? Notice that your hands are firmly on the wheel, that your feet are where they belong and that you are functioning perfectly well. Remember, your feelings are frightening, but not dangerous. You won't do anything you don't want to do.

PP: What if I get onto the road and want to run out of the car?

FM: That's OK. I'll take over the wheel.
(PP takes deep breath and drives to end of the first house.)

PP: I can't believe I did it, but it's really no big deal.

FM: It's terrific and it is a big deal. A few minutes ago you didn't think you could drive at all and now you have driven. Let's go three more houses and then you can turn back.

PP: I can't do that.

FM: You didn't think you could get this far and you did. You're OK.

PP: OK, three more houses and that's all. Keep talking to me.
(PP goes three more houses.)

PP: I'm scared. I want to go back. You promised.

FM: OK. We'll go back, Try to count to 20 first (allow anxiety to pass).
(PP counts to 20 and feels better. Still wants to go back. Does so and is immediately encouraged to move forward again. This time, goes directly to third house and is surprised at feeling comfortable. Looks carefully at FM for any indication of impatience. Sees look of support and encouragement. Continues on to end of block and then end of second block. Repeats whole process several times before ending session.)

The phobic person was able to achieve the goal and a sense of satisfaction because:

1) Specific goals were set.
2) Goals were approached one step at a time.
3) "Outs" were clearly defined and permitted.
4) Achievements were reinforced.
5) Progress, no matter how small, was acknowledged.
6) Patience and commitment were evident on the part of the family member, with no evaluative judgment.
7) Reality was tested.
8) Phobic let family member know exactly what would be helpful.
9) Phobic was encouraged to remain in situation until high anxiety level diminished, but was not forced or humiliated into staying.

10) Phobic was not made to feel weak and/or helpless.

Phobics have a hard time feeling good about their achievements, especially since phobias often develop in areas in which they previously had no difficulty. For example, a business executive who developed a fear of elevators found it difficult to get excited about going three floors in an elevator when he used to ride up and down all day without even thinking about it. It is critical, however, that every step forward, no matter how small, be acknowledged as progress and looked at relative to the beginning of treatment. The businessman's wife was instructed to help him realize that two weeks ago he was unable to go into the elevator at all and today he was able to go three floors. He was encouraged to feel proud of himself and not to feel inhibited about sharing his accomplishment with his wife and other family members.

CHANGING ROLES AS A RESULT OF TREATMENT

Prior to treatment phobics are preoccupied with phobic thinking, often to the extent that other emotions are ignored. Much of the time and energy of phobics is spent trying to avoid and manipulate people and situations which they fear will trigger a panic attack. Because they feel guilty for being so demanding and dependent, phobics often feel that they have no right to assert themselves in other areas. Thus, some emotional needs are ignored and the resulting frustration further perpetuates anxiety and adds strain to their relationships. During treatment, phobics are taught to increase their awareness of their emotional needs and to become more assertive. As this change takes place, the nonphobic family member often feels less needed, more threatened and confused, and sometimes attempts to keep the phobic passive and dependent.

Case I

Mrs. A had been unable to leave her house for nine years without her husband, who appeared to be very supportive. Following her eighth week of treatment and two successful shopping trips with her therapist, Mrs. A decided to attempt to go shopping on her own. She was so excited about being alone and not feeling panicky that she stayed in the store much longer than she had anticipated. When her husband came home from work and did not find her at home, as usual, he became frantic. When Mrs. A arrived home 20 minutes later, expecting Mr. A to be as excited as she was about her accomplishment, she was, instead, confronted with anger and hostility.

Comment

Clearly, Mr. A was frightened that something might have happened to his wife. During the following week's group session, it was suggested to Mrs. A that a phone call to her husband, explaining where she was and that she might be late, could have easily avoided the unpleasant situation and might have resulted in his sharing her excitement. It was further suggested that Mrs. A needed to recognize the potential effect the changes she was going through may have on her husband and the importance of her being aware of his feelings, as well as expecting him to be aware of hers.

Case II

Mrs. B had been housebound for three years and after nine weeks of treatment excitedly announced to her husband that she accepted a part-time job as a typist. Mr. B was outraged and threatened to "cut the wires" in her car if she tried to go to work. He argued that her "role" was to be home and take care of him and their children and not to be out working around other men all day.

Comment

During her next individual therapy session, it became obvious that part of Mr. B's reaction had to do with the way Mrs. B told him about her acceptance of a job. Rather than being honest and saying that, now that she was able to go out, she did not want to stay in the house all day and that she felt the need to do something for herself, Mrs. B told her husband that she was taking a job because they needed the money. Mr. B, a very proud and traditional man, interpreted this as her telling him he was not a good provider. This brought up many of his own insecurities and resulted in his feeling embarrassed and humiliated by the thought of his wife having to work. Once both partners became aware of this miscommunication, the issue was resolved. They decided to put the money Mrs. B earned into a special bank account and use it to take a vacation, something they had been unable to do previously because of her agoraphobia.

Case III (Relating to Children)

For 42 years Mrs. C had been phobic relative to elevators, driving, and thunderstorms. During a conversation with her eldest child, now 37 years old, Mrs. C mentioned that she was being treated for her phobias. Her daughter said she was shocked to find out her mother had suffered all these years. She had no idea. She then recalled being a youngster in grade school and feeling angry and neglected when there would be a rainstorm and all the mothers except hers would come to pick up their children. Mrs. C always seemed to be waiting for some delivery, cooking something on the stove, or having a headache. Her daughter remembered thinking that if her mother really loved her, she wouldn't make her walk home in the rain. Mrs. C, on the other hand, talked about the pain and guilt she felt when her fear of thunderstorms and driving was so great that even the thought of her loved ones walking home in the rain couldn't get her to confront her fears. She was too humiliated and embarrassed to ask her neighbors to pick up her children because, as is typical of phobics, Mrs. C was sure that if she did ask they would think she was crazy.

Comment

Mrs. C was afraid to tell her children the truth for fear they might "catch" the fear or that they might make fun of her. She now realized that the negative effect which this had on her relationship with her children was much more devastating than if she had told them the truth. Telling children of their parents' fears and how it affects their behavior may be less damaging than allowing the children to think they are unloved.

In relating to children, phobics are encouraged to explain the fear in terms of fears children can relate to, i.e., fear of the dark, the "bogey man," or strange noises. It should be explained that grown-ups are also sometimes afraid of things which they really do not have to be afraid of, and that things may be frightening to some people and not to others. This often helps children to understand their parents' fear, and to feel better about their own fears. Children are often much more accepting and tolerant than adults imagine and can be helpful to phobics if they are included in the practice sessions. Children can help set goals, participate in reality-testing exercises and help phobics find simple, manageable tasks that can help the phobics to focus on the present.

CONCLUSION

The amount of progress phobics make during treatment is often dependent upon the degree of support they receive from their spouse or other family members. By including these support people in the group sessions and teaching them how to become supportive, they are able to share the excitement of progress rather than feel left out and confused by the changes that may occur in their relationships as a result of treatment. It is important for phobics to realize that, even if family members are supportive, it is difficult for non-phobics to recognize when phobics are experiencing panic or for them to fully understand what phobic fear is like. Therefore, phobics are taught to take responsibility for letting others know when they are feeling phobic so they can get the help, support, and encouragement that are so vital to their progress.

REFERENCES

1. DuPont, R.L. *Profile of a phobia treatment program: first year results.* Paper presented at the 132nd annual meeting of the American Psychiatric Association. Chicago, Illinois, May 18, 1979.
2. Ross, J. *The use of former phobics in the treatment of phobias.* Paper presented at the 132nd annual meeting of the American Psychiatric Association. Chicago, Illinois, May 18, 1979.
3. Milton, F. and Hafner, J. The outcome of behavior therapy for agoraphobia in relation to marital adjustment. *Archives of General Psychiatry,* 36: 807-811, 1979.
4. Hardy, A.B. *The role of the spouse in the treatment of the agoraphobic patient.* Paper presented at the 132nd annual meeting of the American Psychiatric Association. Chicago, Illinois, May 18, 1979.
5. Zane, M.D. Contextual analysis and treatment of phobic behavior as it changes. *Am. Journal of Psychotherapy,* 32:338-356, 1978.
6. Marks, I. *Living with Fear.* New York: McGraw-Hill, 1978.
7. Weekes, C. *Simple Effective Treatment of Agoraphobia.* New York: Hawthorn Books, 1976.

5

An Integrative Approach to Agoraphobia: Centrum—A Model Program

Marvin R. Cohen

At the Centrum Phobia Clinic in Oak Park, Illinois, we have combined two historically opposite modalities of treatment, behavioral and psychodynamic, along with pharmacological intervention if necessary, in order to deal with the complex issues of the agoraphobic condition. The primary treatment modality for this integrative approach is the longer-term, process-oriented group therapy model.

The initial interview with a client consists of a diagnostic assessment and the gathering of a psychosocial history. A profile of present phobic responses is established, as well as developmental patterns of fear-avoidance behavior.

Behavioral strategies are used initially to aid the individual in attaining some immediate level of success in coping with space-distance fears. This is essential for building some degree of confidence, morale, and commitment to treatment. Mobility has often been severely restricted by years of avoidance behavior. Panic, the most disturbing symptom of agoraphobia, is a most powerful conditioner which needs only to occur infrequently in order to produce entrenched patterns of avoidance behavior. The difficulty in accomplishing tasks and fully moving about, which were formerly so much an ordinary and automatic part of the person's repertoire of everyday responses, spawns feelings of low self-confidence and diminished self-worth.

In all of our cases this inhibition of mobility is related to the individual's fear of panic in an environment felt to be unsafe, due to the distance from home or from a familiar person. The client's limitations in spatial movement prohibit the individual from entering shopping areas, interfere with work or job responsibilities, inhibit commitments where performance expectations are required, and, in general, narrow the individual's world to a circumscribed area of safety.

Early in treatment, specific areas and parameters of limitations are established so as to begin to design with the client a hierarchy of in vivo tasks which will gradually expose the individual to the phobic settings. Graduated levels of accomplishment, made up of in vivo goals and steps, become an ongoing process and are an intrinsic part of the group work. These steps progress from easily attainable (with some expected discomfort) to relatively more difficult tasks associated with higher fear levels.

Weekly in vivo homework assignments, progressively structured, are planned with the client, along with the individualized and group in-vivo field practice accompanied by the therapist. The sense of increased physical autonomy and independence enhances the individual's self-esteem and establishes a pattern of new responses. Our observation has been that, for optimal desensitization and integration of the in vivo experience, exposure must be gradual and each goal must be manageable and yet stimulate a moderately high arousal level in the individual. We also stress that duration of time in a moderate-to-high arousal setting is of greater treatment value than distance from safe object. It is the ability to deal with the internal pressure which allows for a general sense of confidence, and not the physical and mechanical conquering of every square of space. Space and distance are the media through which we work and not the actual goal. The goal is to begin to feel more confident in dealing with internal arousal levels. The in vivo tasks are established by the client with staff and group input. Group in vivo field trips are significant because of the modeling and supportive group behavior, which has a very positive effect in directly influencing the individual member's attempt to confront extremely phobic situations. Group exposure in outings also tends to increase group cohesiveness and intimacy through the mutual sharing of one's vulnerable self.

An inevitable and coexisting problem along with panic, a problem perpetuating the client's avoidance behavior, is anticipatory anxiety, which is triggered in most cases by the mere thought of venturing out. Anticipatory anxiety alone can inhibit movement and can be attenuated through group reassurance and encouragement, and by accustoming individuals to expect the presence of anxiety prior to and during an in vivo experience. Progress in in vivo experiences is contingent on dealing with anticipatory anxiety.

In order to aid the individual in confronting his fears in the real setting, coping strategies, that are mainly centered in cognitive restructuring and relaxation methods, are introduced to the client. These techniques, which vary in effectiveness, include educating the individual in recognizing secondary thought processes which generate multiple arousal stimulation, helping the person alter thoughts to positive and calming imagery, and diverting attention to positive cues in the immediate environment.

Another method employed to help an individual handle fear is to encourage him to monitor fear levels on a numerical rating from 1-10 while exposed to the phobic situation. This procedure, as Zane (1) has pointed out and which we have found to be extremely helpful, enables the agoraphobic to recognize the wave-like pattern of fear and panic, reassuring the individual that these seemingly uncontrollable emotions do have upper limits and do have falling as well as rising properties. Along with this, we encourage clients to allow the panicky feelings to arise and not attempt to fight back these feelings. Maintaining a lid on these emotions creates greater pressure, tension, and explosive-like sensations. For the patient, changing this behavior is extraordinarily difficult, given the desperate need for control which is endemic to the panic feeling itself. I often use the metaphor that, like a beachball held under water straining hard for the surface, suppressed panic builds in intensity, and pressure will decrease when the panic is allowed gradually to surface.

Along with this latter technique, relaxation and paradoxical intention methods are introduced to the client. Because the therapist is seldom in the phobic situation with the client to observe behavior and listen to expressed thoughts, we use a technique developed by Zane, in which agoraphobics use a tape recorder to record their experience while exposed to the phobic setting. These tapes are subsequently evaluated with the client to identify patterns of phobic thought and frightening imagery that tend to increase tension. Methods designed to help maintain thought in the manageable present and distract catastrophic imagery can then be discussed with the client.

I have observed that the tape recorder not only is a means of feeding information back to the therapist or group, but also effectively acts as an instrument of communication representing a connection with a comforting and empathic figure. This tends to help the individual feel less isolated when being exposed alone to the phobic setting, and it helps neutralize anxiety through the incorporation of positive imagery. In effect, the tape recorder acts as a transitional object imbued with a magic-like security function. The tape recorder becomes an extension of the safe and protective person or group, and is similar to the young child's need for transitional objects in order to function alone without mother's presence, bridging a very harrowing and significant passage of human development.

It is my impression that a great deal of the success attributed to coping strategies or techniques can be better understood in light of their associative and connective qualities with the safe object or person. Many of the tape recordings and process notes of in vivo experiences brought back to the group for evaluation are filled with comments and personal asides, as though the group members were present at the time as intimate listeners. This need of the agoraphobic to seek connectedness with the familiar objects, in order to experience inner security and avoid psychic separation, gives rise to theoretical considerations described later in this chapter. It is important here to point out that in the use of behavioral and relearning techniques, one should not underestimate the significance of the positive association to the therapist, or in some cases, to the group itself. It may be that the positive imagery and associations connected with the coping or communication method may be of greater therapeutic benefit than the method or technique itself.

With continued involvement in the treatment program, higher levels of anticipatory anxiety and fear appear as the patient begins to challenge the more difficult space-distance endeavors, especially if unaccompanied by a companion. Also, the high expectations and suggestive or placebo effect of the new program wane in light of the realistic demands, often exhausting, of continuously confronting the phobic stimuli. Periodically during treatment sustained high levels of discomfort and panic, seemingly washing away future possibilities and past gains, can create a plateau effect. It is important to stress throughout the program that setbacks are a phenomenon endemic to the deconditioning process and that acceptance and tolerance of these setbacks are necessary for therapeutic change to take place. The polarization of thought around failure and success creates a sense of being on a fragile tightrope which, if not perfectly traversed, is disastrous. This kind of thinking is the prototype of phobogenic thought. An empathic understanding of the discouragement and frustration around setbacks and the fear of taking another step must be combined with firm encouragement and planned structuring around new in vivo goals. In reiteration, it is important to understand that we are not only deconditioning fear of a situation, but also helping a person deal with relatively high internal arousal levels while using the setting as the medium.

Of great help to the agoraphobic is the group support and positive reinforcement around each step gained. We have found the group to be a powerful therapeutic tool in reducing the individual's isolation, enhancing member gratification of accomplishments, stimulating efforts through modeling and ways of handling new situations, and providing a forum for the sharing of mutual experiences.

At the Centrum Clinic we have found that long-term systematic desensitization in vivo, as an essential part of the ongoing group work, allows for the gradual integration of spatial ability, as well as helping the individual to internalize a more positive and constructive attitude regarding the phobic condition. However, we must also recognize the existence of psychological motive behind behavior and that behavior is not just a haphazard pattern of conditioned responses. The interpersonal dynamic is a determining force in the structuring of personality and ultimately affects the way an individual responds to his or her environment. These issues need to be addressed. My theoretical model is based within an object relations framework, placing the roots of the agoraphobic syndrome within the first three years of life, or what Mahler (2) describes as the separation-individuation phase of development. I am particularly interested in the 15th to 24th month of life, Mahler's rapprochement phase, because of its similarity to the adult agoraphobic syndrome.

During this process of psychological growth, rapid development of cognitive and motor functions enables the child to become aware of movement and distancing, along with the realization of his own separateness from mother. This revelation goes to the roots of the child's security system, causing extreme feelings of separation anxiety. An acute vigilance with focused and, at times, frantic concern regarding mother's whereabouts is demonstratively observable. Mahler emphasizes that the mother's support of the child's exploratory behavior, plus her emotional availability as a need-satisfier in reducing anxiety and enabling the child to internalize a sense of inner security, are of critical importance to the normal development of more independent functioning.

If a disturbance occurs in the child-mother relationship during this early and critical stage of life when the mother is realized as separate and having her own self-integrity, the child will experience a grave ambivalence and will have a great difficulty in broaching the psychological process of differentiation and separation. This disturbance interferes with a basic necessity of human psychological growth, or what

Hartmann (3) has described as object constancy, the ability to maintain an image of the mothering object in her absence, leading to an internalized sense of well-being.

There is evidence to indicate that the adult agoraphobic experienced trauma in early childhood interfering with the process of development leading to object constancy, such as the loss of a significant person, a sudden emotional decathexis by mother, an entrapment by mother's overly dependent or possessive needs and ensuing fears of being alone, or the presence of severe ambivalence on the part of one or both parents. The phobic-depersonalization syndrome in adulthood, characterized by the agoraphobic's fear-panic response when venturing away from a safe place or securing person, can be viewed as paradigmatic of the disturbance in the child-parent relationship and of the child's ensuing feelings of disconnection and disruption during the critical individuation stage of psychological growth.

The dynamic part of our treatment approach stemming from object relations theory postulates that the adult agoraphobic syndrome represents a primary interpersonal disorder, with roots in the rapprochement period of development. We view the initial sudden onset of panic occurring while alone and under stress as reestablishing the intrapsychic self-object separation crisis and separation-autonomy conflicts. The original interpersonal disturbance preventing object constancy is played out in adulthood in the external physical arena of pan-phobic responses. The agoraphobic disorder is not only a fear of leaving or of being left, but an intense anxiety around psychic separation, a morbid existential concern with a disconnectedness from the primary comforting other. Because of this early interpersonal disturbance, a pattern of behavior develops which is largely motivated by the unconscious need to maintain a bond with a parent figure or symbolic substitute. This behavior does not stem from isolated needs, but is symptomatic of a characterological structure designed to repress experience associated with the individual's aggressive and assertive feelings. This repression is in the service of maintaining a connectedness with the securing significant objects by the vigilant mediating and placating of one's environment.

Patients in the group often describe feelings of inhibition and anxiousness, or even paralyzing caution (a feeling of constantly having to walk on egg shells), in discussing early relationships with one or both parents or present relationships with a spouse or partner. These feelings are often accompanied by a diffuse sense of guilt or wrongdoing, with a pressing need to make amends or placate the other, in order to avoid disturbing or alienating the perceived object of security.

The need for security from objects creates a need-hate ambivalence in relationships stemming from the original primary dyad. The anger and rage of the agoraphobic toward the object of dependency are internalized as a chronic sense of self-disgust and shame. Treatment in the therapy group must also deal with these underlying issues of primary ego integrity involving conflicted emotions pertaining to loss, separateness and self-esteem. Helping the individual to identify and express these emotions is important because it goes to the heart of the interpersonal conflict, the avoidance of feelings which, if acknowledged and communicated, would provoke archaic fears of abandonment and annihilation. Because of the existential nature of the fear, it is of particular importance that the therapist's responses be empathic, accepting, and noncontrolling and that the therapist convey an emotional availability as the individual begins to deal with conflicted space-distance and interpersonal issues.

Validation and support in the group through evolving stages of intimacy provide the agoraphobic with positive mirroring experiences which appear to help neutralize anxiety and intrapsychic tension, enabling the individual to begin to internalize a sense of greater inner security. Fragmented experiences and feelings—split-off, polarized, and avoided—can gradually become expressed and a more integrated part of the self through the validation and acceptance by the group. Only with this sense of the group as "safe object" will the individual begin to reality-test perceived dangers inherent in the direct expression of inner experiences, thereby dealing with the interpersonal phobia, as well as confronting more symbolic space-distance fears. This process of internalizing the group as a securing image is an essential goal of treatment and a major factor necessitating a relatively long-term group experience.

With an increased sense of security, more material related to significant and object-dependent figures will come up in the group. Initially these figures are portrayed as model supportive persons, while the client's self-portrayal is of an ineffectual partner. With the surfacing of repressed material, the individual begins gradually to share with the group conflicted and ambivalent feelings regarding these relationships. Feelings of dissatisfaction are expressed toward the partner's and family members' lack of responsiveness and understanding, and their inconsistent and "imperfect" responses. Anger, severe disappointment, and grief are emotions often observed with this realization. In time, individuals begin to vent angry feelings regarding the imperfect and insensitive responses of the therapist and the group itself. This is a major step for the agoraphobic because it implies a diminution of fear in expressing split-off and usually well-defended material and a willingness to risk group condemnation. The feelings of anger and disappointment can then be dealt with directly and emphatically within a safe therapeutic context.

Inevitably, the individual begins to become aware of the placating and submissive nature of the involvement in relationships in exchange for security from the needed object. It becomes evident that placating behavior and suppressive defenses take on a pattern that telescopes back historically in the person's life. The agoraphobic adult in childhood and adolescence was often seen as a "model child" or "model pupil," precociously adult-like in demeanor. This behavior is often mistaken for healthy development rather than compensation for deep-seated feelings of insecurity and a basic attempt to maintain connectedness with the maternal figure.

In adulthood the placating behavior often serves to reduce or postpone conflicts around separation in the individual's marriage or relationship. But then conflict is experienced between the need to secure the dependent relationship and the wish for autonomy. The result is often a feeling of resentment and ambivalence toward the partner or object of dependency. This ambivalence is experienced as a fear of entrapment, an apprehension around object attachments. Any commitment to a relationship or any situation representing phobic safety (a partner, a house, or a job) can become established as a phobic cue stimulating habitual fears of separation. The wish to experience one's autonomous self is countered by archaic feelings associated with separation and object loss and a morbid uncertainty as to whether the individual can function without an outer auxiliary ego. The active need to experience this sense of separateness and independence is often underestimated and unappreciated by those close to the individual, including professionals, because it is so well covered by phobic thought and behavior. It must be recalled that Mahler's toddlers actively initiated the movement away from mother as though there is innate motivation to autonomously extend one's boundaries. This movement is quite natural unless inhibited by the early interpersonal disturbance.

The autonomy-attachment or wish-fear dilemma is often unconscious, especially early in treatment. We see in our clients a nagging and chronic discontent with themselves or vague generalized feelings of entrapment. This inner conflict is often manifested either by an open ambivalence to making a commitment to the group or an overzealous enthusiasm masking resistance to change. Recognition and expression of walled-off affect, whether within the group context or with the individual's family and/or social environment, disrupts a delicate pattern of being, designed to maintain external protection. To become angry—to bare one's assertive, aggressive, and competitive nature—risks the vengeance of and disillusion with those figures relied on for survival. Competitive statements and comments directed toward significant figures are quickly retracted, minimized, or apologized away as a rush of guilt is felt. This guilt signals to the person that his or her excessive boldness in expression has disrupted that delicate balance, placing the individual in danger of severance by angering those who have the power to leave the agoraphobic in isolation—the same frightening isolation experienced in the multitude of space-distance phobic settings.

A primary task in the group is for the individual to confront the interpersonal phobia, i.e., the morbid fear of exposing one's inner experiences and feelings, thereby risking rejection and ultimate abandonment. The therapist's task in the group is to help identify and interpret patient responses and resistance patterns that germinate from archaic fears and to communicate a sense of availability while encouraging some risk-taking in efforts toward greater non-phobic and autonomous functioning. Through this process of reality testing we have observed the client gradually begin to experience an increased sense of security, greatly enhancing ego functioning and strengthening ego boundaries. This is reflected in decreased inhibition of direct and assertive expression of feelings within the group as well as with the spouse and family, a more active participation in the group with increased receptivity to listening and empathy, and a greater facility to differentiate and separate out one's own inner experience without the intrusion of falsely perceived expectations of others.

The integrative approach emanating from object relations theory allows for a frame of reference within which the observation, understanding, and treatment of patient behavior is on a multidimensional level. Patterns of responses can be evaluated and treated with greater specificity in light of symbolic space-distance, intrapsychic self-object, and interpersonal issues.

CONCLUSION

The Centrum Phobia Clinic in its treatment of agoraphobia utilizes an integrative approach. We combine behavioral techniques, principally gradual exposure in vivo, with a long-term group therapy modality. Both space-distance goals and psychodynamic and interpersonal material are discussed and processed in the group.

The program's theoretical consideration is couched in object relations theory postulating that a disturbance in the child-mother relationship in the separation-individuation phase of early development inhibits the internalization of secure and autonomous ego functioning. This disturbance in the young child causes grave concern around psychological separation and extreme ambivalence regarding space-distance movement from the mothering object. It is thought that the adult agoraphobic's space-distance fear-panic response is symbolic of this early interpersonal conflict.

The space-distance panic disturbance reflects the core pathology, a fear of psychological separation from a significant object, and is rooted in the pathogenesis of the original interpersonal experience. Fear and avoidance of acknowledging and expressing a part of one's inner experience and feelings occur, in order to preserve what is perceived as a very fragile connectedness with the securing object. It is of prime importance to work with both the space-distance fear and the interpersonal phobia. The long-term nature of the therapy group allows for the development of the psychodynamic and interpersonal process, as well as the establishment, through behavioral means, of patterns of responses leading to increased autonomy of movement.

REFERENCES

1. Zane, M. Contextual analysis and treatment of phobic behavior as it changes. *American Journal of Psychotherapy,* 32: 338-356 1978.
2. Mahler, M.S. On the significance of the normal separation-individuation phase: with reference to research in symbiotic child psychosis. In: *Drives, Affects, and Behavior,* Schur, M., Ed., 2: 161, New York: International Universities Press, 1965.
3. Hartmann, H. The mutual influences in the development of ego and id. *Psychoanalytic Study Child,* 7: 9, 1952.

PART II

Alternative Treatment Approaches

These two chapters describe alternative treatments for the phobic person. The first, and more important, is the chapter by Charlotte Marker Zitrin, entitled "Combined Psychological and Pharmacological Approach to the Treatment of Phobias." This chapter, written by one of the pioneers in the psychopharmacological approach to the treatment of phobias, not only outlines the therapeutic approach of the use of antidepressant drugs such as imipramine in the treatment of phobias, but also clearly states the need to integrate this pharmacological approach within the context of the supported exposure treatment. While many in the field generally do not express enthusiasm for the use of minor tranquilizers or antianxiety drugs such as Valium in the treatment of phobias, there is considerable support for the use of antidepressants in selected patients who are failing to respond to the supported exposure approach alone. This chapter by Dr. Zitrin presents in a readable and yet highly scientific fashion the results of a series of important research studies.

Jane Miller's excellent chapter, "Phobics of Branford," outlines the treatment of phobic people in a public mental health center in a small town. Provision of services through public facilities and especially in smaller communities has been one of the most important unmet needs of phobic people in recent years.

6

Combined Psychological and Pharmacological Approach to the Treatment of Phobias

Charlotte Marker Zitrin

In order to understand the rationale for combining psychological and pharmacological treatment in certain phobias, one must first understand the two main types of phobic disorders.

The first type consists of those patients who have panic attacks that come "out of the blue." We have called these "spontaneous" panics because they do not seem to be caused by any discernible stimuli. That doesn't mean that the stimuli aren't there, just that we do not know what they are. These panic attacks, patients tell us, come without any warning and not necessarily in phobic situations. They can come any place, any time. Some people experience them even at home, for no apparent reason.

Patients who experience spontaneous panic attacks are divided into two groups. The first consists of agoraphobic patients, who have severe travel restrictions, that is, great difficulty in travelling away from home, especially alone. The second group consists of mixed phobics, who are like agoraphobics in that they have spontaneous panics, but are like simple phobics in that they have discrete phobias, for example, claustrophobia or acrophobia.

Typically, the illness starts with one or more spontaneous panics. A common story from patients is that they were feeling fine when, one day, without any warning, while driving the car or in a store or walking on the street they suddenly experienced a severe panic attack. The attack usually consists of palpitations, difficulty in breathing, sweating, sometimes dizziness, sometimes nausea or an urge to urinate or defecate and a feeling of impending doom, which is terrifying. The panic attack is the first stage of this disorder. As a result of this panic attack or a series of panic attacks, patients begin to fear going into the situations where they have experienced them, or in which they expect to experience them.

This leads to the second stage of the illness, the stage of anticipatory anxiety. An example of this type of anxiety is seen in people who fear flying but know they must take a plane trip in several days. As they think about it, they start to get "nervous." The nervousness or anxiety increases more and more as D-day approaches, in anticipation of the trip. The longer the interval between knowledge of the trip and actual embarkation, the greater the anticipatory anxiety on the day of the trip. In some people, this leads to the third stage, that of phobic avoidance.

At first, patients avoid places in which they have experienced panic. Rather rapidly, they begin to avoid more and more places that become associated in their minds with the possibility of a panic attack and their lives become increasingly circumscribed. Thus, the phenomenon of phobic generalization has occurred. For example, if originally they were afraid to drive on highways, they later became afraid to drive on side roads five miles from home, then four, then one. Finally, they can drive only in the immediate neighborhood or perhaps they give up driving entirely. Initially, they may be afraid to go into large, crowded stores. This soon spreads to large stores at any time, then to medium-sized stores, and finally they may be unable to enter any store. Often, these patients can tolerate going into these situations if they are accompanied by someone they feel they can trust to take care of them, like their spouse or another close family member. Some patients, who cannot go out of the house alone, can go anywhere if accompanied.

The other main group of phobics are the simple phobics. These patients do not experience inexplicable panic attacks. They have panic attacks only when confronting phobic situations. For example, if they are afraid of flying, the only time they will have a panic attack is when they are actually about to board a plane. If they are afraid of heights, the only time they panic is when they are in that situation or about to enter it. Thus, their lives are not circumscribed by their phobias; they function well and lead relatively normal lives.

Simple phobics are afraid of a specific situation, whereas the agoraphobic and mixed phobic patients, who experience spontaneous panics, are more afraid of getting a panic attack then the specific situation. Naturally, the situations become associated in their minds with the panic attacks, leading to fear of those situations, but their primary fear is of the panics. Interestingly, agoraphobics with spontaneous panics have good days and bad days. On good days, they often can go into many more situations than on bad days. They also tend to have remissions or partial remissions and exacerbations of their symptoms. We don't know why these occur but there are indications that, in some patients, internal stimuli may trigger panics which, in turn, may cause an exacerbation of phobic symptoms.

We do know that some patients have vulnerabilities that may predispose them to the development of phobias. For example, we found a high incidence of separation anxiety during childhood and we believe that this may be a predisposing factor. In addition to the predisposition, often there is a precipitating stress. We have found a fairly high incidence of mitral valve prolapse in agoraphobic women. We also have found that about 10% became phobic within a year of developing hyperthyroidism. Both of these groups experience palpitations as part of their physical illness. In a vulnerable person, it is possible that palpitations will precipitate a panic attack, particularly if the cause of the palpitations is unknown at the time. Another large group of our patients became symptomatic following a loss, either real or imagined, in their lives. There may be other internal stimuli, both psychological and physiological, that trigger panic attacks, but further study is required to investigate this.

We have found that, in those patients with spontaneous panic attacks, tricyclic antidepressant drugs are effective in blocking the panic. The original drug on which this observation was made is imipramine (1) and it is this drug that we have used in our studies. Subsequently, monoamine oxidase (MAO) inhibitors were also found to be effective (2, 3).

I am going to describe results of three studies on the combined psychological and pharmacological treatment of phobias. The first is one that compared treatments in agoraphobic, mixed phobic and simple phobic patients (4, 5).

EXPERIMENTAL DESIGN OF FIRST STUDY

Patients were grouped according to diagnosis. Each diagnostic group was divided, by random selection, into one of three treatment groups: behavior therapy + imipramine; behavior thearpy + placebo; supportive psychotherapy + imipramine. Supportive therapy was a control for behavior therapy. The behavior therapy groups were double-blind for drug condition (i.e., neither patient nor therapist knew whether patient was getting drug or placebo). Supportive therapy was single-blind for drug condition (i.e., patients did not know whether they were receiving drug or placebo). Behavior therapy consisted of systematic desensitization, assertiveness training, and in vivo homework assignments. Supportive psychotherapy was dynamically oriented and nondirective.

Our prediction was that agoraphobic patients would behave like mixed phobic patients in all treatment conditions, since both of these groups have spontaneous panic attacks. We predicted that in these two groups, behavior therapy with imipramine would be superior to behavior therapy with placebo, because the drug would block the panics. Further, we predicted that behavior therapy would be superior to supportive therapy, because it focuses systematically on phobic situations and is more structured toward helping patients to confront these situations.

In simple phobics, who do not experience spontaneous panics, we did not think that the drug would have any value and therefore predicted that behavior therapy with imipramine would be equivalent to behavior therapy with placebo. We also predicted that behavior therapy would be superior to supportive psychotherapy for the reasons given above.

Table 1 is a summary of patients' characteristics. Note that there are many more females than males in the agoraphobic and simple phobic groups (about 70% to 30%). The mean age at evaluation is 33-35 years. Simple phobics have a significantly longer duration of illness because their phobias usually start in childhood, whereas the others start in adolescence or early adult life. The simple phobics also have significantly more education than the other groups. Perhaps this is because they haven't been so compromised by their phobias.

Table 2 illustrates the dropout rate in the different groups. There are no significant differences among groups with regard to dropouts, but the reasons for dropping out are of interest. Most of the dropouts refused medication, even though some of them were on placebo. (The latter complained of medication side effects.) These patients tend to be afraid of medication and some of them are medication sensitive.

Figure 1 shows a page of the Wolpe-Lang Fear Inventory. There was a total of 102 fears which were to be checked off in one of the columns, from "none" to "terror."

Medication Effects

Imipramine is a tricyclic drug, used extensively as an antidepressant. In 1962, Klein (1) found that it blocked the spontaneous panics of phobic patients. That led to its use in this study. We start with 25 mg per day, which is a low dose, and increase it gradually up to 150 mg or more, if panic attacks do not subside. The maximum dose is 300 mg. We soon discovered that about 20% of our phobic patients are exquisitely sensitive to imipramine. When we start medication, some patients will call the next day or the day after and say, "I'm flying, I can't sleep, I feel very nervous and jittery, I'm all wound up and have a tremendous amount of energy." Those who have taken amphetamines before say, "It's as if I am taking an amphetamine" or, "It's like taking dexedrine." In short, the drug has a stimulant effect. With these very sensitive patients, we decrease the dose to 10 mg, and, if 10 mg is still bothersome, we go down to 5 mg or even less. Amazingly, these patients respond to the

Table 1
Patient Characteristics

	Agoraphobic ($n=46$)	Mixed ($n=25$)	Simple phobic ($n=40$)	Total ($n=111$)
Sex				
Male (%)	24	48	28	31
Female (%)	76	52	72	69
Age at screening (yr)				
Mean	37	34	34	35
Range	22–46	23–46	20–47	20–47
Marital status				
Never married (%)	6	20	15	13
Married (%)	78	76	78	77
Remarried (%)	6	4	5	5
Separated, divorced, or widowed (%)	9	0	2	5
Education				
Mean number of years	13.4	14.8	14.8	14.2
College graduate or beyond (%)	22	60	50	41
Less than college graduate (%)	88	40	50	59
Duration of illness				
Mean (yr)	10.8	11.6	14.9	12.4
Range	1.5–35 yr	11 mo–38 yr	8 mo–34 yr	8 mo–38 yr
Prior treatment for phobia				
% Patients who had prior Rx	74	60	40	59
Mean duration of Rx for these	3.03 yr	1.9 yr	1.5 yr	2.4 yr
Range, duration of Rx	1 mo–8 yr	2 mo–4 yr	2 mo–6 yr	1 mo–8 yr

Table 2
Dropout Rate by Treatment Group and Diagnosis

Diagnosis	Supportive Rx-imipramine	Behavior Rx-imipramine	Behavior Rx-placebo	All imipramine
Agoraphobic				
Number of dropouts	4	4	2	8
Number completed	13	14	19	27
% Dropouts	24	22	9	23
Mixed phobic				
Number of dropouts	4	3	4	7
Number completed	7	9	9	16
% Dropouts	36	25	31	30
Simple phobic				
Number of dropouts	5	6	2	11
Number completed	7	15	18	22
% Dropouts	42	29	10	33

Figure 1

The items in this questionnaire refer to things and experiences that may cause fear, nervousness, or anxiety. Place a check mark in the column that describes how much it disturbs you.

	None	Very Little	A Little	Some	Much	Very Much	Terror
1. Sharp objects							
2. Being a passenger in a car							
3. Dead people							
4. Suffocating							
5. Failing a test							
6. Being a passenger in an airplane							
7. Worms							
8. Arguing with parents							
9. Rats, mice							
10. Life after death							
11. Hypodermic needles							
12. Roller coasters							
13. Death							
14. Crowded places							
15. Blood							
16. Heights							
17. Being a leader							
18. Swimming alone							
19. Illness							
20. Stores							
21. Illness or injury to loved ones							
22. Driving a car							

very small doses. Some of them can never tolerate more than 10 mg per day, yet their panic attacks subside.

We had a 26-week course of therapy (one session weekly) and Table 3 illustrates that most of the therapeutic benefit occurred in the latter half of treatment. Note that at the midpoint (13th session) very few patients are markedly improved whereas, at the final session, almost half or over half, depending on the rater, are markedly improved, that is, virtually symptom-free.

Figure 2 is a graph showing patient ratings of global improvement, according to an analysis of variance. For agoraphobic and mixed phobic patients, the imipramine-treated groups, i.e., supportive therapy + imipramine (ST-1) and behavior therapy + imipramine (BT-1), do equally well, whereas the placebo groups (BR-P) show significantly worse results. On the other hand, in the simple phobic group, there are no significant differences among the three treatment conditions.

Figure 3 is a graph of patient improvement ratings shown as a percentage of overall improvement, divided between marked and moderate improvement. (The portion of each bar below the horizontal line is moderate improvement and the portion above the bar is marked improvement.) In agoraphobic and mixed phobic patients, imipramine groups are significantly more improved than placebo groups, even though placebo groups show good improvement (67-85% moderately or markedly improved). Further, more patients are markedly improved in the imipramine than in the placebo groups. In simple phobics, there are no significant differences between imipramine and placebo or between supportive therapy and behavior therapy.

Table 3
Comparison of Global Ratings at 13th Session and at Completion of Treatment

	Therapist's rating (n=111)		Independent evaluator's rating (n=86)[b]		Patient's rating (n=111)	
	13th session	Final session	13th session	Final session	13th session	Final session
% Marked improvement	2	45	3	42	18	54
% Moderate improvement	45	40	42	28	51	32
% Minimal + no improvement	53	15	55	30	30	14

[b]The independent evaluator's ratings at 13 weeks were discontinued after the first two years of data collection, since the pattern with respect to rate of progress appeared clearly established.

Figure 4 shows therapist ratings at baseline and endpoint. These are analyses of covariance, with the baseline as covariate. Again, there is considerable improvement at the endpoint in all groups. Note that ago-

Figure 2

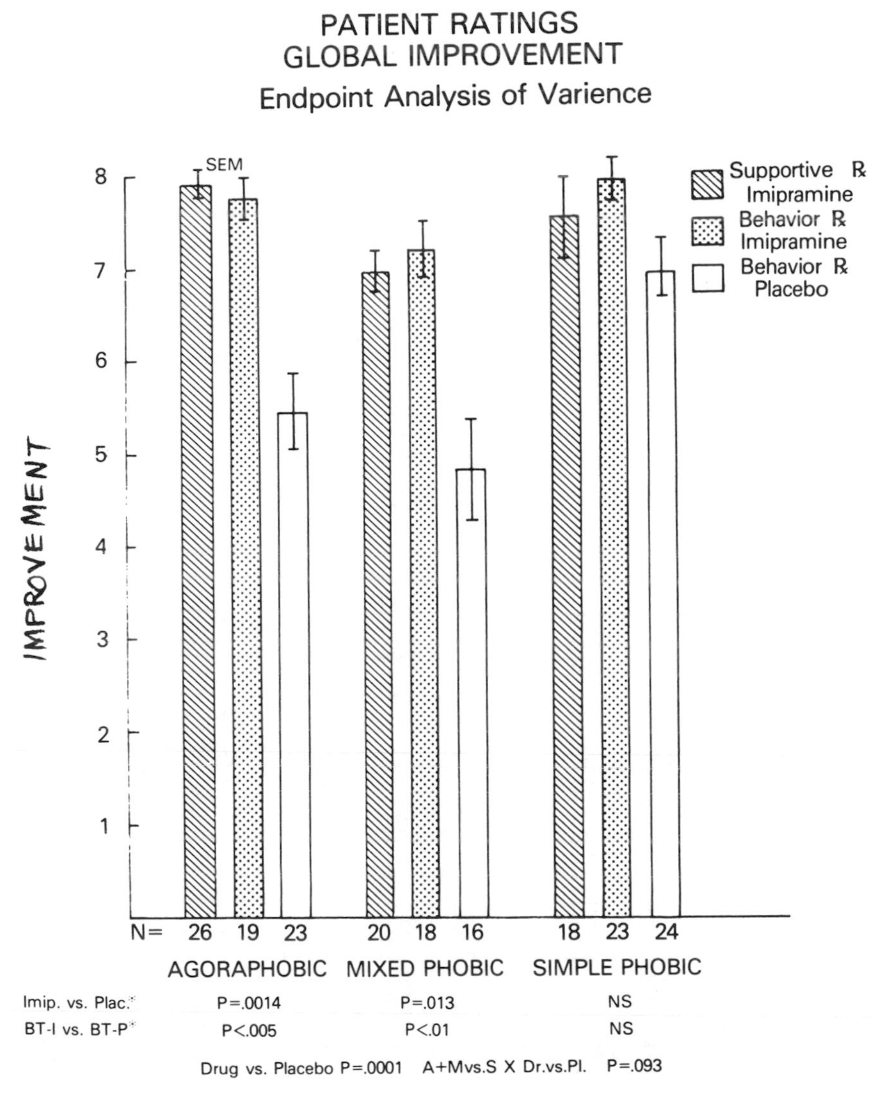

Figure 3

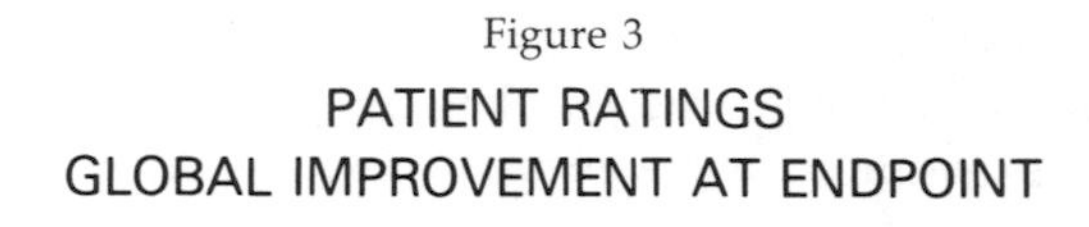

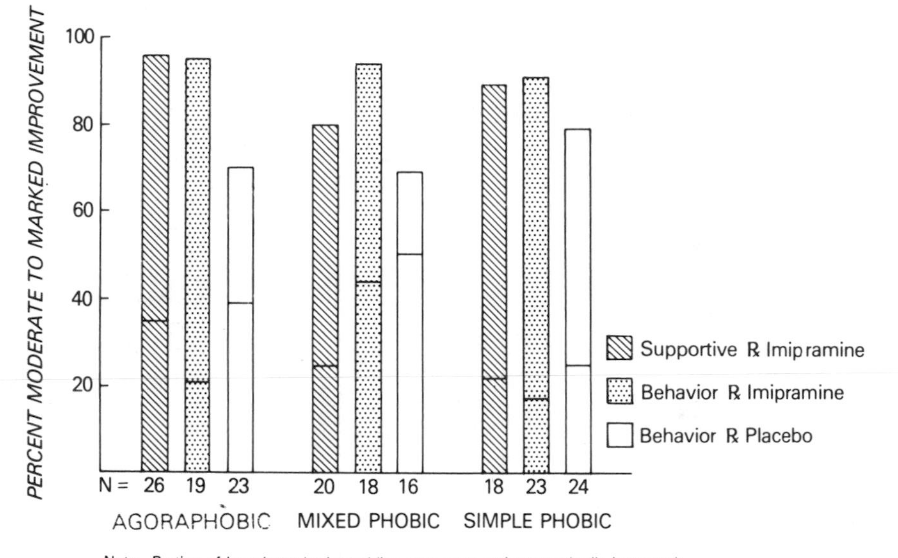

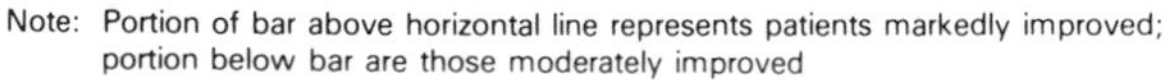

Figure 4

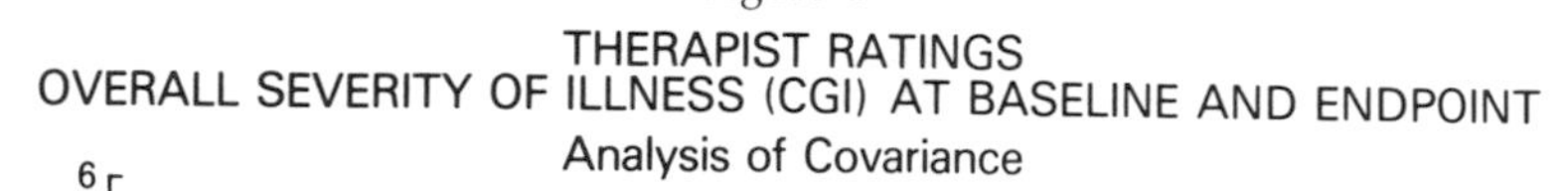

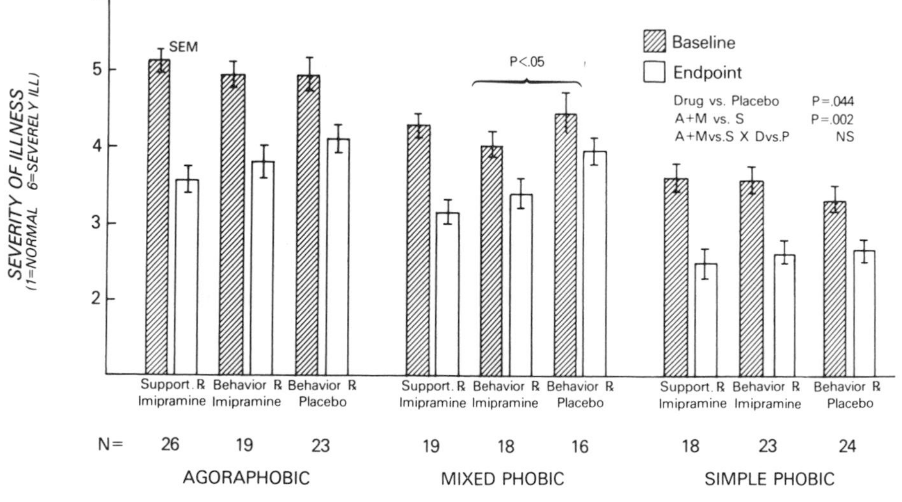

Table 4
Patient Ratings
Acute Panic Inventory

Analysis of Covariance for Drug Effect (Behavior Rx- Imipramine vs. Behavior Rx- Placebo)
Probability Values for Significant Variables

	Drug x Diagnosis Analysis				Within Diagnosis Analysis					
	*Drug Main Effect		*Drug x Diagnosis Interaction		*Agoraphobics		*Mixed Phobics		**Simple Phobics	
	C	E	C	E	C	E	C	E	C	E
Frequency of anxiety attacks in past month	—	<.05	—	—	<.0025	<.0025	—	—	—	—
Frequency of anxiety attacks in past month compared to previous month	<.005	<.01	—	—	<.005	<.025	—	—	—	—
Severity of anxiety attacks in past month compared to previous month	<.00025	<.0025	<.05	—	<.00025	<.025	<.01	<.01	—	—

Note: C = completer analyses, E = endpoint analysis; dash indicates not significant;
*p values in this column are one – tailed
** p values in this column are two – tailed

Table 5
Therapist and Independent Evaluator Ratings—Completer Analysis of Covariance

	P VALUES—one tailed	
	Drug Effect	Interaction*
Therapist (N=170)	.014	NS
Clinical Global Imp. - Status	.034[a]	.002
Phobia I - Improvement	.023[a]	NS
"Spontaneous" Panic	.023	.013
Acute Panic related to Phobia	.007	
Independent Evaluator (N=156)	.024	.01
Clinical Global Imp. - Status	.008	.047
Phobia I - Improvement	.043	NS
"Spontaneous" Panic	NS	NS
Acute Panic related to Phobia		

* Agoraphobic + mixed vs. simple x drug vs. placebo
[a] NS on endpoint analysis

Table 6
Therapist and Independent Evaluator Ratings

Behavior Therapy—Impiramine vs. Behavior Therapy-Placebo
Completer Analysis of Covariance—Dunnett T Test

	P VALUES—one tailed		
	Agoraphobic	Mixed Phobic	Simple Phobic
Therapist			
Clinical Global Imp. - Status	NS	<.01	NS
Phobia I - Improvement	<.05[a]	<.05[a]	NS
"Spontaneous" Panic	<.005[a]	NS	NS
Acute Panic related to Phobia	<.025[a]	<.05[a]	NS
Independent Evaluator			
Clinical Global Imp. - Status	NS	<.05	NS
Phobia I - Improvement	<.05	<.05	NS
"Spontaneous" Panic	NS	NS	NS
Acute Panic related to Phobia	NS	<.05	NS

[a] NS on endpoint analysis

raphobics are the sickest to start with and remain the sickest patients, that is, they have greater overall psychopathology than the other groups. Simple phobics are the healthiest to start with and they are the healthiest at the endpoint. All groups showed considerable improvement but agoraphobic and mixed phobic patients receiving imipramine showed significantly more improvement than those on placebo. In the simple phobics, there were no differences in improvement among the three treatment groups.

Table 4 shows results of the drug-placebo contrast on acute panic. Three of the four variables show a drug effect, greatest in the agoraphobic patients.

Table 5 gives therapist and independent evaluator ratings of the four most important variables. All show a drug effect, according to therapist ratings, and three out of four show a drug effect on independent evaluator ratings.

Table 6 gives within-diagnosis analyses of the same variables. Most show a drug effect for agoraphobics and mixed phobics, but there are no drug effects in simple phobics.

Figure 5 shows relapse rates over a two-year period after completion of treatment. Although there was more relapse among agoraphobics and mixed phobics (22% and 25%) than simple phobics (about 14%), these differences are not statistically significant.

SECOND STUDY

In this study (6), agoraphobic women were treated with either group exposure in vivo plus imipramine or group exposure in vivo with placebo. The drug condition was double-blind. Patients started with four weeks of medication, then had ten exposure in vivo sessions once weekly, while continuing medication. Exposure sessions consisted of going into actual phobic situations with the therapist. These were graded so that in the first week patients went to a local shopping center, whereas by the final exposure session they were going by bus and subway to large, crowded department stores in downtown Manhattan (in New York City). After completion of in vivo therapy, medication was continued for 12 more weeks, to make a total of six months of medication.

Table 7 shows that there was no significant difference between the two groups in percentage of dropouts. As in the previous study, medication refusal is the most common reason for dropping out in the imipramine group but, in the placebo group, most patients dropped out because they couldn't keep up with the group.

Table 8 contrasts baseline severity of illness and impairment of func-

Figure 5

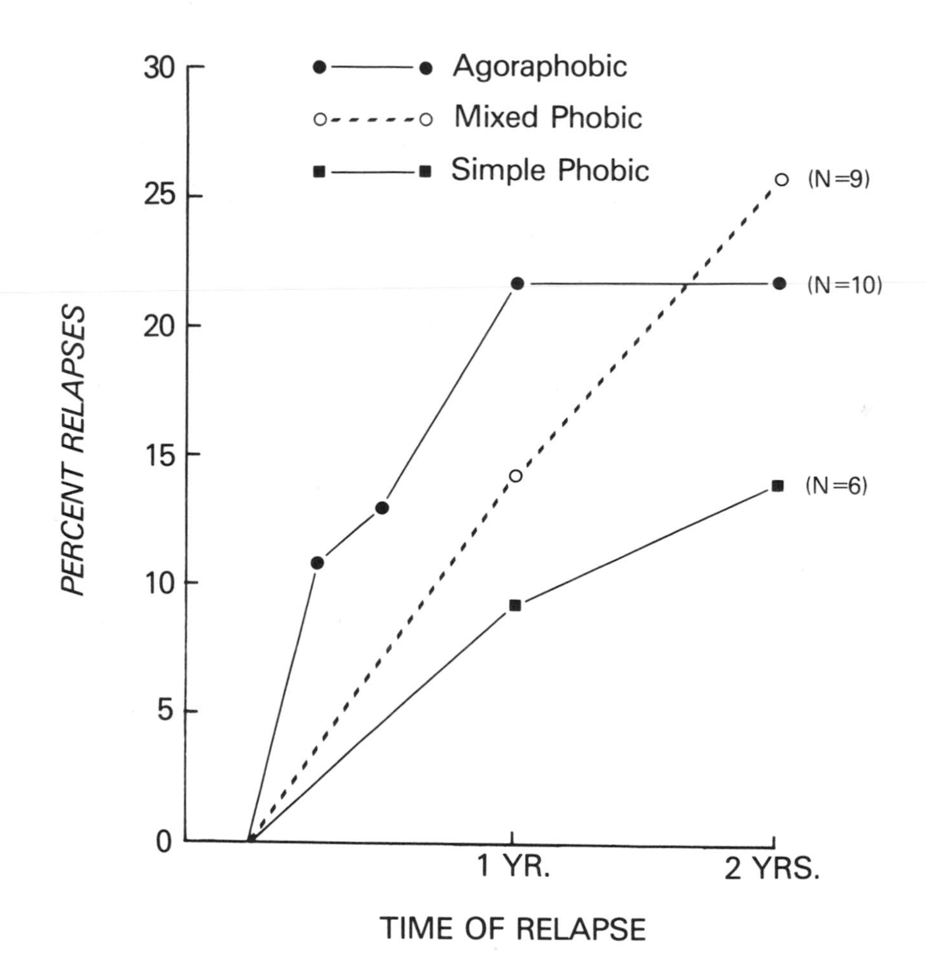
RELAPSES
DURING TWO YEAR PERIOD
AFTER TREATMENT
Agoraphobic
Mixed Phobic
Simple Phobic
(N=9)
(N=10)
(N=6)
30
25
20
15
10
5
0
PERCENT RELAPSES
1 YR.
2 YRS.
TIME OF RELAPSE

Table 7
Dropouts and Their Reasons for Dropping Out of Treatment

	Imipramine Group No. (%)	**Placebo Group No. (%)**
Reason for dropping out		
Medication refusal	8 (66.7)	3 (30)
Inability to keep up with group	1 (8.3)	5 (50)
New job	1 (8.3)	0 (0)
Moved away	1 (8.3)	0 (0)
No transportation	0 (0)	1 (10)
Depression	0 (0)	1 (10)
Time inconvenient	1 (8.3)	0 (0)
Total No. of dropouts	**12** (29)	**10** (29)
Total No. of patients entering treatment	41	35

tioning in dropouts and completers. It is interesting that in the placebo group, the sickest patients dropped out because they couldn't keep up with the group, whereas in the imipramine-treated group, there was no difference in severity of illness between dropouts and completers. Thus, imipramine did keep the sicker patients in treatment.

Table 9 shows results of therapist improvement ratings at the end of exposure in vivo treatment. There is a significant drug effect on all variables. Table 10 shows independent evaluator ratings of improvement at the end of exposure in vivo therapy (14 weeks) and the end of medication (26 weeks). There was a drug effect on all four variables which was greater at 26 weeks than 14 weeks, except for functioning.

Some people have said that the reason we get good results with imipramine is due to its effect on depression. To test that hypothesis, we did a correlation between depression ratings and outcome of treatment. We found that, as can be seen on Table 11, the more depressed the patients, the worse they did in treatment. Thus, there was an inverse correlation between depression and outcome.

THIRD STUDY

Another study in which drugs were contrasted to placebo, by Sheehan et al. (7), compared 57 agoraphobic patients randomly assigned to imipramine, phenelzine (an MAO inhibitor), or placebo. All patients were seen in supportive group therapy every two weeks. Patients in both imipramine and phenelzine groups showed significant improvement

Table 8
Baseline Measures of Severity of Illness: Comparison of Patients Completing Treatment and Dropping Out by Analysis of Variance

Independent Evaluators' Ratings		Treatment Group: Imipramine Completed Treatment	Treatment Group: Imipramine Dropped Out	Treatment Group: Placebo Completed Treatment	Treatment Group: Placebo Dropped Out	F Tests: Comparison	*F*	*P**
Severity of illness (CGI)† scale	Mean	4.34	4.50	4.38	5.00	Completers vs dropouts	3.86	.053
	SD	0.72	0.90	0.82	0.67	Imipramine vs placebo	1.78	NS
	n	29	12	24	10	Interaction of dropping out × drug treatment	1.40	NS
Spontaneous panic scale‡	Mean	4.12	4.90	4.13	4.90	Completers vs dropouts	4.12	.046
	SD	1.48	0.99	1.71	0.88	Imipramine vs placebo	0.00	NS
	n	26	10	23	10	Interaction of dropping out × drug treatment	0.00	NS
Functional impairment scale‡	Mean	5.00	4.80	4.86	5.70	Completers vs dropouts	1.45	NS
	SD	0.96	1.48	0.94	0.48	Imipramine vs placebo	2.09	NS
	n	27	10	22	10	Interaction of dropping out × drug treatment	3.84	.054
Primary phobia scale‡	Mean	5.93	6.30	6.04	6.00	Completers vs dropouts	0.60	NS
	SD	0.68	0.67	1.11	0.00	Imipramine vs placebo	0.18	NS
	n	27	10	23	10	Interaction of dropping out × drug treatment	0.96	NS

*Indicates that the *P* values are two tailed.

†The numerical values for the Clinical Global Impression (CGI) scale are as follows: 1 indicates normal; 2, borderline mentally ill; 3, very slight impairment; 4, moderately ill; 5, markedly ill; 6, severely ill; and 7, among the most severely ill patients.

‡The numerical values for this scale are as follows: 1 indicates better than normal; 2, normal; 3, very slight impairment; 4, slight impairment; 5, moderate impairment; 6, marked impairment; and 7, total impairment.

Table 9
Therapist Improvement Ratings at End of In Vivo Therapy (14 wk)

	Imipramine Group (N = 29)	Placebo Group (N = 25)	*t* Test*
Clinical Global Impressions Scale			
Marked improvement	6 (21)†	2 (8)	
Moderate improvement	21 (72)	16 (64)	
Minimal improvement	2 (7)	5 (20)	
No improvement	0 (0)	2 (8)	
Mean	1.86	2.28	$t = 2.44$,
SD	0.52	0.74	$P < .01$
Primary phobia scale			
Marked improvement	18 (62)	9 (36)	
Moderate improvement	10 (35)	8 (32)	
Minimal improvement	1 (3)	5 (20)	
No improvement	0 (0)	3 (12)	
Mean	6.59	5.92	$t = 2.98$,
SD	0.57	1.04	$P < .002$
Spontaneous panic scale			
Marked improvement	22 (76)	10 (40)	
Moderate improvement	5 (17)	8 (32)	
Minimal improvement	2 (7)	1 (4)	
No improvement	0 (0)	6 (24)	
Mean	6.69	5.9	$t = 3.19$,
SD	0.60	1.2	$P < .001$
Functioning scale			
Marked improvement	22 (76)	10 (40)	
Moderate improvement	5 (17)	10 (40)	
Minimal improvement	2 (7)	4 (16)	
No improvement	0 (0)	1 (4)	
Mean	6.69	6.16	$t = 2.67$,
SD	0.60	0.85	$P < .005$

*Indicates that the *P* values are one-tailed.
†The numbers in parentheses are percentages.

over placebo treated patients on all outcome measures. Phenelzine was superior to imipramine on two measures (the Work and Social Disability Scale and the Symptom Severity and Phobic Avoidance Scale). They also found that drug effects were not due to their effect on depressive symptoms.

When imipramine is ineffective or difficult to tolerate because of side effects, another tricyclic may often be effective, since the action on panic is similar. In addition to phenelzine, other MAO inhibitors have also been found to affect panic attacks. As long as patients adhere to the

Table 10
Independent Evaluators' Ratings of Improvement at 14 and 26 Weeks*

Independent Evaluators' Ratings		Baseline Covariate		Period 14 wk		Period 26 wk		F Tests		
		Imipramine	Placebo	Imipramine	Placebo	Imipramine	Placebo	Comparison	*F*	*P* Value†
CGI scale‡,§	Mean	4.34	4.38	1.90	2.29	1.48	2.04	Imipramine vs placebo	6.30	< .008
	SD	0.72	0.82	0.62	0.91	0.69	0.86	14 vs 26 wk	16.83	< .0001
	N	29	24	29	24	29	24	Drug × period interaction	1.02	NS
	Adjusted Means	...	...	1.90	2.29	1.49	2.04	...	...	...
Primary phobia scale‡,‖	Mean	5.92	6.05	6.16	5.71	6.64	5.81	Imipramine vs placebo	7.64	< .004
	SD	0.70	1.12	0.75	1.06	0.49	0.98	14 vs 26 wk	8.29	< .003
	N	25	21	25	21	25	21	Drug × period interaction	3.71	< .03
	Adjusted means	...	...	6.15	5.72	6.63	5.82	...	...	...
Spontaneous panic scale‡,‖,¶	Mean	4.79	5.21	6.37	6.00	6.95	5.86	Imipramine vs placebo	7.95	< .004
	SD	1.03	0.80	0.96	1.04	0.23	1.03	14 vs 26 wk	1.80	NS
	N	19	14	19	14	19	14	Drug × period interaction	4.94	< .017
	Adjusted means	...	...	6.37	5.99	6.95	5.85	...	...	...
Functioning scale‡,‖	Mean	5.08	4.90	5.92	5.60	6.36	6.00	Imipramine vs placebo	2.46	< .062
	SD	0.91	0.85	0.81	1.10	0.64	1.03	14 vs 26 wk	14.68	< .0001
	N	25	20	25	20	25	20	Drug × period interaction	.03	NS
	Adjusted means	...	...	5.94	5.58	6.38	5.98	...	...	...

*The ratings were analyzed by a 2 × 2 analysis of covariance with baseline impairment ratings as the covariate.
†Indicates that the *P* values are one tailed; NS indicates that the *F* value is not significant.
‡The baseline scale is the same as in Table 3.
§The numerical values for the Clinical Global Impression (CGI) scale at 14 and 26 weeks are as follows: 1 indicates markedly improved; 2, moderately improved; 3, minimally improved; 4, no change; 5, minimally worse; 6, moderately worse; and 7, markedly worse.
‖The numerical values for these scales at 14 and 26 weeks are as follows: 7 indicates markedly improved; 6, moderately improved; 5, minimally improved; 4, no change; 3, minimally worse; 2, moderately worse; and 1, markedly worse.
¶ Indicates that only subjects with spontaneous panic attacks at baseline were included in the analysis.

dietary restrictions necessary when taking MAOIs, hypertensive crises have not been a problem. Since many patients learn to cope with panic attacks through psychological therapy (i.e., placebo-treated patients in the studies cited above), it seems reasonable to start treatment with a trial of psychological therapy alone. If panics continue to disrupt the lives of these patients, with perpetuation of phobic behavior, then the addition of a tricyclic or MAO inhibitor seems indicated.

To conclude, I would like to restate the findings that in phobic patients who have spontaneous panics (agoraphobics and mixed phobics), we find tricyclics and MAO inhibitors to be very effective in combination

Table 11
Correlations of Independent Evaluator Baseline Depression Ratings*
with 14- and 26-Week Outcome Measures

	Imipramine Group			Placebo Group		
Improvement Ratings	**n**	***r*†**	***P*‡**	**n**	***r*†**	***P*‡**
14 wk						
Independent evaluator						
CGI§	27	.37	.06	23	.44	.034
Phobia 1	27	.28	NS	23	.23	NS
Spontaneous panic	27	−.20	NS	23	−.26	NS
Functioning	27	.39	.046	23	.10	NS
Therapist‖						
CGI§	27	.35	.07	23	.55	.008
Phobia 1	27	.44	.02	23	.425	.044
Spontaneous panic	27	.43	.026	23	.01	NS
Functioning	27	.25	NS	23	.12	NS
Patient self-rating	27	.58	.002	23	.27	NS
26 wk						
Independent evaluator						
CGI§	5	.40	.04	22	.58	.006
Phobia 1	25	.25	NS	20	.22	NS
Spontaneous panic	25	−.22	NS	20	−.25	NS
Functioning	25	.32	.12	20	.44	.054
Patient self-rating	27	.47	.014	21	.44	.048

*The distribution of baseline depression scores was as follows: in the imipramine group, 12 were rated 2 (normal), seven were rated 3 (very slight), 11 were rated 4 (slight), seven were rated 5 (moderate), and none were rated 6 (marked); in the placebo group, 12 were rated 2, four were rated 3, 11 were rated 4, seven were rated 5, and two were rated 6. The last two patients were rated moderately depressed at the time of screening.

†Positive correlations indicate that greater depression is associated with worse outcome.

‡Indicates that the *P* values are two-tailed.

§CGI indicates Clinical Global Impressions Scales.

‖Indicates that the last contact with patients was at 14 weeks.

with a psychological therapy. In patients who do not have spontaneous panics, like simple phobics, we find that various psychological therapies are very effective and that these medications are not useful. Although these drugs have long been used as antidepressants, we find that their effect in these patients is not due to their antidepressant action. In fact, we found a negative correlation between depressive symptoms and treatment outcome.

REFERENCE NOTES

Tables 1-3 are reprinted with permission from Zitrin, C.M., Klein, D.F., and Woerner, M.G. (1978). *Arch. Gen. Psychiatry*, 35: 307-316, 1978. Copyright 1978, American Medical Association.

Figures 1-5 are reprinted with permission from Zitrin, C.M., Woerner, M.G., and Klein, D.F.: Differentiation of panic anxiety from anticipatory anxiety and avoidance behavior. In: *Anxiety: New Research and Changing Concepts*, D.F. Klein and J. Rabkin (eds.). New York: Raven Press, 1981, pp. 27-42.

Tables 6-11 are reprinted with permission from Zitrin, C.M., Klein, D.F., and Woerner M.G.: Treatment of agoraphobia with group exposure in vivo and imipramine. *Arch. Gen. Psychiatry*, 37: 66-69, 1980. Copyright 1980, American Medical Association.

REFERENCES

1. Klein, D.F. Delineation of two drug-responsive anxiety syndromes. *Psychopharmacologia*, 5: 397-408, 1964.
2. Kelly, D., Guirguis, W., Frommer, E., et al: Treatment of phobic states with antidepressants. *Brit. J. Psychiatry*, 116: 387-398, 1970.
3. Lipsedge, J.S., Hajjoff, J., Huggins, P., et al. The management of severe agoraphobia: a comparison of iproniazid and systematic desensitization. *Psychopharmacologia*, 32: 67-80, 1973.
4. Zitrin, C.M., Klein, D.F., and Woerner, M.G. Behavior therapy, supportive psychotherapy, imipramine, and phobias. *Arch. Gen. Psychiatry*, 35: 307-316, 1978.
5. Zitrin, C.M., Woerner M.G., and Klein, D.F. Comparison of imipramine and placebo treatment of phobias: a controlled study. Submitted for publication.
6. Zitrin, C.M., Klein, D.F., and Woerner, M.G. Treatment of agoraphobia with group exposure in vivo and imipramine. *Arch. Gen. Psychiatry*, 37: 60-72, 1980.
7. Sheehan, D.V., Ballenger, J., and Jacobsen, G. Treatment of endogenous anxiety with phobic, hysterical, and hypochondriacal symptoms. *Arch. Gen. Psychiatry*, 37: 51-59, 1980.

7

Phobics of Branford

Jane Miller

This chapter deals with outpatient treatment of phobic anxiety in a small community-based mental health center, the Branford Counseling Center. This environment presents the following special problems for phobic clients and the therapist: 1) Our clinic has limited funds and a small clerical staff; 2) there is only one staff member trained to deal with phobics; 3) because the clinic is free, there may be a lack of client motivation; 4) there is no clear-cut, time-limited contract between client and therapist; and 5) the style of treatment is somewhat informal. Nevertheless, it would appear from an encouragingly high rate of success, which I plan to document, that there are some unique qualities in this treatment model not found in more sophisticated programs. Guidelines for treatment in a small community-based center have not, to my knowledge, been addressed in the literature.

For many years Branford was a suburban bedroom community, but in the last few years there has been a marked increase in light industry, and more local people experience panic when they have to go from the Town of Branford to the city of New Haven crossing over the Quinnipiac Bridge in the process. This unassuming bridge which spans the mouth of the Quinnipiac River has become a bête noir for phobics. Not statistically significant, but perhaps noteworthy, this new light industry in

Branford, with available jobs for local people, appears to be reinforcing the phobic avoidance of the notorious "Q" Bridge.

Since my career as a phobic specialist at the Branford Counseling Center began four-and-a-half years ago, I have worked with over 50 phobic clients. This work has included individual sessions, in vivo desensitization, open-ended group work, home visits, treatment by telephone, and work with family and significant others. A training program was initiated for doctors, dentists and ministers as well as other mental health professionals, to become familiar with the problems and treatment of phobic anxiety.

In contrast with the accepted professional model espoused by most practitioners, it has been my experience that clients with phobic anxieties respond best to an eclectic, individualized approach, based primarily on the therapeutic alliance between client and therapist, rather than a particular model. Support for this approach is given by Strupp (1), who states that "the bulk of evidence points to the overriding importance of the collaborative relationship" in the therapeutic setting, and "there is scant evidence that therapeutic method per se determines therapeutic outcome" (p. 590). I believe that the therapeutic alliance, particularly in treatment of phobics, is determined by certain variables: 1) the clients' motivation for treatment; 2) the clients' suitability for psychotherapeutic or behavioral techniques; 3) the effectiveness or counterproductiveness of the clients' support system; 4) the clients' investment in secondary gain; and 5) the clients' "neurotic style." Equally important are the personal commitment, clinical skill, persuasiveness, plausibility, and human qualities of the therapist.

Results of my treatment of 50 phobics also indicate that the usual category "agoraphobia" is not particularly helpful. It can often be counterproductive, and after the initial intake, diagnosis is better disregarded. This population, I suggest, is best described as a group of people having common symptoms of phobic anxiety, each being classified with single, clustered, or generalized phobias.

My "informal" unstructured clinical practice is based on the fundamental belief that avoidance of the phobic situation compounds the apprehension, whereas exposure to the situation is essential. The phobic person is predominantly a non-assertive person; therefore, my treatment always incorporates learning assertiveness skills. Further, this treatment stresses the motivation, needs, and goals of each individual client. This may involve addressing and dealing with specific problems generally around early separation anxiety issues. Finally, an open-ended, open membership group is always maintained, for I believe that group experience for the phobic is almost always indicated.

I have conducted a group for three years, comprising 34 clients—8 men and 26 women who have been exposed to the phobic situation. They are all encouraged to return after any interval, or for any reason. Approximately 25% of the total have done so.

My group treatment model involves selecting, carrying out, and sharing specific goals; practicing relaxation techniques and learning to distinguish and deal with common symptoms of single, clustered, or generalized phobias; familiarizing the group with various alternative techniques for reducing anxiety and panic, such as monitoring SUDS (Subjective Units of Discomfort) levels, using what Dr. Manuel Smith (2) calls the "automatic orientation reflex"; considering and understanding the use of paradoxical intention; and, finally, incorporating a buddy system or peer self-help group. Comparing medication treatment or swapping frightening symptoms is discouraged.

I sent a four-page Phobic Anxiety Questionnaire (see Appendix) of my design to the 44 phobic people who were accessible, and whom I have treated in various ways in the last four-and-a-half years. I was interested in determining the results of this treatment, whether treatment results had been sustained, and the clients' current level of functioning. The first section, with 27 situations, was an Avoidance Index in which I set out to determine how the client responded to certain situations before and after treatment at our Center. There were two columns marked "Before" and "After," with a 1 to 4 scale (1 = Never Avoids, 2 = Sometimes Avoids, 3 = Almost Always Avoids, 4 = Always Avoids). Next was a comprehensive set of Yes and No questions about medication, job, previous therapy, etc. Finally, there was a list of the most helpful sorts of treatment, e.g., group session, individual therapy, assertiveness training, reading, medication, relaxation techniques, etc. Because of the nature of the treatment and the unorthodox sampling procedure, a statistical analysis would not be appropriate. Some phobics I talked with only on the phone, some I saw for only three times, some I have seen for over a year, and others I treated four-and-a-half years ago and have not seen since. Also, I sent out a personal covering letter with each Questionnaire which might invalidate my data. Table 1 shows data from 41 responses (7 male, 37 female) to questionnaires sent to 44 clients ranging in age from 10 to 62 years, with the majority (25) between 20 and 40 years of age. The duration of their phobic symptoms was from 2 months to 33 years.

As shown in Table 1, 29 people felt they were functioning better as a result of treatment, 10 indicated "much better" (their comment, not on the questionnaire), and 2 in the early stages of treatment said "about the same." None indicated they were "worse." When asked which of

Table 1
Data Obtained from 41 Responses (7 Male, 37 Female) to 44 Questionnaires

Phobias	*Number*
Single	3
Clustered	11
General	27
Previous Treatment	
None	11
Helpful	10
Not helpful	20
Marital Status	
Married	27
Unmarried	14
Posttreatment Functioning	
Better	29
Much better	10
No change	2
Worse	0

10 modes of treatment were "most helpful," 22 checked "individual" treatment in the top three modes; 20 checked "group sessions" in the top three modes; and 26 checked "talking to other phobic people" in the top three modes. The "helpful" use of medication was at the bottom of the list. The use of relaxation techniques and reading pertinent material were important to many, but not in the top three. In the section "other ways that have helped," "using humor" and "getting mad" had high priority; next most helpful was "being with a friend" or "physically touching someone or something." In the last section, "other remarks," almost everyone responded with thoughtful, imaginative and often very moving comments. Finally, it was impressive to note that out of 27 clients with generalized symptoms, 11 indicated they were completely phobic-free. In other words, they had no "Always Avoids" and not more than two "Almost Always Avoids."

The following case histories will illustrate my style of treatment, and will focus in general on the individualistic eclectic approach. The three cases I will discuss can be categorized as people having common symptoms of the generalized or diffused phobic pattern. The first case, Mary B., is characteristic of many of the women I treat although somewhat older than the majority. Their presenting problem, excessive anxiety leading to uncontrollable panic attacks, leaves these women functioning at a very low level and avoiding situations in which they feel they may lose control. Most have responded well to treatment and are now comfortably going into supermarkets, restaurants, hairdressers, elevators, over bridges, etc. The other two cases, though atypical in terms of age and onset of symptoms, aptly illustrate some of my treatment techniques.

Mary B. is a 49-year-old married middle-class woman with a family. She has been in sporadic therapy at the Branford Counseling Center with five different counselors for ten years. Eleven years ago she presented herself as a chronically depressed, despondent, non-assertive woman with meager self-esteem, expressing frequent feelings of guilt, anxiety and inadequacy as a wife, mother, neighbor and person. She was referred to me in August 1975 by her last therapist who felt discouraged about her prognosis and felt she presented severe symptoms of phobic anxiety which had not been addressed. Her acknowledged fears included a pathological fear of death and dying, and, if at all possible, she avoided germs, bridges, restaurants, being alone, being in groups, and the hairdresser. She described her panic attacks as frequent as three or four times a day, and as coming unpredictably, like a "bolt out of the blue."

When I first saw her she was a heavyset, whiny, serious woman—a reluctant Weight Watcher with a pretty face and lovely smile, which she used infrequently. There was always a suggestion of genuine warmth, humor, and hope. She characterized herself as a 1 on the 0 to 10 self-esteem scale, and said she was "a failure at everything." She was initially relieved to be diagnosed as an agoraphobic, but later we referred to her generalized phobic symptoms. I saw her eight times in individual treatment, and urged her to go into the phobic group. I persuaded her finally to join my eight-week Woman's Assertiveness Group as her only other option for treatment. Her progress was remarkable, and she soon felt comfortable enough to join the phobic group, and became a reliable phobic group member. After participating in the two groups for several weeks she became more self-confident, and her fine earthy humor and engaging manner surfaced and she became a champion of assertive behavior. Predictably, with such a long history of pathology, she experienced setbacks, mostly around her inability to lose weight, but in general her progress was rewarding, and she now no longer avoids bridges, restaurants, living alone, being in a group, etc.

She related with great style a story about an intimate medical operation performed on her favorite pet mallard called "Boy Duck." This pet's need for immediate medical attention, and her motivation to save his vital part, catapulted her over the formidable "Q" bridge and into New Haven to see the veterinarian. After successful surgery and her return home, she realized she had never before been over the bridge without panic, and never alone. She was astonished by her accomplishment, and realized that motivation was the key.

After eight weeks of the workshop, Mary became the assertive pillar of the phobic group. She was an excellent model and an inveterate propagandist—a tribute to the effectiveness of assertive behavior for phobic people.

I recently got in touch by telephone with Mary B. She had subsequently decided to terminate with the phobic group, and we had stopped our individual treatment. She said, "I'm okay and doing well. I no longer have that dreadful fear of death, and do most things with relative ease." Her parting words, however, were, "I wish I had more control over my weight. It sets me back sometimes, and I get very discouraged and depressed."

Linda G. is a 21-year-old woman who was prohibitively limited by her phobic fears. A year ago she was living in her boyfriend's home with his family in a town 30 minutes from Branford. Until six months before that, she had been living at home with two alcoholic parents who were divorced, but living together for reasons of expediency. I started treating her by telephone, and we probably logged over 100 telephone hours. Her boyfriend and her minister came to see me to learn how they could be supportive. They were only moderately effective.

Linda was a passive, dependent, non-assertive, obsessional, but likable young woman. She said she was angry and obdurate, and could not deal with criticism. She appeared motivated for treatment, but was actually very resistant.

She had her first two episodes of panic in high school and thought she was going "crazy." After this she never went back to school and became completely housebound with her two destructive, unreliable, alcoholic parents. After an excruciating year and a step-by-step desensitization procedure, she moved out of her parents' house into her boyfriend's house, which was a major accomplishment for her. However, what seemed utopian at first presented her with a new set of problems.

My treatment method was to relentlessly nudge her forward, admonishing her with hope and humor. She had frequent setbacks, and was very negative, a characteristic of most phobics. She could not see her substantial progress. Interviewing her mother and father also proved only moderately productive. I then saw her twice a month privately over a period of three months, and she responded well to a treatment technique we initiated. Using a bundle of small sticks and starting to count backwards from 10 with each step, we walked away from the house exposing her to her fears—dropping sticks and counting and dropping and so on. Today she carries a bundle of sticks with her everywhere, and now using the "automatic orientation reflex" she can orient herself to the game rather than to her mounting fears.

Linda's progress has been impressive. She has become more assertive and has lost some of her emotional dependency on others, including me. She now sees herself as a person able to make and carry out positive decisions. She is presently married to Bob, her former boyfriend, and they live in a cottage by the ocean. With Bob's help, she planned and orchestrated their wedding against formidable odds. Linda still has limitations, but they are not as formerly prohibitive. She also occasionally becomes discouraged with her progress, which always seems "too slow." She needs frequent reminding of how far she has come from that once "desperate imprisonment."

It appears, also, that she is responding to the phenomenon of secondary gain, which seems to compound her problem and makes her difficult to treat. She would deny with self-righteous indignation that she is getting substantial negative reward from the people around her, particularly her boyfriend. I feel she has assumed the position of stage front (albeit the villian, not the protagonist) and is using her phobias to manipulate and control her immediate environment. This plays a major role in her pattern of avoidance. I agree with Harley Shands (see Chapter 10) that although the phobic's feeling of loss of control is paramount, the paradox of the phobic is, "There is no one in the world who is more likely to be a domineering, contrary person in the system, whether negatively or positively, than the phobic patient."

Also, Linda G. has not been exposed to the phobic group, nor has she ever talked face-to-face with another phobic person. This supports my contention, reinforced by my questionnaire, that, for effective treatment, participation in a phobic group is indicated.

June R. was referred to me by a colleague who had been treating the family, consisting of a mother and two young daughters by different fathers, neither present, for approximately seven months. June was ten and white; her sister was eight and black. The counselor felt June presented some severe symptoms which suggested phobic anxiety. I started seeing her individually, on a weekly basis. She said she felt terrified when she had to read aloud in school, although she knows she is a "good reader." Her reading marks were deteriorating and everyone was concerned. She also described irrational fears around heights, thunder and lightning, germs, blood, fire engines, etc., but as her primary panic she described the feeling of being trapped in an elevator, or any other enclosure where she had the sensation of being imprisoned.

June was an unusually engaging and sensitive child. She wanted desperately to please, and become pathologically dependent on those she cared about. She described her mother as a person with many of her own fears and overly protective. Some evidence of physical abuse by her mother was noted. June expressed anger at her sister who "can do anything and is not afraid." When apprehensive she cried excessively, had severe stomachaches, and threw up. She frequently expressed bitterness because she had never seen her natural father whom she felt had intentionally let her down, and her sister's black father whom she loved had also abandoned her, she felt.

June and I decided to confront the reading phobia, as it was her highest priority, and caused most frequent stress. She felt immediately reassured when I told her the symptoms she was experiencing were quite common, and she was not "going crazy" or "going to die." I said these were feelings she had learned, and what she had learned, I would try and help her "unlearn." We practiced a special relaxation exercise with a Raggedy Ann doll whose natural floppiness we tried to imitate. After five sessions, she began reading to me without the "scary" symptoms, and eventually learned to "go limp" like Raggedy Ann. At present, in school, she is reading aloud effectively without panic.

Next, we decided to confront her fear of high places. Together we started up an alarming-looking three-floor metal fire escape. She eased up on her bottom a few steps at a time, experiencing dizziness, rapid heartbeat, and terror that her legs would give out. For June the process of desensitization was unusually rapid, and she started overcoming her excessive fear after about three tentative attempts. Today she is irrepressible, and alone she often scrambles to the top as if she were skipping up a few friendly stairs. I attribute her accomplishment to her own remarkable motivation, my lack of fear and confidence in her, and her newfound relaxation skill.

Deciding to tackle her phobic bête noir, the elevator, was a big decision for her. She said she was terrified, and procrastinated with the skill all phobics master. One day she courageously agreed to try. Fortunately there is an elevator at her school and after 45 minutes of my using a combination of friendly persuasion, paradoxical intention, detailed explanations of the workings of an elevator, and tenacity, we finally got off the ground. She pushed the buttons and opened the doors over and over, and finally learned that she, not the "moving monster," was in control.

June agreed to participate with me in a peer-counseling experiment; we both became involved in working once a week with another 11-year-old school phobic who also experienced classic phobic symptoms, "panicky feelings" in church, the movies, the circus, large stores, and high places. We successfully helped her to confront her fears, and June was able to teach her some special relaxation and fear reduction exercises. June was a remarkably effective model, but I would be hard pressed to judge which little girl gained the most from our treatment.

She still possesses many fears, and she will unquestionably have major setbacks as phobics are prone to do. She will probably continue to live in a complex and stressful home environment, and learning to adapt to this will always be a challenge for her. Also, it is possible that the extreme separation anxiety she experienced in her early years may prove to be irrevocably damaging. However, she will hopefully continue learning skills that will give her some control over her life. More important, perhaps she will learn that she is a lovable little girl, and that there are those in this world who will love her, not abandon her.

The principal conclusion I can reach, based on my clinical impression and reinforced by data from the questionnaire, is that the individualized, eclectic approach with emphasis on the therapeutic alliance is effective, and a substantial percentage of the client population I have treated report less avoidance, higher functioning, and positive change. A significant number are phobia-free.

In addition, despite its possible shortcomings, a small community-based center has some unique qualities with demonstrable advantages: 1) easy access for the phobic to the center, and to other town professionals, i.e., doctors, dentists, and ministers now familiar with the nature of phobic anxiety; 2) free, on-going individual and group treatment, which appears to be essential for the majority of clients; 3) in vivo desensitization procedures and home visits; and 4) an informality that does not appear formidable to fear-ridden phobics.

I would like to conclude with one of the comments, from the many, I received on the questionnaires. "As I learned about the other phobic people in my group, I don't feel so alone anymore. Assertiveness training and other exercises of treatment, such as SUDS-level monitoring, and medication to maintain my functioning level have reassured me. I, in turn, took on more responsibility and now consider things more of a challenge, rather than a fear. Now I have become good at this, and see things in better perspective. I have a job, I went back to my church, and I'm being a better mother."

REFERENCES

1. Strupp, H.H. Psychotherapy: Assessing methods. *Science,* 207: 590, 1980.
2. Smith, M.J. *Kicking the Fear Habit,* New York: Bantam Books, 1978, p. 307.

APPENDIX

PHOBIC ANXIETY QUESTIONNAIRE

In the column marked Before, indicate the way you felt before you had any treatment (whether individual, group or by telephone) using Numbers 1-4.

In the column marked After, indicate the way you felt after treatment or feel today, using Numbers 1-4.

*Note: The word "treatment" refers to any kind of treatment you have received at the Branford Counseling Center. It does not refer to previous treatment.

How much do you now, and did you before, try to avoid these situations:

Never	Sometimes	Almost Always	Always
1	2	3	4

	Before	After
1. Participating in a group	______	______
2. Being alone	______	______
3. Traveling alone by bus or train	______	______
4. Driving a car alone	______	______
5. Driving with someone else	______	______
6. Going out to a social event with other people	______	______
7. Going to a restaurant alone	______	______
8. Going to a restaurant with others	______	______
9. Walking alone on a busy street.	______	______
10. Going into large crowded stores	______	______
11. Going alone far from home	______	______
12. Sexual contact	______	______
13. Large open spaces	______	______
14. Going to the doctor	______	______
15. Going to the dentist	______	______
16. Going to hospitals	______	______
17. Going to the hairdresser or barber shop	______	______
18. Going to church	______	______
19. Undertaking something new	______	______
20. Riding in elevators	______	______
21. Being watched or stared at	______	______
22. Talking to people in authority	______	______
23. Flying in an airplane	______	______

24. Being in large crowds of people	_______	_______
25. Thunder and/or lightning	_______	_______
26. Being in or on high places, i.e., bridges, buildings, mountain roads, looking up fire escapes (Underline that which applies)	_______	_______
27. Dogs, cats, snakes, spiders, etc. (Underline or write in other) ____________________	_______	_______

	Months	Years
Approximately how long have you had phobic anxiety?	_______	_______

	Yes	No
Have you had previous therapy or counseling?	_______	_______
Did you find it helpful?	_______	_______

	Months	Years
How long were you in treatment before Branford Counseling Center?	_______	_______
Are you working now?	_______	_______

	Yes	No
Do you go to school or attend special classes?	_______	_______
Before Branford Counseling Center did you go to school or attend special classes?	_______	_______
Do you do any volunteer work?	_______	_______
Are you a full-time parent or spouse?	_______	_______
Is medication for anxiety part of your treatment?	_______	_______

Please specify____________________

____

Were you taking any medication prior to treatment?	_______	_______

Please specify____________________

____

Do you feel you fully understand the nature of phobic anxiety?	_______	_______
Do you feel that those close to you fully understand phobic anxiety? (Some)_______	_______	_______

Do you feel in general you are now functioning

Better__________ Worse__________ About the same__________

What do you think was most helpful to you?
Check by marking 1, 2, 3, etc.
(1 = most helpful, 2 = next most helpful, etc.)

________ Participating in group

________ Individual sessions

________ Medication

________ Assertiveness training

________ Encouragement by telephone

________ Relaxation exercises

________ Confronting phobic situation with me or other understanding person

________ Monitoring your SUDS levels

________ Reading material, books, articles about phobic anxiety. Please specify:

____

________ Talking to other phobic people

Any other ways that have helped you (Please underline)

Counting boxes, signs, etc.

Carrying rocks, rabbits foot or other talisman

Getting mad

Using humor or levity

Religion

Your own special words or sayings

Someones else's special words or sayings

Being with a friend or family member

Physically touching someone or something

Other____

This space for other ways that have helped (be as specific as you are willing) or for any other remarks you would care to make.

Thank you very much,

Jane Miller

PART III

Theoretical Issues

This section reviews some of the fundamental theoretical issues in the treatment of phobias. The first chapter, by Arthur B. Hardy, entitled "Phobic Thinking: The Cognitive Influences on the Behavior and Effective Treatment of the Agoraphobic," gives a description of the patterns of thinking which underlie the phobic experience. Martin N. Seif's sensitive review of the therapy process, entitled "Going Solo: From External Support to Self-support," gives one of the clearest accounts of the treatment process in the supported exposure approach. Harley C. Shands and Natalie Schor's article, "The Modern Syndrome of Phobophobia and Its Management," reviews the theoretical aspects of phobia treatment with a literary and psychoanalytic bent. By contrast, George Curtis' short but important chapter, entitled "Psychobiology of Exposure In Vivo," outlines the state of our knowledge about the biological basis both for the phobic experience and its successful treatment through supported exposure.

Nancy Jane Flaxman's fascinating and insightful paper, "The Correlation Between Quantity of Fears and the Ability to Discriminate Among Similar Items," opens a major door to understanding the cognitive underpinnings of the phobic disorder, as well as clarifying one of the most fundamental aspects of successful treatment, that is, helping phobics change the way they think about fearful feelings and fearful thoughts. David Charney, in "Depression and Agoraphobia—Chicken or the Egg?", explores the interplay between depression and agoraphobia and different treatment approaches.

Bella H. Selan deals with one of the most important issues in the treatment and understanding of phobias in her chapter, "Phobias, Death, and Depression," pointing out that many phobic people have lost significant people in their lives, usually a parent, at an early age, thus sensitizing them to feelings of loss and abandonment at a time when their magical thinking predominates over more reasonable thought processes.

Less theoretical is the paper by Gerald T. O'Brien, David H. Barlow, and Cynthia G. Last, entitled "Changing Marriage Patterns of Agoraphobics as a Result of Treatment." This paper reviews the significant literature on a vital subject and raises issues of importance to all clinicians working with phobic people. Robert Ackerman explores the important relationship of women's issues and phobias, and Maralyn L. Teare's chapter, while not theoretical, outlines a teaching strategy to help phobic people achieve symptomatic relief.

8

Phobic Thinking: The Cognitive Influences on the Behavior and Effective Treatment of the Agoraphobic

Arthur B. Hardy

This chapter will briefly outline some of the more prevalent thinking patterns which clinically have proven, over the years, to be a problem in the recovery process of many of our patients.

As therapists, it has been easier and quicker for us to change behavior patterns than to change thinking patterns. It is true that if we can change the behavior patterns, the thinking patterns will change. But, from each therapy group that we work with, there is always a percentage of people suffering from phobias and anxiety who retain residual problems and it seems to be in this group that the maladaptive thinking patterns tend to persist.

I will mention some of the thinking patterns, but not necessarily in the order of their importance.

AVOIDANCE

In the study entitled, "Avoidance vs. Confrontation of Fear" (1), the behavior of avoiding fears vs. confronting fears was compared as to which was the most effective in overcoming fears. In the studies, one-half of the patients were asked to keep a diary and to avoid all things which were fearful to them for one week. The other half of the group were asked to confront the fears for one week and also to keep a diary. As might be expected, the avoidance group showed an increase in anxiety while the confrontation group showed a significant improvement.

It is important to consider what this means to phobic people and what it does to their thinking. All people are naturally pleasure-seeking and pain-avoiding, with a tendency to make decisions on the basis of short-term comforts and to overlook, or ignore, the long-term deleterious effects. If some stimulus is likely to arouse some negative feelings, some fear, or something uncomfortable, the tendency is to make efforts to avoid that situation. This type of thinking is the most characteristic for phobics. It is a thinking error which can have devastating effects upon their lives. There are thousands of examples. The phobic thinks, "I believe I'll take a Valium now because later I might get into a situation which will arouse some anxiety and I'll hope that the problem won't exist when the effects of the Valium wear off." More healthy thinking would be: "I'm upset now. I'll analyze my upsetness, now—try to do something about it—try to resolve or change the situation. Then it is solved for the long term. This may mean some discomfort now, but that discomfort will motivate me to solve this problem and when the problem is solved, I won't need Valium or any short-term relief."

The first level of avoidance is in the mind. The phobic goes to great lengths to avoid having phobic thoughts enter the mind. Since the mind can only be concerned with one thing at a time, one method of avoidance is to develop obsessions to avoid the central issue or fear. The most common obsessions are dirt, contamination, germs, and poisons. These are generally a protection, by avoidance, of thoughts of death, loss, or separation. At some point along the way, the avoidance process for phobics becomes so all-pervasive that it is almost totally mind-consuming. From the time they get up, they begin to plot how they are going to avoid thinking about distasteful things, seeing distasteful things, hearing about distasteful things, avoiding luncheons, avoiding invitations, avoiding anything that might arouse some anxiety. This avoidance spreads to social situations, and it spreads to certain areas, such as stores, supermarkets, bridges, and highways.

EXTREMIST THINKING

Next to avoidance, the biggest thinking error is "all or nothing." Phobics have great difficulty thinking in different shades of grey or half-way measures. All phobics are extremists. They have a flare for the dramatic and they have a tendency to exaggerate situations. This is evident in their language—things are the "greatest" or the "worst" or the "most miserable." I have often heard the remark, "I am the *worst* phobic you have ever had. No one has ever had agoraphobia as severely as I have had it."

To phobics perfection or success becomes indispensable and failure becomes catastrophic. It becomes extremely difficult to convince phobics that mistakes are universal, and human, and that they can be a learning opportunity.

Phobics feel that the façade they erect must be protected at all times. One aspect of this feeling of particular importance to therapists is that, if a task involves several different instructions, phobics may become overwhelmed. It is as though, if they cannot *complete* the entire task to their own satisfaction, then they cannot even *try*. For example, a woman calls me on the phone and says she can't get out of bed. I ask her what she has to perform during the day and she says she has to get out of bed, take a bath, get dressed, eat breakfast, get in the car, drive the freeway, go to work, work to noon, and then attend a luncheon. Now, what she is saying is that this is too much for her in one day. As a consequence she is overwhelmed and feels she can do nothing. I tell her, "OK, take a bath and get dressed and then call me on the phone." I give her one instruction, and she does it. When she calls back, I tell her, "Eat your breakfast and drive to work [two instructions—she can take two]. Call me when you get to work." At work she calls me and says, "I can't go to lunch." I say, "You do your work and wait until lunch time and then call me." She did her work, waited until lunch time, and then called me. I say, "Now you can go to lunch." What I've done is to break the tasks down into individual instructions, one at a time, rather than give them all at once.

PERFECTION

Universally, the phobics appear to be frustrated idealists. Their ideals mostly encompass the ideal, the happy, the fun, the pleasant and they hope to eliminate the distasteful, sad, and unhappy aspects of life which we must all suffer through. This eventuates in great difficulties in decision-making. Phobics feel that whatever decision is made must be right because it is made forever; there is no margin left for error. Items or gifts purchased must be in mint-perfect condition, or they are totally unacceptable. Phobic or anxious people have great difficulty in accepting people, the world, and themselves, the way they really are—with imperfections and weaknesses. They have been criticized and they are sensitive about the criticism. They will do to others and to themselves what was done to them, and thus perpetuate the process of criticism. If the therapist can promote greater acceptance of situations "as is," the demands for perfection are alleviated.

SECURITY AND PREDICTABILITY

There is security in predictability. Therefore, phobics look for stability, permanence, and regularity in life. They feel that there is security in marriage, family, home, and friends. When any changes occur, their world is shaken up. They feel insecure and being insecure means they are fearful and fear begins to color their thinking. Phobics need to accept change as a way of life. If they do not, they develop a rigidity of thinking which produces a closed mind and fosters fear.

Their fear of change is also part of their resistance in therapy. They would like things to remain the same, and feel better. When they do change it takes a period of time for them to accept the change and learn to live a new and different life.

SUBJECTIVE TRUTH vs OBJECTIVE TRUTH

Phobics tend to accept their subjective thinking as true and factual without any further objective evidence. They go to great lengths to defend "subjective" truth. They all feel they are clairvoyant and highly intuitive. Since subjective truth contains a very high percentage of error, phobic thinking is frequently very inaccurate. Objective thinking requires mental effort and experimentation, and is far more difficult than subjective thinking, which means we can just do and think as we feel and believe it to be the truth. Along with this, subjective thinking is more impulsive, based on how one feels at that particular moment. Thus, emphasis is placed on short-term comfort or short-term solutions to the problem rather than more logical, objective points of view which would bring into consideration long-term solutions and what the consequences will be of a decision made in the present. We have a little cliché for that in which we say: "Comfort is not our primary goal—getting well is our primary goal."

Reliance on drugs is typical of the short-range point of view solution to a problem. People who are uneasy and want immediate relief reach for a Valium instead of trying to determine what is causing the difficulty and what they might be able to do to alleviate their problems. If decisions are made based on subjective truth, the chances of developing good judgment are small. Using objective truth, the percentage of better results increases greatly.

DISCRIMINATION

Different people vary in their ability to discriminate. Many things look, feel, and sound similar to each other, but some people are able to discriminate more finely among them. In the case of phobics, it seems to be easy for them to see similarities in situations and thereby make generalizations, such as all holidays are weird, or all New Year's Eve parties are awful. Colors, dates, time of day, weather, etc. are other examples. However, they have many difficulties discerning differences. For example, a patient in the hospital sees a new patient brought into the ward. Having heard that this woman has terminal cancer, the patient says to herself, "This woman looks like my mother and therefore my mother is dying of terminal cancer." When her husband comes to visit, she asks him, "Doesn't that woman look like my mother?" He looks at her and says, "Well, she looks about the same age. She does have grey hair, but other than that, I don't see any similarities." He was able to distinguish between the two. The patient did not clearly distinguish between the two and became upset, fearing that her mother was dying of terminal cancer. A thinking pattern frequently seen is, "I am sick—you are well. Therefore, I am entitled to preferential treatment because I have suffered and you haven't. And you owe me that preferential treatment." Phobics also feel great shame—so much shame that they hide themselves. The shame comes to them because they feel that they must have committed some horrendous crime, since other people seem to be able to control their feelings—they seem to be able to be less impulsive, explosive, and volatile. They feel humiliated and begin to hate themselves, feeling fearful that they are unable to perform like "normal people." Consequently, they erect a façade of "normalcy," while never feeling completely acceptable underneath the surface.

MATURITY vs IMMATURITY

Phobics are often immature. One of the most common thinking fallacies of phobics is that it is important that everybody in the world likes them. Consequently, they are extremely concerned about what other people think, to the extent that they are self-conscious and guided by what others think rather than taking control of their own lives. They want what they want, when they want it. They are self-centered rather than other-centered. They have a "me first, gimme" attitude. They have difficulty sharing. They have difficulty accepting "as is." They manipulate rather than negotiate; they will jump to conclusions, rather than test a situation out.

One of our next directions needs to be toward working with people to help them modify their thinking patterns and to be more adaptive in coping with the world.

REFERENCE

1. Griest, J.H. et al. Avoidance vs. confrontation of fear. *Behavior Therapy,* 11: 1-14, 1970.

9

Going Solo: From External Support to Self-support

Martin N. Seif

The method I use to treat phobic people at both the Phobia Resource Center and the Roosevelt Hospital Phobia Clinic is based on contextual therapy (1), a treatment approach that shares similarities with a variety of other forms of in vivo psychotherapy. As a result of my experiences with this therapy, I have found that the successful treatment of phobias is a process which shows considerable similarity from one patient to another, and which, allowing for modifications in intensity and duration, can be divided into four identifiable phases. I call these four phases conceptualization, introspection, introjection, and assimilation.

The first phase—that of adequate *conceptualization*—involves teaching patients how to conceptualize the phobia. My patients learn that the phobogenic, or fear-spiralling, process can be understood as the product of a rapid interplay between future-oriented, terrifying cognitions, on the one hand, and the perception of bodily—especially visceral—sensations, on the other (1). This conceptualization is logical and comprehensible, and allows the phobics to realize with some comfort that their overwhelming and seemingly inexplicable panics have a readily understandable basis.

The second phase I call *introspection*. By this I mean that phobics must learn to adequately attend to their relevant thoughts and sensations which comprise the phobic response. Many phobics initially have great difficulty with this task, and part of our therapy is to teach techniques which help patients learn adequate skills in the technique of self-observation of inner life, or introspection.

Let us skip the third, or *introjection* phase of treatment for the moment, as this will comprise the main body of this chapter.

The fourth phase of treatment—*assimilation*—refers to the gradual, sometimes laborious process whereby patients take the formerly foreign activities of coping in the phobic situation and become familiar and comfortable with them, and, in effect, make them part of themselves. The analogy here is to eating food, where the "unlike" is made into the "like," and the original structure of the food is changed to become part of the individual. In the assimilation phase, patients take what they have learned up until that point, and make it part of themselves—part of their thinking, acting, and feeling. Just as children, whose initial steps are awkward and self-conscious, must successfully assimilate these movements in order to walk gracefully, so must phobics assimilate newly learned, yet still unfamiliar, means of coping in phobic situations before therapy can be considered complete.

The third phase of therapy can be expressed through the analogy of learning to walk, specifically, the development of those first awkward steps. This phase, which I call *introjection,* encompasses the transition from environmental support to self-support. This transition commences at the point where phobics need the presence of the therapist in order to accomplish a task and ends when patients are reliably, even if self-consciously, accomplishing the phobic task alone, unaccompanied by the therapist, and without the overwhelming anxiety which characterized prior attempts. This attainment I call "going solo." Going solo is the point where patients can rely entirely on their own resources to accomplish the task; this is a rewarding and exciting part of every successful therapy.

An integral part of contextual therapy is the patients' gradual contact with the feared situation while accompanied by the therapist. It is precisely at these times—while phobics are experiencing some degree of phobic anxiety—that the therapist is most able to help patients identify the various factors which appear on the one hand to exacerbate and on the other hand to ameliorate the phobic anxiety. The identification and subsequent manipulation of these factors help phobics to manage their anxiety as it arises, and, in so doing, provide a basis for further improvement.

By placing themselves in situations with which they are least able to cope, patients force themselves initially to rely on the therapist for guidance and support. This focus on acting on difficulties, rather than talking about them, demands that patients believe that the therapist can help cope with any encountered problem. In this way, contextual therapy encourages the patients to develop a trusting, highly charged, and somewhat dependent emotional involvement with the therapist. It is only within this emotional context that we can begin the crucial introjection phase of the therapeutic process. What follows is a description of how this works.

As a rule, whenever a patient is able to perform unaided a phobic task that previously required accompaniment, I ask that person to provide a description of the factors which accounted for that accomplishment. I am fascinated by the remarkable similarity among patients in terms of these descriptions as therapy progresses. Let me quote excerpts from the case of a 26-year-old female patient I will call Sally. Sally's fear was of walking in open spaces and especially of crossing streets. The quotations which I excerpt are stereotypical.

The first description is from the eighth week of her treatment, when Sally reported that she had crossed a main street unaided. I asked her how she did it, and she responded, "I imagined you walking with me as I crossed the street. When my fear level got way up there I imagined your beard, your blue jacket. I could see you there. I concentrated on that and it helped me get across."

This response is typical of the first part of the introjection phase. In effect, Sally carries with her a mental image of the presence of her therapist which is replete with visual cues and is remembered with a clarity, richness, and intensity which is eidetic, even hallucinatory, in quality. This vivid mental representation of the therapist functions to provide support to the patient and provide a comforting presence, even in the therapist's absence.

As Sally began to cross additional streets on her own, it became evident that a gradual but distinctive change was occuring in the manner by which she accomplished these tasks. At the 16th session she reported becoming anxious while crossing a street. I asked her how she had managed her anxiety there and she responded, "I imagined you were talking to me. Like you were with me, talking to me, and you were saying what you always talk about, about how the sensations didn't always mean fear, and to concentrate on the present, and I could feel myself start to relax."

This is an example of the second part of the introjection phase. In this quotation it becomes clear that Sally is no longer describing a visual mental representation of the therapist. Rather, she is recounting clear, vivid auditory memories which frequently are sufficiently detailed to include the therapist's distinctive vocal characteristics. Notice also that the verbal content of the memory now takes predominant importance, so that the memories have become more discriminating, less global, and involve the specific functions of support and encouragement that the therapist performs.

In the third and final part of the introjection phase, when the patient is indeed going solo, the process of transition from external support to self-support has been completed. During the 27th week of treatment, Sally spoke about a recent shopping trip in downtown Manhattan. "I sort of keep up an inner conversation with myself. Sometimes I think, 'Hell, what if my legs start to go on me when I'm in the middle of the street?', and then I say to myself, 'Come on, Sally, you can do it; stay in the present; take one step at a time.' I give myself pep talks. I feel sometimes like my own best friend."

It is clear that Sally is now stating to herself the identical statements of technique, support, and encouragement which had previously been told to her by her therapist. Her memory is no longer of the therapist making these statements, but rather the statements and their functional aspects themselves, which can be freely manipulated by the patient. This independent means of managing anxiety as it arises is also a constant connection with the therapist.

These, in summary, are the characteristics of the introjection phase leading to going solo: first, a visual memory of the therapist with eidetic, hallucinatory-like vividness; then, the auditory memory of the therapist's supportive and encouraging words; and, finally, the internal manipulation of the therapist's suggestions, rules, and emotional support. In addition, this process is occurring within the context of an intense, often idealizing emotional involvement felt by the patient towards the therapist—an involvement that has been called positive transference in other psychotherapeutic systems. Also, and importantly, there is a concomitant translation of these internal psychological changes into observable improvements in the phobic symptoms, and, more universally, into a more general ability to cope with anxiety in all aspects of the phobic's life. Finally, these improvements have come about without attending to any presumed underlying defensive dynamics—that is, without analyzing the unawares or unconscious conflicts which are often assumed to underlie the development and maintenance of the phobia.

With regard to a theoretical framework to understand these observations, I believe that we can view the introjection phase as a microcosmic model of personality development, namely, a recapitulation of that aspect of development which leads to the capacity to be and function alone. Furthermore, it apears that contextual therapy provides an optimal therapeutic environment for this development to take place.

To be specific, Winnicott (2), writing on the origins of the individual's capacity to be and function alone, states that this capacity requires the experience "*of being alone, as an infant and small child, in the presence of a mother*. Thus, the basis of the capacity to be alone is a paradox; this basis is the experience of being alone while someone else is present" (p. 30). It requires a confidence in the future, and a belief that the mother, or mother-figure, will be available if needed. If these conditions are met, the supportive mother is gradually "introjected and built into the individual's personality, so that there comes about a capacity actually to be alone" (p. 36), and "This has been referred to in such terms as the establishment of an 'internal environment' " (p. 34).

It is precisely this "internal environment," or internal representation of the supportive figure, which develops during the introjection phase: from global, hallucinatory-like memory of the therapist, to vivid content memory of the therapist's words and actions, and, finally, to self-manipulation of the therapist's advice and suggestions in the form of internal speech.

It appears now that we can conceptualize the therapeutic mechanism of the introjection phase as a necessary present restoration of prior developmental deficiencies. That is, our patients come to us with insufficient confidence in their ability to cope independently with present and future phobic situations (hence, the characteristic catastrophic expectations of the phobic) and they develop this confidence, in part, through the progressively more discriminating introjecting of the characteristics of the idealized but legitimately competent, trustworthy, and caring phobia therapist.

A more detailed description of this early development is provided by Mahler, Pine and Bergman (3) in their elucidation of the separation-individuation process. This is the process whereby the developing infant originates and consolidates a sense of healthy and comfortable individuality. Mahler states that in this stage of personality development, "the characteristic fear is separation anxiety" (p. 9). That is, when the child is sufficiently physically developed to locomote away from the mother, but is not yet sufficiently emotionally developed to function separately from the mother, a form of "organismic panic" (p. 10) ensues, a panic whose characteristics are very similar to the phobic anxiety described by my patients.

Mahler and her colleagues point out that the normal growth of separation-individuation "depends upon the gradual internalization of a constant, positive image of the mother" (p. 109). This internalized image allows the child to function separately.

This achievement, the authors continue, "is a complex and multidetermined process involving all aspects of psychic development" (p. 110). Two essential prior determinants are, first, the development of trust and confidence through reliable support provided by the mother. This support is at first attributed to the mother and is then transferred by means of internalization to the intrapsychic representation of the mother. The second prior determinant is the cognitive acquisition of the inner representation of the mother, or mother-figure. This process allows for the "mother during her physical absence [to] be substituted, at least in part, by the presence of a reliable internal image that remains relatively stable. On the basis of this achievement, temporary separation can be lengthened and better tolerated" (p. 110).

If we compare this normal separation-individuation process to the attainment of going solo, we can note a number of similarities. Furthermore, the use of this model allows us to speculate on the specific areas in developmental deficiencies which are restored during successful therapy.

Mahler identifies four subphases of the separation-individuation process. The first of these subphases, which she calls differentiation, involves the development of a specific and intense bond with the mother. I have already pointed out how the particular methods of contextual therapy serve to maximize this bond.

In the second subphase—which Mahler calls practicing—the internal representation of the mother grows while the child is still "in close proximity to her" (p. 65). Explorations occur at first while still touching the mother, but gradually the practicing brings the child into contact with an ever-wider segment of the world, as the child learns to function at greater and greater distances from the mother. Certainly, here, the similarities to the specifics of in vivo psychotherapy are obvious. The essential point, however, is that exploration and practice take place as an enjoyable, exciting experience only when the explorer—be it the child, the phobic, or, for that matter, any individual—feels a close-enough connection to the supportive figure, a connection that need be not only with the figure itself, but also with its internal representation.

Finally, during the third subphase, which Mahler calls rapprochement, the child's need for mother to share his newly acquired skills and experiences is intensely expressed. This need for closeness, concern, and genuine interest from important others is also a characteristic of the phobic during the introjection phase. Furthermore, it is a compelling reason to include group therapy as an integral part of phobia treatment, for the group members provide an opportunity for rapprochement and emotional refueling which cannot be matched by the therapist alone.

This formulation of the introjection phase easily lends itself to contemporary psychoanalytic theory, especially those theories concerned with the development and analysis of the self. Kohut (4, 5), for example, calls the processes which result in the formation of a reliable sense of self "transmuting internalizations." This sense of self is an essential component of the individual's ability to function independently, with confidence and relative freedom from anxiety. Kohut writes that it is the function of the therapist to create a context which combines proper maturity, receptivity, and optimal frustration, so that transmuting internalizations of the therapist can take place which lead to the formation of a healthy sense of self in the patient. Kohut notes that during therapy, there is a shift in emphasis from the introjection of the entire personality of the therapist towards more and more discriminating introjections, until only a selection of the therapist's specific functions are internalized. This process forms an internal structure which yields a more reliable sense of self and which performs the functions which the therapist at one time performed.

This description is remarkably similar to the phenomenology of the process leading to going solo. In effect, Kohut is stating that an individual's internal environment is formed by a series of progressively more discriminating introjections, so that the resultant internal representation performs the same functions as the external figure, while excluding its more general or irrelevant personality characteristics. This is evident with respect to my phobic patient, Sally, who first remembered my general presence and later my specific words and functions as a means of coping with the anxiety which arose as she crossed streets. Kohut writes that it is the function of psychotherapy to create the conditions for optimal receptivity and frustration so that the necessary "transmuting internalizations" can occur as a *present* restoration of *prior* deficiencies in the formation of a sense of self. And it is precisely these conditions and events which have been described as occurring during the introjection phase of contextual therapy.

Finally, in my search to describe the inherent paradox of the introjection phase—the paradox of needing the presence of another person in order to develop the capacity to be and function alone—I cannot omit the psychological insights of our literary heritage. Kierkegaard (6) describes the child's need for his mother's emotional support at the point where the child starts to walk freely. In his description, Kierkegaard sets forth, in terms of the mother and the child, the precise relationship that the therapist must establish with the phobic who is going solo. He states:

> The loving mother teaches her child to walk alone. She is far enough from him so that she cannot actually support him, but she holds out her arms to him. If he totters, she swiftly bends as if to seize him, so that the child might believe that he is not walking alone . . . And yet, she does more. Her face beckons like a reward, an encouragement. Thus, the child walks alone with his eyes fixed on his mother's face, *not* on the difficulties in his way. He supports himself by the arms that do not hold him, and constantly strives towards the refuge in his mother's embrace, little suspecting *that in the very same moment that he is emphasizing his need of her, he is proving that he can do without her,* because he is walking alone (p. 85).

REFERENCES

1. Zane, M.D. Contextual analysis and treatment of phobic behavior as it changes. *American Journal of Psychotherapy,* 32: 338-356, 1978.
2. Winnicott, D.S. *The Maturational Process and the Facilitating Environment.* New York: International Universities Press, 1965.
3. Mahler, M., Pine, F., and Bergman, A. *The Psychological Birth of the Human Infant.* New York: Basic Books, 1975.
4. Kohut, H. *The Analysis of the Self.* New York: International Universities Press, 1971.
5. Kohut, H. *The Restoration of the Self.* New York: International Universities Press, 1977.
6. Kierkegaard, S. (1846) *Purity of Heart.* New York: Harper and Row, 1938.

10

The Modern Syndrome of Phobophobia and Its Management

Harley C. Shands and Natalie Schor

The syndrome usually called *agoraphobia* has attracted widespread interest in recent years. We believe that this is because the syndrome is a modern emergent, geographically most prevalent in urban centers in which the various contexts of precipitation of symptoms (subways, buses, limited access highways, public speaking requirements, elevators, crowded banks and supermarkets, etc.) occur. When the symptom-picture is carefully examined, it appears that the preferable name for the syndrome is *phobophobia* or even *panicophobia,* since the anxiety experienced is that panic once experienced in the past as a kind of bolt out of the blue might recur. In the state of panic, the level of disorganization is extreme (approximately Freud's *primary* anxiety [1]) and appropriate behavior almost unavailable.

Phobophobia has appeared relatively recently as diseases go. Søren Kierkegaard and Emily Dickinson appear to have been literary harbingers announcing their own symptoms (cf. Shands [2]); Kierkegaard's title *The Concept of Dread* (3) is clearly relevant. A major event in the history of phobia is Freud's 1894 paper on anxiety neurosis (4), in which the clinical descriptions are precisely appropriate to the modern condition. Thorkill Vanggaard (5) describes the occurrences of anxiety neurosis in Denmark during the past 50 years and makes the assertion that this collection of symptoms has been known in Japan only since World War II. The distinguished list of patients suffering from phobic anxiety includes, among many others, the modern masters of psychology William James (6) and Sigmund Freud (7).

The identifying feature of phobophobia is the characteristic pathological anticipation (8) of panic or other disaster. Upon better acquaintance with people who suffer from this disorder, it is repetitively shown that their symptoms are closely related to the capacity for thinking ahead and planning. The most highly developed capacity in modern, as opposed to traditional, societies is that of predicting. For example, many commentators point to enhanced predictive ability as the most significant attribute of the scientist. John Dewey once defined intelligence as the prospective control of the environment; reciprocally, Freud (9) speaks of secondary or signal anxiety as "vor Etwas," i.e., before something, with the emphasis on the vagueness of the "something." Phobophobia patients seem to be hampered by the very context-independence that gives other educated persons a considerable freedom of action in planning.

The typical and closely correlated reportable self-observation in phobophobic patients is an exquisite sensitivity to the visceral components of symptoms and feelings. They are introspective experts, being able to describe significant changes in almost every organ system and region of the body. The two abilities, that of thinking ahead and introspecting deeply into one's own "insides," are closely related to each other. Since it had been found that large numbers of relatively uneducated persons can neither think ahead nor describe inner feelings (10), it seems that paradoxically phobophobics suffer from a hypertrophy of educational experience.

Phobophobic patients are characterized by a high level of development of cognitive skills. The correlation of cognitive sophistication, introspection, and future-anticipation with suitability for psychotherapy has been of major interest for several decades (11, 12, 13). More recently, a widespread preoccupation with cognitive factors in psychotherapy has developed in this country. The characteristic differentiation of the psychoneurotic from the psychosomatic patient on the basis of inability to describe feelings in the latter has been repeatedly noted (14). The recognition of this relationship was greatly increased through the popular neologism invented by Peter Sifneos (15), i.e., alexithymia or "no words for feeling." Both Sifneos and John Nemiah (16) have emphasized that interpretative psychotherapy is contraindicated in working with psychosomatic patients.

The requirement that patients being considered for psychoanalysis must be highly educable was stated by Freud in 1905 (17), along with his opinion that the discipline is an educational process. The correlation is that it becomes of the greatest importance to select patients appropriately for any form of interpretative psychotherapy. Both Sifneos (15) and Otto Kernberg (18) have emphasized that patients familiar with signal anxiety and capable of tolerating it are likely to do well in psychotherapy whereas their non-anxious fellows are not.

It is fascinating, if one begins with the idea that the selection of the patient is the most important variable, that Christopher Jencks and his associates (19) have made the same statement with relation to the process of education in school. They state quite bluntly that the only basis upon which to predict success in school is that of the characteristics of the child upon entrance: In other words, education (like psychoanalysis) is primarily for the educable.

In one other comment about the psychoanalytic system, it is possible to find in Freud's (20) paper on instincts a precise definition of an instinct as an introspectively observable sensory experience. For example, he defines the instinct (or drive, a perhaps preferable translation) as a "gnawing" that "makes itself felt in the stomach" (p. 61). Before the sensation can be described, it is "unconscious." Much of the training undergone by patients in the psychoanalytic process is training in introspection, in learning how their viscera are involved in their feelings.

In the method we have used, we emphasize more than any other one technique the identification of sensations, the interpretation of those sensations as feelings, and the thoughts that can be found to have significant correlation with both sensations and feelings. Since, in general, there is a major gap between behaviorist and psychoanalytic ways of thinking, it is of interest to compare the psychoanalytic method of "making the unconscious conscious" with what Skinner (21) speaks of as the exploration and description of a "private world" of experience available only to the individual in whom it occurs. Skinner notes the particular problem of externalizing sensations so that they can be publicly described in terms of reinforcements from a verbal community, a point to which we will return below.

In another parallel with classical psychoanalytic theory, we find Freud's comments (1) precisely applicable to the method of contextual therapy we have used. This method was pioneered by Manuel Zane (22), who, while he was treating patients in rehabilitation medicine, discovered the importance of working directly with the patient in the significant context. The method, as noted above, focuses primarily upon detailed repetitive training in introspective observation of ideational, visceral, and proprioceptive events. Freud (9) emphasized in his technical comments in 1914 how much patients must be encouraged to examine their own situation:

> The very beginning of treatment above all brings about a change in the patient's conscious attitude toward his illness. He has contented himself with . . . regarding it as nonsense. . . . (He) does not rightly know what are the conditions under which his phobia breaks out. . . .He must find the courage to pay attention to the details of his illness. His illness must no longer seem to him contemptible, but must become an enemy worthy of his mettle, a part of his personality . . . out of which things of value for his future life have to be derived (p. 372).

The core of the method is its recognition of the importance of feedback in both a pathological positive sense and a therapeutic negative sense. Phobic patients are so much preoccupied with the unbearably intense experience of severe anxiety that the threat of becoming panicky acts to produce the very panic predicted. By inducing anxious self-observation in a phobic spiral, the positive feedback effect becomes a self-fulfilling prophecy. By training patients in detached, self-observational techniques leading to objectification, it becomes possible for them to reduce the anxiety through learning negative feedback techniques. Patients quickly learn that the method of objectification is itself a therapeutic technique.

An interesting feature of this method is that it appears not to interfere with other treatments at the same time. Because of its educational nature, we do not prescribe drugs; some patients use varying quantities of minor tranquillizers prescribed by other physicians on an ad hoc basis. In general, along with the emphasis upon learning new strategies of self-observation, we have encouraged patients to use as little medicine as possible.

In our work, we find it uniquely possible to construct a verbal community (cf. Skinner above) dealing with private data in phobia groups because the experience of one phobophobic is astonishingly 1) similar to that of another; and 2) dissimilar to that of a non-phobic person. By comparing and contrasting reports of inner experience, the phobics in our groups find it possible to identify in depth with each other, thus establishing a community in which all can claim membership on the basis of similarly describable inner experiences. This formation of a community leads in many instances to the maintenance of groups in an effective self-help continuation of the experience.

Although we have not had the opportunity to examine our own results in a statistical fashion, DuPont (23) (working with a co-therapist who is an alumna of our program) has reviewed the first 67 cases seen in their own highly similar treatment program. He reports that "92% of the patients thought the phobia program helped them" with "25% saying the program 'totally changed my life for the better'." Our experience supports this conclusion.

Contextual therapy is cognitively oriented and takes place in a classroom-like atmosphere. Two co-therapists work with groups of 10 patients, more or less, in series of one-and-a-half hour sessions lasting eight to 12 weeks. In addition, each patient has a private session each week with a therapeutic aide or helper, whose function resembles that of the teaching assistant in college classes. The T.A. and patient go out together into one or more of the contexts in which the symptoms tend to occur, and the attention of both is focused upon the application in situ of the principles and techniques learned in the group (classroom) sessions.

The first step taken is to emphasize to the patient that anxiety is a symptom that is impossible to avoid completely. The response of the patient is often one of surprise or distress, since the universal hope held is that of finding some complete cure. Many patients remember nostalgically a life without anxiety, sometimes a life of counter-phobic exploits and feats, and they find it difficult to accept that a permanent change has taken place. Concurrently, it is pointed out that the goal is learning how to manage anxiety and to reduce it to the lowest possible level. It is essential to work with these patients at the very beginning in the effort to accept and tolerate anxiety, and to work against their very strong tendency to try to avoid all situations in which anxiety might occur. The patient is usually greatly helped in the group by finding others to whom the notion of "accepting and allowing" anxiety to occur is less distressing.

The next step is the essential operation of objectification, that is, providing the observer (in this case the self-observer) with a set of numbers through which to quantify and differentiate different occasions of anxiety. The scale we use is the familiar one of 0 to 10; patients are instructed to think back to the worst anxiety attack ever experienced and to describe that numerically as a 10. The other end of the scale is the state of total relaxation with no trace of anxiety; many phobic patients say that this never (or no longer) occurs. Coupled with the quantification, patients are given definite homework assignments, in the pattern of the schoolroom. They are encouraged to keep a diary or notebook (in a manner forbidden by many dynamic psychotherapists) in which to make a record, several times a day, of the level of intensity of the feeling and even to chart it in the manner of a vital signs record of temperature, pulse and respiration in a hospital chart. In doing this, patients learn that the symptom varies in relation to the context throughout the day.

Secondly, homework is based upon the use of the common phobic strategy of arranging always to be accompanied when outside. A therapeutic aide trained to accompany patients and to keep them constantly reminded of the "accept and allow" instruction as well as the quantification instruction provides the often essential personal accompaniment as well as the in situ teaching that supplements the group learning—as noted, in the familiar alternation of classroom and field trip.

The next step in this method of treatment involves a further correlation technique. Patients learn to examine the relation between the level of anxiety as now quantified and the time-orientation of the thoughts they perceive themselves to be having at the same time. By classifying thoughts into past, present, and future, it becomes possible to note carefully which kinds of thoughts are associated with higher levels of anxiety. The immediate discovery made is that anxiety is associated with "future thinking," that is, with anticipation of some unpleasant or drastic occurrence. The patient learns that a common response to the discovery of a heightened pulse rate with palpitation is, "What if I am having a heart attack . . . a stroke, or. . . a brain tumor?" It is notable that the hypochondriacal element in the phobic state is often high.

Phobic patients learn to begin to manipulate their own level of anxiety by choosing to think about different topics, running the level up and down. By concentrating upon something as irrelevant as reading very carefully the label on a tin can in a supermarket, patients learn that anxiety can be strikingly reduced by "remaining in the present." Other techniques include counting the pulse at different levels of anxiety while noting how the count changes with distressing or reassuring thoughts, to correlate one variable with another in a multidimensional context. Patients learn to recognize that if they can raise the level of anxiety through the "what if. . .?" method, it is also possible to lower the level by turning off certain kinds of anticipation.

Formally, the method seems to substitute directed introspection for speculative involvement in possible future disaster (the "Chicken Little Syndrome"). Phobophobic patients, more than any other group we know, are able to call the roll of their symptoms: Dizziness, dry mouth, difficulty swallowing, blurring of vision, "butterflies" in the stomach, "rubbery" knees, and feelings of instability are perhaps the most frequent.

The training process in introspection involves detailed discussion of the various somatic and visceral components of the feelings of which they complain. In two commonly used senses of the term, feeling in terms of butterflies in the abdomen tends to be interpreted as feeling in the sense of anxiety. We find it useful to differentiate between sensations or data ("raw feelings") and emotions (initial interpretation of probable behavior). Human beings have to learn this correlation—in common with other forms of correlational thinking.

The technique often succeeds in transforming the condition of anxiety from a hostile invasive experience to a state of familiar companionship ("no longer contemptible," as Freud wrote [9]). Patients learn that, in appropriate intensity, anticipation is a highly effective help in planning (and in the delay of gratification involved in prolonged intensive education). The correlation with self-consciousness immediately apparent in our groups is the very high level of social and educational success displayed, even with the handicap of the phobic neurosis.

CORRELATIONAL THINKING

In scientific work, as the anthropologist Schweder (24) has recently emphasized, the crucial method is that of thinking correlatively. Schweder emphasizes that intuitive thinking tends to rely heavily upon likeness: He uses the example of a primitive treatment of ringworm in which a type of fowl excrement that resembles the form of the ringworm lesion is applied as an example of the erroneous use of likeness.

In our patients, we work intensively with the lack of correlation between breathlessness that may come with exercise and the dyspnea associated with heart disease, or the lack of correlation between the transient dizziness or unsteadiness associated with anxiety and the vertigo that sometimes goes along with a brain tumor. Again and again, phobic patients leap to distressing and highly improbable conclusions on the basis of a superficial similarity in symptoms.

Schweder emphasizes that correlation data-processing depends upon learning the statistical techniques involved in accurate assessment of probability. As we have worked with patients in this method we find consistently that correlational data-processing tends to be utterly lost in the panic state. Phobic people know quite well—and can usually tell an interviewer so—that the subway train is not likely to stop, nor is an elevator likely to get stuck, even though in the news and newspaper reports we do read of certain kinds of accidents on the subway and elevators. Normal people take for granted that many of their activities are dangerous: Crossing the street is not unknown to be a lethal action, for example, but, relying upon the probabilities, people accept the occasional accident as unavoidable. Phobic people often remember clearly the nonchalance with which, not too long ago, it was possible for them to drive, to fly, to take the elevator or subway when it is now quite impossible.

While intuitive thinking relies upon large similarities, correlational thinking begins with local similarities abstracted through sampling techniques. For example, in the common biological example, a fish and a whale look very much alike, and a whale and horse look very different; a bat looks more like a bird than like either a whale or a horse. Thus, it is a major change when the scientist begins to examine whale, horse, and bat from the standpoint that all three suckle their young. This kind of sampling process allows us to make the category of "mammal" and to place these three creatures—aquatic, terrestrial, and aerial—in the same large group. When the deep structure of the skeletons in these three kinds of animal is studied, the anatomist finds that the arrangement of similar bones is isomorphic from the one to the other species. The outward appearance is then called an analogy and differentiated from the inner reality, and the latter is given the term homology.

Taking this method back to the phobic situation shows the importance of sampling in the way it becomes possible for patients to learn to look inside, using the help of the therapist or aide to find the details of the anxiety reaction and to subject that descriptive entity to the numeration procedure through which today's sample becomes comparable with yesterday's and tomorrow's in stochastic fashion.

Instead of finding themselves in a recurrently novel situation of panic, trained phobic people discover a universe replete with correlations. Visceral feelings can be increasingly accurately observed with training; sensory data can be rank-ordered according to a numerical scale. The self-observers learn that the sensory data become more and less intense in rhythmic variation; even the most severe panic is fleeting in its duration. The dreaded situation is an expectation, projected into the future, that some previous experience will reoccur in an unbearable form—the recipe for that very dreaded event to occur.

SUMMARY AND CONCLUSION

In our adaptation of Zane's contextual therapy for phobophobia, the steps involve accepting and describing the condition as an alternative to trying to avoid it, then learning self-observational (introspective) techniques through which it is possible to quantify sensations and the emotions they indicate. It then becomes possible to develop a stochastic self-definition incorporating routine daily and occasional precipitated variation. Through learning the major correlation with pathological anticipation, the patient learns how to increase as well as to decrease the intensity of anxiety. The method can be described as an intensive exercise in self-objectification or, in paradoxical form, as objectification of subjectivity. In our experience, results with this technique (emphasizing intellectual insight) have been far better than with any other therapy we have used previously.

REFERENCES

1. Freud, S. *The Problem of Anxiety*. New York: Norton, 1936.
2. Shands, H.C. Malinowski's mirror: Emily Dickinson as Narcissus. *Contemporary Psychoanalysis,* 12: 300-334, 1976.
3. Kierkegaard, S. *The Concept of Dread* (1844). Walter Lowrie (ed.). Princeton, NJ: Princeton University Press, 1946.
4. Freud, S. The justification for detaching from neurasthenia a particular syndrome: The anxiety-neurosis (1894). In: *Collected Papers,* Vol. 1. London: The Hogarth Press, 1948.
5. Vanggaard, T. *Phallos, a Symbol and Its History in the Male World*. New York: International Universities Press, Inc., 1974.
6. James, W. *The Philosophy of William James*. Ed. Horace M. Kallen. New York: Modern Library, 1925.
7. Henry, G.W. Freud's pathography and psychoanalysis. Fundamentals of Psychology: The psychology of self. *N.Y. Academy of Sciences,* 96: 823-830, 1962.
8. Shands, H.C. Pathological anticipation. *McLean Hospital Journal,* 1: 4-16, 1980.
9. Freud, S. Recollection, repetition and working through. *Collected Papers,* 366-376 (1914).
10. Shands, H.C. and Meltzer, J.D. Unexpected semiotic implications of medical inquiry. In: T. Sebeok (ed.), *A Perfusion of Signs,* Bloomington: Indiana University Press, 1977.
11. Shands, H.C. An approach to the measurement of suitability for psychotherapy. *Psychiatric Quarterly,* 32: 500, 1958.
12. Shands, H.C. *Thinking and Psychotherapy: An Inquiry into the Processes of Communication*. Cambridge, MA: Harvard University Press, 1961.
13. Shands, H.C. Suitability for psychotherapy II: Unsuitability and psychosomatic disease. *Psychotherapy and Psychosomatics,* 28: 28-35, 1977.
14. Shands, H.C. How are psychosomatic patients different from psychoneurotic patients? *Psychotherapy and Psychosomatics,* 26: 270-285, 1975.
15. Sifneos, P.E. The prevalence of 'alexithymic' characteristics in psychosomatic patients. 9th Eur. Conf. Psychosom. Res., Vienna (1972). *Psychother. Psychosom.,* 22: 255-262, 1973.
16. Nemiah, J.C. and Sifneos, P.E. Psychosomatic illness. A problem in communication. *Psychother. Psychosom.,* 18: 154-160, 1970.
17. Freud, S. On psychotherapy (1905). *The Standard Edition of the Complete Psychological Works of Sigmund Freud,* Vol. III. London: The Hogarth Press, 1953.
18. Kernberg, O.F. Psychotherapy and psychoanalysis. *Bulletin of the Menninger Clinic* 1/2: 181-183, 1972.
19. Jencks, C., Smith, M., Acland, H., Bane, M.J., Cohen, D., Gintis, H., Heyns, B., and

Michelson, S. *Inequality: A Reassessment of the Effect of Family and Schooling in America.* New York: Basic Books, 1972.
20. Freud, S. Instincts and their vicissitudes (1915). *Collected Papers,* IV: 60-85.
21. Skinner, B.F. Behaviorism at fifty. *Science,* 140: 951-958, 1963.
22. Zane, M.D.: Contextual analysis and treatment of phobic behavior as it changes. *American J. of Psychotherapy,* 32: 338-356, 1978.
23. DuPont, R.L. Personal Communication, 1979.
24. Schweder, R.A. Likeness and likelihood in everyday thought: Magical thinking in judgments about personality. *Current Anthropology,* 18(4): 637-658, 1977.

11

Psychobiology of Exposure In Vivo

George Curtis, Randolph Nesse,
Oliver Cameron, Bruce Thyer,
and Michael Liepman

Successful treatment of a phobia results in a dramatic change in an individual's response to stimuli that previously produced great anxiety. This suggests a change in the brain's handling of these stimuli, and hence a change in the brain itself. Identification of these brain changes would provide an important key to better understanding and treatment of phobias, and perhaps of anxiety in general.

If phobias are treated by exposure in vivo, these changes take place rapidly and predictably in response to a specifiable set of operations. Among the current non-invasive methods for inferring brain mechanisms are the measurement of peripheral autonomic and neuroendocrine responses and the use of drugs as probes.

DESYNCHRONY OF THE FEAR RESPONSE

Most of what is known about the physiological events during in vivo exposure is compatible with the concept of "desynchrony" (1, 2, 3). This means that some components of the fear response occur in the absence of others and that during treatment the different components change at different rates. This finding is somewhat at variance with Cannon's concept of a stereotyped all-or-none "fight-flight" reflex in which all components—subjective, behavioral, and physiological—change in unison.

During exposure treatment the typical course of events is that avoidance behavior diminishes first (since the therapist requests it), heart rate diminishes somewhat later, and subjective anxiety diminishes still later (4, 5). However, individuals may deviate markedly from the typical pattern. Subjective fear may persist longer than heart rate response, or avoidance behavior may persist longer than subjective fear (6).

Endocrine responses appear to follow a similar principle. Of the subjects studied to date, most have shown either suppression or no change in plasma cortisol levels despite substantial subjective anxiety (7, 8). Those who do increase their cortisol levels have tended to require more prolonged treatment than those who do not. By contrast, about two-thirds of the patients studied have shown significant elevations of plasma growth hormone levels during exposure therapy, while one-third have shown no growth hormone response at all (9). No subject has shown significant changes in plasma levels of prolactin or thyroid stimulating hormone (10).

A speculative, but tenable interpretation of the above findings is that the various aspects of the anxiety response do not all extinguish at the same rate. Behavioral avoidance, subjective fear, and increases in heart rate and plasma levels of cortisol, growth hormone, prolactin, and thyroid stimulating hormone may all be part of a "normal" full-blown anxiety response. During exposure to anxiety-evoking phobic stimuli, the usual order of extinction of the component responses seems to be: 1) prolactin, 2) thyroid stimulating hormone, 3) cortisol, 4) avoidance behavior, 5) heart rate, and 6) subjective fear. However, individual subjects may deviate markedly from the usual sequence. Some exposure to anxiety-evoking stimuli occurs in ordinary living prior to any formally defined treatment. Consequently, phobic patients appear for treatment with various components of the full-blown fear response already extinguished, either partially or completely. The more of the full-blown response previously extinguished, the easier and shorter the treatment.

FAINTING

A puzzling psychophysiological observation is fainting during in vivo exposure. As Connolly et al. (11) have noted, although many phobics report feeling faint in the presence of anxiety-evoking stimuli, actual fainting appears to be limited to persons with "blood, injury, and illness" (B-I-I) phobias; in fact, all persons in their series with this type of phobia gave a history of fainting in these circumstances. Of six persons with B-I-I phobias whom we have seen, only two gave a history of fainting. Both did so while being treated, and in both we were able to document that the fainting was of the "vasovagal" type characterized by a fall in blood pressure and a reduction in heart rate, in contrast to "hysterical" fainting which occurs without any detectable physiological change.

DRUG EFFECTS

The main drug probes used thus far to modify exposure therapy have been drugs of the sedative-hypnotic class which reduce subjective anxiety (12). Probably the "drug" used more commonly for this purpose is not a prescribed medication at all, but ethanol, which is also a member of class of sedative-hypnotics. However, even though these agents may reduce subjective anxiety, they may promote desynchrony and actually impede the desensitization process during in vivo exposure by preventing progressive behavioral approach. We found that subjects with simple phobias who were treated with in vivo exposure after a placebo experienced both reduced subjective anxiety and augmented behavioral approach. However, those treated while intoxicated with ethanol experienced decreased subjective anxiety but *no* increase in behavioral approach after two hours of treatment. In other words, ethanol intoxication produced a desynchrony or dissociation between subjective anxiety and an objective measure of anxiety, that is, approach toward the phobic object.

This finding suggests that treatment under moderate or high (but not necessarily low) doses of sedative-hypnotics may be counterproductive, and supports the finding of Marks et al. (13) that behavioral treatment under the effects of "waning" diazepam may be more beneficial than under "peak" diazepam. And it also suggests, contrary to data reviewed by Marks (14), that the experience of some anxiety may be necessary for effective behavioral treatment (although other interpretations of these data are possible).

REFERENCES

1. Rachman, S. and Hodgson, R. Synchrony and desynchrony in fear and avoidance. *Behavior Research and Therapy*, 12: 311-318, 1974.
2. Hodgson, R. and Rachman, S. Desynchrony in measures of fear. *Behavior Research and Therapy*, 12: 319-326, 1974.
3. Grey, S., Santory, G. and Rachman, S. Synchronous and desynchronous changes during fear reduction. *Behavior Research and Therapy*, 17: 137-147, 1979.

4. Watson, J., Gaind, R. and Marks, I. Physiological habituation to continuous phobic stimulation. *Behavior Research and Therapy,* 10: 269-278, 1972.
5. Thomas, M. and Rapp, M. Physiological, behavioral and cognitive changes resulting from flooding in a monosymptomatic phobia. *Behavior Research and Therapy,* 15: 304-306, 1977.
6. Borkovec, T. The role of expectancy and physiological feedback in fear research: A review with special reference to subject characteristics. *Behavior Therapy,* 4: 491-505, 1973.
7. Curtis, G., Buxton, M., Lippman, D., Nesse, R., and Wright, J. "Flooding in vivo" during the circadian phase of minimal cortisol secretion: Anxiety and therapeutic success without adrenal cortical activation. *Biological Psychiatry,* 11: 101-107, 1976.
8. Curtis, C., Nesse, R., Buxton, M., and Lippman, D. Anxiety and plasma cortisol at the crest of the circadian cycle: Reappraisal of a classical hypothesis. *Psychosomatic Medicine,* 40: 368-378, 1978.
9. Curtis, C., Nesse, R., Buxton, M., and Lippman, D. Plasma growth hormone: Effect of anxiety during flooding in vivo. *American Journal of Psychiatry,* 136: 4A, 1979.
10. Nesse, R., Curtis, C., Brown, G., and Rubin, R. Anxiety induced by flooding therapy for phobias does not elicit prolactin secretory response. *Psychosomatic Medicine,* 42: 25-31, 1980.
11. Connolly, J., Hallam, R. and Marks, I. Selective association of fainting with blood-injury-illness fear. *Behavior Therapy,* 7: 8-13, 1976.
12. Marks, I.M. Psycholopharmacology: The use of drugs combined with psychological treatment. In: R.L. Spitzer and D.F. Klein (eds.), *Evaluation of Psychological Therapies, Psychotherapies, Behavior Therapies, Drug Therapies and their Interactions.* Baltimore, MD: John Hopkins University Press, 1976.
13. Marks, I.M., Viswanathan, R., Lipsedge, M.S. and Gardner, R. Enhanced relief of phobias by flooding during waning diazepam effects. *British Journal of Psychiatry,* 121: 493-505, 1972.
14. Marks, I.M. Cure and care of neurosis. I. Cure. *Psychological Medicine,* 9: 629-643, 1979.

12

The Correlation Between Quantity of Fears and the Ability to Discriminate Among Similar Items

Nancy Jane Flaxman

Over the years we have noticed that people with agoraphobia are very quick to see similarities and connections among things, but have great difficulty seeing the differences. This leads to a great deal of generalization, and "all-or-nothing," "either-or" thinking. Most agoraphobics can easily classify apples and oranges as fruit, but do not think about the differences in taste, texture, etc. Worse than that, they do not even discriminate between one kind of apple and another, or one kind of orange and another.

They tend to classify people with the same lack of differentiation, and this leads to thoughts, such as, "All people are good or perfect except me," or, "Everyone will criticize me," or, "No one could possibly understand me." Many of them speak and think in superlatives—"I am the *worst*," "This is the *best*"—and their thoughts and vocabulary are filled with superlative generalities such as "all," "everything," "never," "nothing," "always," "no one," and "everyone." These thoughts and vocabulary trigger a chain reaction which is usually negative and often catastrophic. Thinking, such as, "Because I once had a bad day when it was raining, I will always have a bad day when it is raining," is very common.

The people we see are highly creative and have very active imaginations. We call these active imaginations "phobic power." A simple thought will start a chain reaction of thoughts in miniseconds. For example, the thought, "My husband is late," can start a chain in the phobic's imagination that will probably be not only negative but extremely frightening. The chain might go like this:

> He's late—he had an accident—he's going to die—I'll be a widow—how will I survive—PANIC.

It does not occur to the phobic that many other reasons for her husband's being late are not only possible, but probably more likely, and that she could wait to see what happened before reacting. Positive cognitive processes do not seem to be utilized. Instead, feelings, usually negative because they are influenced by fear, are believed to be true, and the phobic trusts these feelings and acts and reacts upon them without testing them out for reality. The difference between subjective (feeling) truth and objective (logic) truth is not seen by the phobic, which causes this chain reaction and hair-trigger negative emotionalism. The phobic seems to be highly responsive to his *feelings* about himself and the world around him, and takes these feelings as an absolute truth. Since these feelings are usually scary, the phobic is always expecting something terrible to happen and, therefore, is always uptight and anxious.

Agoraphobics also tend to see the *possibilities,* but not the *probabilities.* These possibilities are usually negative and prevent the person from doing many things. "I can't go into an airplane because airplanes crash." Well, that's true, occasionally airplanes do crash, but many more airplanes fly with no mishaps. The probability of the airplane crashing is very small, but it is possible. But phobics see only the possibility and not the probability, and therefore feel that the risk is far greater than it really is. They do not discriminate between negative, subjective thinking of the possibilities, and objective thinking about the probabilities.

It is interesting to note that the "if it happened once, it will always happen again" thinking is almost universally negative. The possitive aspects are not believed and in fact seem to be totally ignored. Again, there seems to be a lack of discrimination between "good" or positive possibilities and "bad" or negative possibilities.

While this lack of discrimination between what the agoraphobic is feeling and the reality of the situation has been clinically observed over a period of 18 years, and seems to apply to all the agoraphobic's emotions, the primary emotion that the agoraphobic is dealing with is *fear.*

The author therefore decided to see whether there is, in fact, any correlation between the amount of fear a person is experiencing at a particular time and the ability or lack of ability to discriminate among similar items.

DESCRIPTION OF STUDY

Participants in this study consisted of 25 women and 15 men, living throughout the United States and Canada, and ranging from 19 years of age to 70 years of age. Twelve subjects knew they were participating in a research project, 28 did not. However, none of the subjects knew the purpose of the project. Thirty participants had been diagnosed as agoraphobic or ex-agoraphobic; 10 had, by their own admission, never suffered from the problem.

Each participant was asked to fill out a shortened version of Wolpe's fear inventory (1), consisting of 35 questions, in order to measure the quantity of fear they were experiencing at the time. Along with this fear inventory, each participant was given a list of 25 questions as follows:

In the following sets of words, one of the words does not bear the same relationship as the other four. Underline the word that doesn't fit.

1. bread, roll, pastry, muffin, toast
2. mistake, criticism, goof, error, wrong
3. silver, brass, copper, gold, platinum
4. rattlesnake, python, garden snake, boa constrictor, cobra
5. willow, spruce, pine, fir, cedar
6. anxious, excite, nervous, uptight, tense
7. coffee, coca cola, wine, tea, milk
8. definitely, possibly, sure, of course, absolutely
9. argue, shout, fight, quarrel, confront
10. alone, lonesome, isolated, separated, abandoned
11. desert, sand, water, thirst, cactus
12. stop sign, red light, green light, crosswalk, freeway
13. obstetrician, pediatrician, optician, psychiatrist, dermatologist
14. breakdown, break into, breakthrough, break up, breakage
15. ABCDE, GHIJK, KLMNO, QURST, DEFGH
16. avoid, withdraw, back off, retreat, leave
17. mayonnaise, ketchup, mustard, lettuce, butter
18. supermarket, department store, restaurant, coffee shop, bakery
19. chair, couch, closet, table, bed

20. laughing, crying, yelling, sobbing, out-of-control
21. lion, tiger, panther, alley cat, leopard
22. escalator, ramp, elevator, height, stairs
23. mother, mother-in-law, son, father, daughter
24. crazy, strange, weird, hysterical, nuts
25. plane, bus, ferry boat, car, taxi

In addition, 15 of the word groupings were classified as possibly threatening in that these words tend to stir up emotions, while ten of the word groupings were classified as non-threatening.

Figure 1 illustrates the correlation between the amount of fears reported and the ability to discriminate. As the authors expected, the ability to discriminate among the non-threatening word groupings was higher (96%-72%, with a mean of 76%), while among the threatening word groupings, the ability to discriminate had a far wider range (94%-50%, with a mean of 59%).

Figure 1

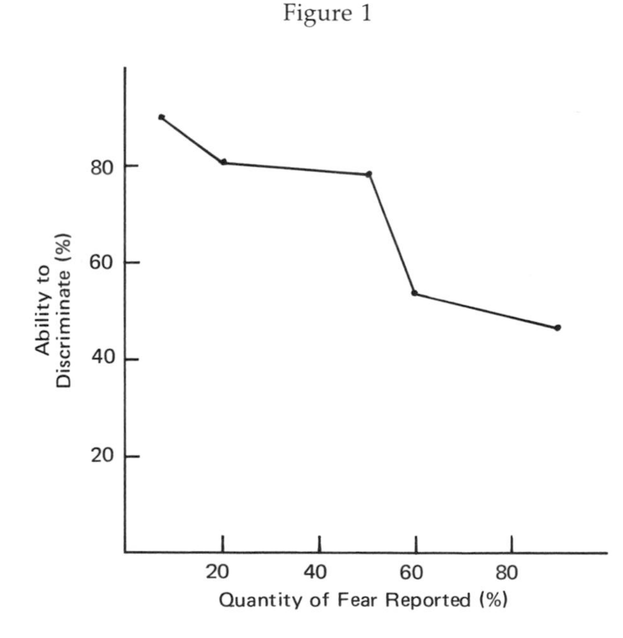

INTERPRETATION

There appears to be a definite correlation between the amount of fear a person is experiencing at a particular time and the ability to differentiate among similar items. No attempt was made in this study to measure discriminatory abilities over a long period of time, when it would be expected that the amount of fear that is experienced would fluctuate.

One interesting factor was discovered in these results. While there did not seem to be any noticeable difference between the amount of fears reported by either men or women, the men were far better able to differentiate among the word groupings, ranging from 88% to 48%. In addition, in a recent study (2), 73% of the 285 agoraphobic participants were women. While these measurements do not indicate any conclusive evidence, it is possible that there is some validity to the hypothesis that men tend to think more logically, while women tend to think more emotionally, and this may account, in part, for the higher percentage of agoraphobic women than men.

CONCLUSION

While systematic desensitization and in vivo exposure have been proven to be very effective in the treatment of agoraphobia (3) and need to be introduced early in our clinical programs, it appears that behavioristic techniques are not sufficient in themselves to produce long-lasting results. While it has been proven that changes in behavior can be effected very rapidly, changes in thinking seem to be achieved far more slowly, and deserve emphasis at this time. The cognitive generalizations and apparent lack of differentiation lead the agoraphobic into unrealistic thinking patterns and a very negative, frightening image of the world. This author believes that procedures which will produce cognitive changes, in conjunction with behavioral changes, need to be developed and introduced into the agoraphobic treatment program.

REFERENCES

1. Wolpe, J. and Lang, P. A fear survey schedule for use in behavior therapy. *Behavior Research and Therapy,* 2: 27-30, 1964.
2. Doctor, R. A large scale survey of agoraphobia. Unpublished manuscript.
3. Bandura, A., Adams, N., Hardy, A., and Howells, G. Tests of the generality of self-efficacy theory. *Cognitive Therapy and Research,* Vol. 4, No. 1, 1980, pp. 39-66.

13

Depression and Agoraphobia—Chicken or the Egg?

David L. Charney

Depression and agoraphobia often overlap. This interplay is seen on several levels. First, at the most basic level the two may be regarded as but different manifestations of the same biological illness. Second, depression may also be present as a psychological reaction in phobics who are experiencing the devastating losses associated with the erosion of their normal lifestyle. Third, depression may appear in depression-prone individuals who happen to be phobic and whose phobia problem so stresses them that it triggers, secondarily, a true endogenous depression. The first case, then, supposes originally a core depressive illness with a coinciding and related phobia; the second and third cases respectively demonstrate depression as being either a psychological or a biological reaction to the stress of living life as a phobic. Sorting out which case holds for any particular patient may become a chicken-or-the-egg proposition.

AGORAPHOBIA AS AN EXPRESSION OF A CORE DEPRESSIVE ILLNESS

That agoraphobia and depression share a common biological root has been postulated by various authors (1, 2, 3, 4). In my own view, mood disorders represent a cybernetic imbalance in the function of certain contiguous midbrain structures, resulting in syndromal depression. Because many key pathways and centers within the central nervous system literally overlap, the Venn Diagram, a model based on overlapping circles, best pictures the notion that the exact expression of any one person's symptoms will reflect which specific centers are affected and which are spared. Hence, we have the "Chinese Menu" notion of depressive symptoms where not all, but some, symptoms in each major category (mood, vegetative, cognitive, etc.) need be present to arrive at a solid diagnosis (5). Utilizing this model, a logical extension would suggest that widening circles would invade additional brain centers and, in a certain percentage of patients, lead to hybrid diagnoses.

The panic response has been linked to separation anxiety (6). Since separation and loss are regularly precipitants of depression, it could be surmised that the brain centers for panic and generalized depression are contiguous. Therefore, it might be predicted that some patients would show a pure depression picture, some a pure panic spell picture (and, ultimately, agoraphobia) and some patients parts of both. In fact, in my practice approximately 20-25% of phobic patients suffer coexisting endogenous depression.

Approximately 10% of depressed patients report panic attacks. This "lumper" (versus "splitter") approach conceptualizes affective illness as being the main unifying core illness and agoraphobia as but one of many possible ensuing complications. Thus, agoraphobia would take its place among a variety of syndromes allegedly correlates of mood disorders, such as alcoholism and other drug addictions, and eating disorders.

What the "lumper" approach loses in specificity it gains in discovering interesting commonalities in clinical phenomenology. For example, factors in depressive and agoraphobic illness which suggest common pathogenesis (7, 8) include:

1) the many cases where the two illnesses coexist in the same patient;
2) the high incidence of depression in the life histories of phobics and their near relatives; and
3) vice versa, the frequency of panic spells occurring during frank depressive episodes;
4) the responsiveness to antidepressant medication by many patients (but not all) who suffer from panic attacks alone;
5) the similar sex ratios with females predominant;
6) the similar ages of onset;
7) the similar sensitivity to hormonal tides, especially in the female;

8) the same long-term cycles of exacerbations and remissions.

This argument does not require depression and agoraphobia to be identical illnesses, merely highly related. If the "panic center" is part of or near the affective illness complex in the midbrain, disturbances in either center would tend to "travel together" much as in genetic illness. (Genetic illnesses determined by contiguous genes "travel together" statistically more frequently the closer together they sit on the same chromosome.)

Furthermore, it would be simplistic to hold that agoraphobia is merely and solely a biological illness. More accurately, the panic attack per se is the biological event which links to depression. The elaboration to an agoraphobic condition depends upon the attention-demanding forcefulness of the panic attack occurring in the psychologically primed individual. The psychological factors set up phobics for the extremes of their avoidance behavior, which in turn develop a life of their own. Since the psychological factors have been very adequately discussed by others, they will not be commented upon here.

The continuing driving force of the biological root of the phobia—the panic attack—may be likened to what happens with a child's swing. Once child and swing are well in motion, all it takes is an occasional extra shove to keep them moving at the same fast clip. So it is with phobic persons who require only occasional panic attacks to remind and reinforce them in their avoidance behavior. The capriciousness of this biological force, the panic attack, and its unpredictable episodic patterning also help explain the exacerbations and remissions seen even in phobics who have successfully completed organized phobia programs and who have truly digested their behavioral and attitudinal lessons. Setbacks with these phobics could be accounted for by supposing that the biological push is temporarily more energetic. This would mirror the situation where a purely biological downswing in mood-cycling can drive a depression-prone person unexpectedly into a frank depressive episode.

The setback can typically occur when during a relatively quiescent period the recovering phobic is lured into a false sense of total cure—and then suddenly the panic attack strikes. Unless phobics are aware of the possibility of a strictly biological setback (which for them may seem irrational in the sense that it is unconnected with events in their life), they may feel all is lost and spiral once more into a chronic state of misery. Thus, long-term undulating cycles in the threshold of alarm of the panic center would be expected to parallel the pattern in affective illness. That is, waves of panic attacks would arise inexplicably during intervals of emotional or environmental calm, their only logic residing in the known propensity of these systems to cycle on their own.

A two-factor model of illness expression would follow for both depression and phobia: The sum of the effects of inner biological vulnerability (one fluctuating variable), and the effects of environmental stress on psychological balance (the other variable), *together* must exceed a certain threshold amount before eliciting an overt episode. Access to the biological variable is available primarily through medication. Access to the psychological dimension occurs through psychotherapy. Both avenues of approach are effective and valid and each has a rationale of its own.

WHY BEHAVIORAL TECHNIQUES ARE EFFECTIVE IN A BIOLOGICALLY-ROOTED CONDITION

The effectiveness of behavioral techniques in agoraphobia results from their capacity to reduce the spiral of anxiety initiated by the panic attack. Behavioral techniques allow phobics to attenuate their psychological contribution to anticipatory anxiety. The anticipatory anxiety may be regarded as a humanly realistic mode of coping with a bewildering condition. However, it is an over-exuberant survival effort resembling the occasional development of a keloid—or excessive scarring—during wound-healing. Carrying the wound metaphor further, feedback loops of biological panic-psychological anxiety are somewhat like scratching at an open wound. The wound here represents the irritable brain panic center. Proper healing cannot take place until the wound is allowed to rest undisturbed. Thus, in time, if the psychological anxiety states are ameliorated through behavioral conditioning and desensitization, the feedback loops are broken and the panic center can settle back into a baseline quiet state. In effect, the behavioral techniques stop the patient from "scratching at the wound."

Behavioral techniques not only help patients to discover for themselves the fundamental illogic of their projecting to an external situation the cause for what, in truth, is an internal event, but also teach them to tune out signals of distress which they come to realize are aberrant and unconnected with a genuinely alarming situation. In other words, they realize that the panic attack is a noise, rather than a signal, and so arrive at an almost philosophical posture which amounts to: "Yes, yes, I hear you; but I'm not listening!" This would parallel the approach of cognitive therapy to depression where inner feelings of depression are not allowed to convince patients that they are unable to function.

THE PURELY BIOLOGICAL TREATMENT APPROACH: ANTIDEPRESSANT MEDICATION

The use of antidepressant medication in agoraphobia underscores the postulated close relationship between agoraphobia and depression at the most fundamental level. Antidepressant medication has convincingly been shown as effective in curtailing panic attacks (9,10), a demonstration that one can "fight fire with fire," a biological diathesis with a biological tool. When panic attacks subside, this therapy holds that the anticipatory anxiety will gradually wither away on its own.

Generally, a low dosage of medication is required, for example, seldom more than 50 mg of imipramine per day, often less, suggesting a relatively hypersensitive organic substrate. Perhaps this generalized hypersensitivity in phobics explains why their panic centers are so prone to discharge with so little provocation. An interesting analogy to seizure disorders can be made here wherein an irritable brain focus (analogous to the panic center) can be subdued through the use of adequate antiseizure medication.

But there are problems with this seductively simple approach. While medication can be quite effective, even as the only modality in many cases, unfortunately a significant percentage of patients (I would guess at least one-third) do not respond at all, or seem to be ultra-sensitive to medication, or become terrified of side effects and ultimately refuse medication outright. For these people the best strategy is to focus primarily on the behavioral techniques. Growth in this dimension of treatment has, in fact, outstripped the use of medication, except among psychiatrists. Phobia treatment centers have sprung up around the country, often upon the initiative of phobics themselves, basing their methods on discovery and elaboration of behavioral techniques, and mutual support groups.

My own inclination in this newer direction followed my failure in successfully treating several patients using only medication and psychotherapy. These patients did not improve as anticipated. Since then, my reliance on medication as the main tool has been supplanted by the group therapy, behavioral techniques model, with emphasis on contextual therapy (or in vivo desensitization). Nevertheless, medication is still called for when the well-trained phobic continues to cycle into setback in a biologically driven pattern.

Now to proceed to the other categories of depression as they relate to agoraphobia.

PSYCHOLOGICAL DEPRESSION AS A CONSEQUENCE OF AGORAPHOBIA

Reactive depression is almost a consistent finding in agoraphobia. This is understandable in view of the massive demoralization which accompanies the phobic's feelings of incompetence, ineffectualness, and sheer loss of self-respect. Phobics feel disappointed and hopeless about themselves, feel weird and different from the common lot of mankind. They are all too aware of their fearful dependency on their spouse or "significant other," feel parasitic and destructive, and cannot help but notice the resentment, bitterness, and anger they arouse in their closest companions. These losses, internal and external, generate the reactive depression. Fortunately, this form of depression can be expected to relent as phobics gain more and more mastery over their problems in the course of treatment.

BIOLOGICAL DEPRESSION AS A CONSEQUENCE OF AGORAPHOBIA

This condition must be theorized to exist in some individuals who are already genetically loaded to depression-proneness. Here we would suppose the usual case, that a person free of frank depression develops a phobic illness through the appearance of free-standing spontaneous panic attacks. In time, the consequences of the agoraphobia complex become such an unbearable stress that finally a biological depression is precipitated when the threshold for such a depression is met.

Differentiating this type of depression from a pre-existing endogenous depression at the time of initial evaluation can be a rather moot point. The exact timing of onset of the depression may help somewhat in determining which came first—the chicken or the egg? But for practical purposes it is enough to make sure that the proper diagnosis is made promptly. It cannot be blithely supposed that all depression will disappear as patients conquer their phobia. After all, biological depressions have lives of their own and may hang on to confound the treatment of the phobia. In fact, on occasion biological depression is so well entrenched on initial evaluation that a decision must be made to postpone the phobia therapy until patients are well enough recovered so that they have at least a minimal amount of energy and attention to devote to learning. Here, medication should be the rule.

CONCLUSION: THE PREFERRED ECLECTIC TREATMENT APPROACH

My own bias now is to utilize primarily the full array of behavioral therapy methods as worked out in practice by most centers: a combination of group therapy, individual contextual therapy and a follow-up self-help program. However, a key decision occurs at initial evaluation which must take into account the message of this paper: Depression in its various guises should be an expected fellow-traveler of agoraphobia. Sorting out which type of depression is present in any particular patient is a clinical challenge which may determine the course of recovery. Clearly, when biological depression is diagnosed, whether it is antecedent or consequent to the agoraphobia, a decision regarding medication is raised. Behavioral treatment, directed at changing the ingrained habitual thought patterns of defensive avoidance, is seen as the essential ingredient of a phobia program. But belief in the primacy of the behavioral techniques need not stand in the way of prescribing antidepressant medication when appropriate.

Today, in the treatment of agoraphobia, there seems to prevail a somewhat doctrinaire gulf between those who espouse behavioral techniques and those who hold with medication. This gulf is artificial, anti-therapeutic, and must be bridged.

REFERENCES

1. Shapiro, K., Kerr, T.A., and Roth, M. Phobias and affective illness. *Br. J. Psychiatry,* 117: 25-32, 1970.
2. Bailey, R.I. and Wooten, L.W. Pain, depression and phobia: A biochemical hypothesis. *J. Internal Med. Res.,* 4(2): 73-80, 1976.
3. Gardos, G. Is agoraphobia a psychosomatic form of depression? Paper presented at conference of American Psychopathological Association, Washington, D.C., April 1980.
4. Klein, D.F. Anxiety reconceptualized. Paper presented at conference of American Psychopathological Association, Washington, D.C., April 1980.
5. Goodwin, F.K. Diagnosis of affective disorders. In: H. Jarvik (ed.), *Psychopharmacology in the Practice of Medicine.* New York: Appleton-Century Crofts, 1977, pp. 219-227.
6. Frances, A. and Dunn, P. The attachment-autonomy conflict in agoraphobia. *Int. J. Psycho-Anal.,* 56: 435-439, 1975.
7. Marks, I.M. The classification of phobic disorders. *Br. J. Psychiatry,* 116: 337-386, 1970.
8. Burns, L.E. et al. Fears and clinical phobias: Epidemiological aspects and national survey. *J. Internal Med. Res.,* 5 (1): 132-139, 1977.
9. Zitrin, C.M., Klein, D.F., and Werner, M.G. Behavior therapy, supportive psychotherapy, imipramine and phobias. *Arch. Gen. Psychiatry,* 35: 307-316, 1978.
10. Treatments for Agoraphobia (editorial). *Lancet,* II: 679-80, Sept. 29, 1979.

14

Phobias, Death, and Depression

Bella H. Selan

A number of psychiatric investigators have noticed the importance of an actual death in the formation of human phobias (1, 2, 3, 4). Seligman (5) thinks that "human phobias are largely restricted to objects that have threatened survival, potential predators, unfamiliar places and the dark." One need not be a Freudian to conclude that dark, unfamiliar places often symbolize death and dying. The question is, just how relevant are past, traumatic events such as death to the type of treatment technique used for the extinction of a phobic response?

Lately, it has become quite unfashionable in psychiatric circles to ponder the *why* of a phobia or other mental disorders. Causal events are increasingly considered as irrelevant to the cure. Behavior therapists claim that phobias are faulty learning patterns which can also be unlearned. Therapists use a variety of behavioral techniques to help phobic clients, such as Wolpe's (6) and Rachman's (7) relaxation and desensitization treatments and Zane's (8) contextual methods. Other practitioners experiment with biofeedback and hypnosis or encourage phobic persons to help themselves by joining support groups which specialize in Claire Weekes' (9) approach to the problem. She calls phobias a nervous illness and advocates thought-changing and other self-help methods for overcoming this illness.

In this chapter, I shall argue that the experience of a real death at a crucial time in life may be an important event in the formation of phobias and phobia-associated depression and, thus, has significance in the selection of treatment techniques. I agree with Hardy (10) that the "basic cause of phobias and the means by which they are perpetuated and maintain themselves provide important clues to the most effective corrective techniques" (p. 27). If behavioral and exposure methods were truly successful in eradicating most phobias, there would be no need to reopen inquiry into original trauma.

According to Richard Stern and Isaac Marks (11), behavior therapists should not be overly enthusiastic about any one method. They caution that although behavior therapy may be a useful technique as part of a general psychiatric management, it does not replace conventional methods. Gelder and Marks (12), like many other researchers and therapists, have also observed that symptomatic treatment is not very successful with severely agoraphobic persons and others who have underlying psychic disturbances.

Single, circumscribed phobias, on the other hand, yield quite well to such treatment. In the past, psychoanalytically oriented therapists spent many years analyzing phobic people without ever helping them overcome the crippling social consequences of their phobias. Despite this remarkable lack of success, many of these therapists still persist in working with a method which gets their patients nowhere except to the therapist's office. Behaviorally oriented therapists need to show that they do not fall into the same self-serving habits.

Death, always a traumatic event, has significant emotional consequences, particularly on the lives and personalities of children. Although death generally causes pain, sadness, and grief, the strength of these reactions often depends on the timing and circumstances. Sudden, unexpected loss by death adversely affects the ability to cope with the finality of separation. An adult whose aged parent dies after having lived a full life or after having suffered from a long, terminal illness is certainly more likely to accept this death philosophically than would a small child whose mother dies suddenly while she is still young. Children have very active fantasies in which death, dying, and abandonment play major roles. Thus, when someone actually does die, some of these fantasies become real and bring about many confusing feelings of guilt, pain, anger, and fear. These ambivalent feelings may result in bewilderment that lets some children succumb to a generalized anxiety about their own security and the security of those who care for them. Uncomfortable feelings of diffuse anxiety when converted to a single phobic symptom become easier to control. In this case, the phobia restores emotional balance to some degree. Being afraid of entering an elevator or a big black bear in the closet does not disorganize a person's life as seriously as the feelings of helplessness and being out of control produced by diffuse anxiety.

Seligman (5) says that those people who feel very much out of control and see themselves as helpless when abandoned also suffer the most severe trauma. This makes sense in the context of our observations. Phobic persons become quite frantic when they think they will lose control in front of others. In such situations, they resort to their phobic rituals, hoping that these maneuvers will once again be effective in restoring control. Paradoxically, these rituals soon become anxiety-producing in themselves, thus defeating their purpose. Therapists are frequently confounded by the variety and rapidity of generalization of phobic behavior. They see a curious dichotomy between the phobics' frantic efforts to remain in control by holding on to symptoms which they say they want to relinquish and by their pathetic dependence and helplessness in the face of seemingly innocuous objects and stimuli.

I have chosen death as an issue in the clinical treatment of phobias because I have found it to be of importance in the lives of many phobic and depressed clients. Seventeen of the 25 phobic clients I have treated in the past year have reported experiences with death and dying which have occurred while they were young or at a crucial age (pre-puberty and adolescence). Most of these clients have also revealed a great preoccupation with death, saying they dream about it often and vividly. The spectre of separation and abandonment is ever present for these clients. A case in point is that of Terry, a 32-year-old client of mine.

Terry first came to see me when she was exactly as old as her mother had been when she died of cancer. Terry had recently seen a TV program on agoraphobia and had recognized that the fears and panics the women discussed were much the same as her own. Until she viewed the program, she had thought she was mentally ill and would soon have to be committed to a psychiatric hospital. Now that she had a tangible name for her symptoms, Terry wanted to be cured. Her biggest fear was that she would lose control in front of others and that she would do crazy things. This fear resulted in social isolation. She only saw her friends when they came to see her; she stayed out of crowded places, like restaurants and supermarkets; and she gave up sports activities she had previously liked. Initially, she thought her panics came "out of nowhere," but lately Terry realized that they could be set off by someone speaking a casual word, by a TV movie, by a book or a newspaper article, or even by an unremembered dream.

Her very first panic occurred several years prior to her entering treatment. She was checking a column of figures at work when she suddenly started to shake, her heart pounded and raced, and her knees became wobbly. She knew that she would have to get up and leave. Outwardly calm, she walked to the restroom where she sobbed and trembled, and put her head against the cool tile hoping the wall would steady her. Someone brought her home and Terry never returned to her job. She had learned to fear the panic.

From then on, life became very difficult. Every time she was forced to leave home, she had torrents of horrible thoughts; even if she stayed in the house, these thoughts would intrude upon her. Rationally, she knew she had little to worry about. Her husband, Joe, was kind and considerate and their marriage was good. The children were doing well at home and at school. The family owned their own home and had no other pressing financial problems.

Concerned about the amount of depression, crying, and disorganization which occurred during the first interview with Terry, I asked her to bring along her husband for the second session. Joe and Terry were informed about the phobia program, were instructed in the use of Dr. Zane's task sheets, and were given a reading list. Joe was extremely supportive of Terry's effort to overcome her problems and offered to help. Terry was also asked to keep a daily diary of her thoughts, sensations, feelings, and actions so we could discuss what happened. After these two sessions, Terry experienced such relief from pressure that she decided to accept a three-hour daily job as a school crossing guard.

Terry, a very compliant and motivated client, never missed an appointment, completed all her assignments as directed, and progressed beautifully. After four meetings, she had resumed going bowling, shopping in supermarkets, and meeting me in restaurants. Although her phobic symptoms were yielding, her underlying fears of "going crazy" were not. She still experienced panics. At this point, I decided on a shift in treatment emphasis toward more traditional psychotherapy. With great difficulty, Terry began to look at her past.

Terry, the oldest of three children, grew up on a Wisconsin farm. Her father, a cold and silent man, was an alcoholic. The family was poor. Although Terry's mother was ill at home for two years prior to dying of cancer, Terry remembers little about her. After her mother's death, Terry, at age seven, was responsible for the care of her younger brothers. She also cooked and cleaned the house and helped with farm chores. Apparently no one gave her recognition or praise for her accomplishments. Several housekeepers came and went until her father remarried several years after his wife's death. The marriage lasted less than two years. Terry described herself as a complacent, quietly efficient child who was always eager to please. Having little time to fritter away on play, she made few friends. After graduating high school, she worked in an office until she met and married Joe, a man who was everything Terry had ever wanted in a husband. He was bright, kind, considerate, affectionate, dependable, fun-loving and nice-looking. Until the birth of her first child, Terry's fears of "going crazy" had been fleeting thoughts. Following this birth, these thoughts became daily preoccupations which intruded on Terry's happiness.

At no time before she entered therapy or immediately thereafter did Terry directly connect her phobias to her mother's death or other childhood events. But neither did she connect these phobias to anything else. They just seemed to be there; her world appeared to shrink day by day. The more anxious she became at the thought of losing control, the more convinced she was that she already was mentally ill. After all, normal, healthy people don't constantly worry about "going crazy"!

The process of delayed mourning was very hard on Terry, particularly because she simultaneously had to face her ambivalence toward her mother who deserted the family by dying and toward her father who did the same by drinking. Like everyone else in her family, Terry believed that she could cope with life without "wasting time" on feelings.

Within a few months, Terry's fear and panic reactions virtually ceased. Her last panic struck in January 1980 after she took Joe to the airport. Although his trip was to be a short one, she felt dejected, abandoned, and deserted. She was able to avoid the worst of the panic by identifying the source and validity of it. She was also able to drive herself home and function fairly well throughout a pretty scary, miserable weekend. Terry terminated therapy in the fall of 1980. Since then she has accepted part-time employment and was able to serve on a two-week jury, getting to the court (15 miles away) by herself.

Hardy (10, p. 33) astutely observed the emotional breakthrough which occurs after some desensitization and exposure therapy. In Terry's case, desensitization and exposure treatments had already stabilized certain frightening parts of her life before we began to explore her painful life history. Terry might have become increasingly despondent and more phobic while exposing her childhood hurts had she not also been reinforced by the success of the exposure and extinction procedures. A purely behavioral program would most likely not have relieved the underlying depression. By the time she had her last panic attack in January, Terry was well aware of the connection between her feelings and her phobia. She wrote me the following letter:

> I was watching a movie on TV today and a thought came to me. I wonder if I have obsessions or a phobia as a wall between me and my feelings? If I have an obsession or phobia, all I can feel is fear—I hardly have any time for other feelings. I know I have always built up walls and walls do not let you feel. I guess I don't want to be hurt. I know I have a lot of feelings but they don't always come out. I would like to take my chances and feel more. I know I must take the risk but if I feel the joy, maybe I have to feel the hurt, too. I want to feel the joy but I am afraid of the hurt. Joe has gotten through my walls; he's always accepted me. I know I take a risk with this, but I have been able to do so with him. Bella accepts everything I say to her and makes me feel everything is not terrible. I like this, but I guess I am afraid to go into my past and just feel it. Maybe that's why I can't remember much about me as a child while my mother was still alive.

Hopefully, phobia therapists and research investigators will direct some attention to the frequent association of death and dying with phobias. These investigators may also want to study phobia-associated depressions which survive so stubbornly even after phobic symptoms have yielded to behavior management. Is it possible that the trauma of death of an important person at a crucial time in one's life is responsible for a majority of depressions compensated for by phobias? Even our enthusiasm for behavioral treatment techniques cannot blind us to the fact that there seem to be certain psychic states like depressions which regularly appear to be linked with severe phobic states. The combination of these two states may well be a signal to therapists to shift to a different treatment strategy to ensure a fair rate of therapeutic success.

REFERENCES

1. Salzman, L. *Treatment of the Obsessive Personality.* New York: Jason Aronson, 1980, pp. 105-122.
2. Arieti, S. *On Schizophrenia, Phobia, Depression, Psychotherapy and Further Shores of Psychiatry.* New York: Brunner/Mazel, 1978, p. 191.
3. Delange, M., Demouchel, A., Poirier, G., et al. A clinical approach to the impulsion phobia. *Annales Medico-Psychologique, 2(5): 821-838, Dec. 1977.*
4. Freud, A. Fears, anxieties and phobic phenomena. *The Psychoanalytic Study of The Child,* 32: 85-90, 1977.
5. Seligman, M. Phobias and Preparedness. *Behavior Therapy,* 2: 307-320, 1971.
6. Wolpe, J. *Psychotherapy by Reciprocal Inhibition.* Stanford, CA: Stanford University Press, 1958.
7. Rachman, S. The treatment of anxiety and phobic reactions by systematic desensitization psychotherapy. *Journal of Abnormal Social Psychology,* 58: 259-263, 1959.

8. Zane, M. Contextual analysis and treatment of phobic behavior as it changes. *American Journal of Psychotherapy,* 32: 338-356, July 1978.
9. Weekes, C. *Peace From Nervous Suffering.* New York: Hawthorn Books, 1972, pp. 1-6.
10. Hardy, A.B. *Agoraphobia: Symptoms, Causes, Treatment.* Menlo Park, CA: Terrap, 1976.
11. Stern, R., and Marks, I.M. Brief and prolonged flooding: A comparison in agoraphobic patients. *Archives of General Psychology,* 28: 270-276, Feb. 1973.
12. Gelder, M.G., and Marks, I.M. Severe agoraphobia: A controlled prospective trial by behavior therapy. *International Journal of Psychiatry,* 112: 309-319, 1966.

15

Changing Marriage Patterns of Agoraphobics as a Result of Treatment

Gerald T. O'Brien, David H. Barlow, and Cynthia G. Last

Agoraphobia, the most severe and disabling type of phobia, can seriously disrupt an individual's ability to function independently. In many cases, the agoraphobic is completely or almost completely unable to leave the house unaccompanied. In more severe cases, the agoraphobic may also be unwilling to travel far from home even if accompanied or to stay at home alone. In addition, most agoraphobics report a wide variety of other fears and other symptoms, such as fear of crowds, fear of losing control, and episodic anxiety attacks. Obviously, such behavior patterns can have a significant impact on the families of agoraphobics as well as on others with whom they may interact. Many mental health professionals have hypothesized that interpersonal relationships may in fact be of critical importance in the development and maintenance of agoraphobia (1, 2, 3, 4, 5, 6). For example, Lazarus (5) presented a case in which the husband seemed to need and want his agoraphobic wife to be excessively dependent upon him. Lazarus suggested that individuals cannot develop an agoraphobic behavior pattern unless someone

This research was supported by Research Grant MH 34176 from the National Institute of Mental Health.

in their interpersonal field submits to their demands and dependency. He concluded that "agoraphobia, then, depends as much upon interpersonal as upon intrapersonal variables both for its origin and its maintenance" (p. 97).

In an important conceptual paper, Goldstein and Chambless (4) postulated that "complex agoraphobia," which is agoraphobia that is not secondary to a drug experience or a physical disorder, virtually always develops in a climate of marked conflict, which is usually interpersonal in nature. They observed that a frequent pattern in the development of agoraphobia is that an individual with low levels of self-sufficiency experiences conflict concerning separation from parents in late adolescence or a desire to escape from an unsatisfactory marriage. This conflict produces anxiety and, if sustained for a sufficient time period, may lead to the experience of acute anxiety attacks. The increased anxiety and panic attacks result in lower levels of self-sufficiency, even greater conflict concerning dependency and independence, and avoidance of situations that potentially may evoke a panic attack. Two other factors also postulated as being critically important in the development of complex agoraphobia are fear of fear, that is, fear of interoceptive sensations of anxiety, and difficulty in appropriately identifying the causal antecedents of unpleasant feelings. Although Goldstein and Chambless' reanalysis of agoraphobia has not yet been empirically validated as a developmental model of agoraphobia, it does seem to be consistent with the clinical picture of many female agoraphobics.

In addition to the interest in interpersonal variables in the etiology and maintenance of agoraphobia, there has been considerable interest in the relationship between interpersonal variables and the treatment of agoraphobia. Some clinicians and researchers have suggested that interpersonal factors, particularly the quality and pattern of the client's marriage, may have an important influence on the client's response to treatment and that, conversely, treatment-produced change in phobic symptomatology may significantly affect the client's marriage and other interpersonal relationships. It seems particularly appropriate to examine the evidence concerning such hypothesized relationships at the present time, since the relatively recent development of in vivo, exposure-based treatments has provided therapists with a powerful tool in the clinical treatment of agoraphobia.

We will first briefly summarize some of the available evidence concerning the influence of clients' marriages on their response to behaviorally oriented treatments. We will then examine more closely the evidence concerning the impact of phobia treatments upon marriage patterns and marital adjustment. We are focusing primarily on marital relationships because most of the evidence concerning interpersonal factors and treatment of agoraphobia is restricted to married agoraphobics and their relationships with their spouses.

In their reports of controlled investigations of the effectiveness of exposure-based treatment programs for agoraphobia, Emmelkamp (7) and Hand, Lamontagne, and Marks (8) noted that marital and family difficulties seemed to interfere with the progress of some of their subjects. Some other studies have attempted to investigate in a more controlled manner the relationship between interpersonal difficulties and treatment response. Hudson (9) classified agoraphobic patients into three groups on the basis of the stability and adjustment of their families. Seven of 18 families were classified as "well-adjusted." Seven were classified as "anxious-patients" families, that is, families that responded to the patient as a highly anxious individual. Four families were classified as "sick" families, in which severe pathology was manifested and the patient's agoraphobia seemed part of a disturbed family system.

All patients received short-term drug-assisted exposure treatment. Three months following treatment, significant improvement (based on a psychologist's global ratings) was displayed by all patients in the well-adjusted families, but patients in the other two family groups displayed only partial improvement or no improvement at all. The poorest treatment response was shown by agoraphobics in the "sick" family group.

In several papers, Hafner (10, 11, 12) has presented evidence of the deleterious effects of marital problems on the effectiveness of behavioral treatments of agoraphobia. For example, Milton and Hafner (12) reported that agoraphobics with unsatisfactory marriages, as determined by median split on a measure of overall marital adjustment, were less likely than patients with satisfactory marriages to improve following intensive, prolonged in vivo exposure treatment. Patients with unsatisfactory marriages were also more likely to relapse during the six-month follow-up period. These studies will be discussed in further detail in relation to the effects of phobia treatments on marriage patterns.

Consistent with the findings of Milton and Hafner (12), Bland and Hallam (13) found that agoraphobics with poor marriages showed somewhat less general improvement in phobic symptoms immediately following in vivo exposure treatment than agoraphobics with good marriages. The agoraphobics with poor marriages displayed significantly greater tendency to relapse during the three-month follow-up. Bland and Hallam speculated that one reason why poor marriages are associated with less favorable treatment response is that the husbands may be less likely to spontaneously provide support and encouragement to their wives during treatment and follow-up and that the wives may be less likely to accept such support, even if it were offered.

To summarize briefly, the findings of Hudson (9), Hafner (10, 11), Milton and Hafner (12), and Bland and Hallam (13) all indicate that when agoraphobia is associated with family or marital dysfunction, it may be more resistant to exposure-based treatments and/or the effects of treatment may be less stable. Some evidence somewhat inconsistent with this conclusion was reported in a pilot study by Barlow, Mavissakalian, and Hay (14) and in a study by Cobb and his associates (15). However, the former evidence is based on only two cases and the latter investigation involved a mixed group of obsessive-compulsives and phobics, only some of whom were agoraphobic. Further investigation of the relationship of interpersonal variables to treatment outcome is still warranted.

We will now more closely examine some of the evidence concerning the impact of therapy on the marital adjustment and marriage patterns of agoraphobics. Milton and Hafner (12) examined the influence of prolonged in vivo exposure on, among other variables, the marital relationships of 14 agoraphobics. Prior to treatment, the agoraphobics were divided by median split of scores on a marital adjustment questionnaire into two groups: maritally satisfied and maritally dissatisfied. As previously mentioned, although both groups improved on phobic symptoms following treatment, the maritally satisfied clients showed greater improvement and their improvement increased following the end of treatment, whereas maritally dissatisfied clients showed no further improvement and some relapse after treatment ended. Milton and Hafner hypothesized that the maritally dissatisfied clients were more dependent than the maritally satisfied clients on the therapist's support and encouragement during treatment. When this support was no longer available following the end of treatment, the maritally dissatisfied clients tended to relapse.

Some information concerning the effect of treatment on marriage is provided by the group means on the marital adjustment self-ratings. Even though the maritally satisfied group reported high levels of marital satisfaction prior to treatment, at the six-month follow-up this group reported significant improvement in self-ratings of both overall marital adjustment and sexual adjustment. In other words, the maritally satisfied clients reported starting off with good marriages and, as a group, showed improvement in their marriages following treatment. In contrast, the patients in the maritally dissatisfied group did not show any improvement in their ratings of either overall marital adjustment or sexual adjustment.

Among the 14 couples in Milton and Hafner's study, eight couples showed some increase in marital dissatisfaction at the six-month follow-up as compared to the pre-treatment ratings. In the other six couples, the marital relationship improved during or following treatment, in some cases substantially. Six clients reported some relapse in phobic symptoms by the six-month follow-up. All of these six clients were in marriages that deteriorated following treatment. Milton and Hafner concluded that there was "a clear relationship between increased marital dissatisfaction and partial relapse during follow-up" (p. 810).

Milton and Hafner (12) identified two distinct types of marital patterns that seemed to be associated with deterioration in marital satisfaction and relapse of symptomatic improvement. The first marriage pattern involves what has been labeled by Fry (2) the "compulsory marriage." In this type of marriage, the agoraphobic partner's symptoms presumably serve to maintain the marriage, even though the marriage may be full of conflict and unsatisfying to one or both partners. Since the wife cannot be alone or travel anywhere unless accompanied by someone, usually the husband, the wife is unable to leave the marriage. Similarly, the husband cannot leave his wife, since she is so completely dependent upon him. If, however, treatment successfully reduces the wife's fears and avoidance behavior and consequently her overdependence on her husband, the compulsory nature of the relationship is changed. The possibility that the spouse may now leave may be very threatening to either or both partners.

Milton and Hafner reported that in one couple that they treated, which was not included in the analyses because of missing data, the husband permanently left his wife three weeks following successful in vivo exposure treatment. In two originally dissatisfactory marriages, the wives began to fear that their husbands might leave them because they were no longer completely dependent on their husbands. In Milton and Hafner's opinion, these "patients partially resumed their phobic behavior in an attempt to protect themselves from fears about the dissolution of their marriages" (p. 810). The resumption of phobic symptoms led to increases in the husbands' dissatisfaction with the marriages, followed by a worsening in the patients' phobias, and a return to compulsory and presumably more secure relationships. In three other marriages, all from the originally maritally dissatisfied group, the husbands apparently began to worry that their wives would leave them as their phobic conditions improved. In these cases, the husbands seemed to interfere with the wives' treatment progress and to weaken their self-confidence. Consequently, the wives relapsed somewhat and reported increased marital dissatisfaction, but the husbands were able to feel more secure in the more compulsory marriage relationship.

A second marriage pattern observed by Milton and Hafner to be related to increased marital dissatisfaction among agoraphobic couples involved marriages in which the husband had some type of problem or inadequacy which had not been recognized or focused on because of the wife's agoraphobic symptomatology. Two husbands had sexual dysfunctions and one husband was socially phobic. As the wives' clinical condition improved, the husbands' problems received more attention, resulting, apparently, in increased marital maladjustment. This pattern had previously been recognized by Fry (2), as well as other clinicians.

Hafner (10, 11) has also identified another, rarer pattern of change in marital relationships following the successful treatment of agoraphobia. This involves the occurrence, or more frequently the recurrence, of extreme jealousy on the part of the husband. In such cases, the husband frequently had been excessively jealous and suspicious of his wife prior to the development of agoraphobia, but this jealousy was relatively dormant when his wife was unable to venture out alone. When the wife became more independent following treatment, the jealousy returned, leading to frequent arguments about his wife's suspected infidelity and her activities when away from home without him. Although the total number of cases of this type that have been reported is small, most seemed to result in at least partial relapse of clinical improvement of phobic symptoms.

In summary, Hafner (10, 11) and Milton and Hafner (12) have identified several marital patterns that seem to be associated with possible relapse following successful treatment of agoraphobia and with increased marital dissatisfaction. It should be recognized that these marriage patterns were identified on the basis of clinical and anecdotal evidence and not through carefully controlled quantitative measurement and research. Nevertheless, such clinical evidence is consistent with previous clinical reports (e.g., 2) and suggests specific hypotheses that can be empirically evaluated in more carefully controlled studies. Also in need of further specification is the nature of the positive changes in the marriages in which marital adjustment improved following behaviorally oriented treatment.

A recent study with considerably more optimistic findings concerning the effects of behavioral treatments on marriage was conducted by Cobb and his associates (15). This investigation involved a comparison of in vivo exposure treatment with behaviorally oriented marital therapy for the treatment of 11 couples with co-existing marital and mixed phobic-obsessive problems. In an unspecified number of these couples, one of the spouses was agoraphobic. The couples were randomly assigned to one of two treatment orders in a crossover design. One group of clients received ten sessions of in vivo exposure treatment for phobic or obsessive-compulsive target problems, followed by ten sessions of behaviorally oriented marital therapy. Marital therapy involved contracting, clarification of difficulties and goals, and, where appropriate, sexual skills training. The other group of clients received marital therapy first, followed by in vivo exposure treatment. Each couple was treated individually, with both spouses present during both exposure and marital therapy.

Marital therapy produced significant improvement on marital target problems, which were individually identified for each couple, but no improvement on phobic-obsessive targets. Exposure treatment produced significant improvement on phobic-obsessive targets. More relevant to the present topic, exposure treatment also resulted in significant improvement in marital target problems. Thus, direct treatment of phobic and obsessive problems via in vivo exposure resulted in some improvement in clients' marital relationships. The authors concluded that exposure treatments are the treatment of choice for phobias and obsessive-compulsive disorders, even when severe marital problems co-exist with the anxiety problems. They suggested that marital therapy may be appropriate if marital disharmony still exists following exposure treatment.

Although the results of Cobb et al. do provide some evidence of the beneficial effects of exposure treatment on marriage relationship problems, their results should be interpreted cautiously. The sample was very small, not all clients were agoraphobics, neither exposure nor marital treatment produced significant improvement on two structured marital adjustment questionnaires, and the crossover design precludes follow-up of either individual treatment. Finally, and most importantly for the present discussion, the results provide no details concerning the types of change in marriage patterns and relationships that may be produced by exposure treatment. This latter criticism can be applied to most other studies conducted to date as well.

Further information concerning the effects of behaviorally oriented treatment of agoraphobia on clients' marriage relationships is available from preliminary data from an investigation currently being conducted by the authors. If, as the evidence seems to suggest, the spouses of agoraphobics may play an important role in the maintenance and treatment of agoraphobia, then it may be beneficial to include spouses in phobia treatment programs.

We are conducting a controlled comparison of behavioral group treatment of agoraphobia conducted with or without the active participation of clients' husbands. The treatment protocol involves 12 weekly group treatment sessions. Therapy sessions involve discussion of agoraphobia, explanation of the importance of exposure and instructions for conducting self-exposure practice sessions, instructions in the application of coping self-statements (16), and a review of clients' progress and problems during the week. Clients receive weekly homework assignments to practice exposure in naturalistic settings to items selected from an individualized hierarchy of fear-eliciting situations. In the "Spouse" groups, clients' husbands attend all treatment sessions and are instructed to participate in some of their wives' weekly practice exposure sessions, to "coach" them in the use of coping techniques, and to support and encourage increasingly independent behavior demonstrated by their wives. In the "Non-Spouse" groups, husbands are not asked to participate and are not given any instructions concerning helping their wives during the treatment program.

Although we are collecting a large number of dependent measures, including behavioral and physiological measures, we will report here on the two measures most closely related to the relationship between treatment response and marital satisfaction. During each weekly group treatment session, clients complete two rating scales. One is a Fear and Avoidance Hierarchy, on which the respondent rates the degree of anxiety and/or avoidance currently exhibited with regard to 10 personally relevant phobic situations. The second scale is the Marital Happiness Scale (17), which provides a single total marital happiness score based on the individual's current satisfaction with 10 dimensions pertaining to the marriage, such as communication and personal independence. Husbands who participate in the Spouse groups also complete these two measures on a weekly basis. (Husbands rate their wives' anxiety and avoidance on the hierarchy ratings and their *own* marital satisfaction on the Marital Happiness Scale.)

Although this investigation is still in progress, data are available from a total of 24 clients, 10 of whom were in the Spouse groups and 14 of whom were in the Non-Spouse groups. The results concerning pretreatment to posttreatment change in marital happiness are presented in Table 1. An increase in self-reported marital happiness from pretreatment to posttreatment of at least 10 points was selected arbitrarily as the minimum level of clinically significant change. Data from the Spouse groups include ratings made by both clients and spouses; that is, a couple from a Spouse group was classified as displaying improved marital happiness if *one or both* of the spouses showed at least a 10-point increase on the Marital Happiness Scale at posttreatment. One couple was classified separately, under "Split opinion," because both partners reported clinically significant change in marital happiness but they differed with regard to the direction of this change. Data from the Non-Spouse groups include reports from clients only, since the Marital Happiness Scale was not scored by their spouses.

As can be seen in Table 1, when treatment conditions are combined, marital happiness improved from pretreatment to posttreatment for 42% of the clients. A 10-point or greater decrease in marital happiness was reported in only 12.5% of the relationships (combining scoring categories 3 and 4). Slightly less than half of the clients reported stability in marital happiness over the course of treatment. Thus, these results suggest that, for a considerable proportion of married women agoraphobics, behavioral treatment was associated with increased marital satisfaction. In only a small minority of clients was there evidence of deterioration in

Table 1
Pre- to Posttreatment Change in Marital Happiness Ratings

Change in Marital Happiness Ratings	Spouse Groups[1]	Non-Spouse Groups	Total
1. Improvement (≥ 10 points)	5 (50.0%)	5 (35.7%)	10 (41.7%)
2. Stable (No change ≥ 10 points)	3 (30.0%)	8 (57.1%)	11 (45.8%)
3. Decrease (≥ 10 points)	1 (10.0%)	1 (7.1%)	2 (8.3%)
4. "Split opinion"[2]	1 (10.0%)	—	1 (4.2%)
Totals	10 (100%)	14 (99.9%)	24 (100%)

[1]Classifications of clients in Spouse groups based on ratings made by both client and husband. Classifications of clients in Non-Spouse groups based on ratings of clients only. See text for details.
[2]"Split opinion" indicates that both partners reported clinically significant changes in marital happiness from pre- to posttreatment, but that the direction of the change differed for the two partners.

the marital relationship, at least as measured by Azrin's Marital Happiness Scale.

Follow-up data at six months posttreatment currently are available from 11 clients. The clients' marital happiness ratings appear to be remarkably stable from the end of the treatment program to the follow-up assessment. No change in marital happiness of more than 10 points was reported by eight (72.7%) of the clients. One client (9.1%) displayed clinically significant improvement in marital happiness at follow-up and two clients (18.2%) displayed clinically significant decrease in marital happiness at follow-up. A similarly stable pattern was shown by most (five out of six) of the husbands for whom follow-up data are available.

The results shown in Table 1 suggest that the Spouse and Non-Spouse groups may have differed with regard to the proportion of couples showing improved and deteriorated marriages. However, it is premature to make any firm conclusions on this issue. First, the sample sizes are still relatively small. Second, as mentioned above, the figures for Spouse groups are based on data reported by both clients and spouses, whereas the figures for Non-Spouse groups are based on reports of clients only. Thus, the figures are not directly comparable. At the conclusion of the study, we will examine in detail differences between the Spouse and Non-Spouse treatment conditions, with regard to marital happiness and adjustment and a wide range of other variables.

Our data permit a finer analysis than merely looking at pre- to post-treatment change in marital happiness. Since clients complete the Fear and Avoidance Hierarchy and the Marital Happiness Scale on a session-to-session basis, we can examine the relationship between weekly change in phobic behavior and change in marital happiness. Inspection of graphs of hierarchy ratings and marital happiness ratings (scores of clients only) across sessions for the 24 clients who have completed treatment so far reveals that one type of relationship is particularly common. This consists of a predominantly parallel relationship between change (increase *or* decrease) in phobic symptomatology and change in marital happiness. For clients showing a parallel relationship between these two variables, decreases in self-reported phobic symptoms were associated with increases in the client's marital happiness ratings. Conversely, increases in fear symptoms were generally associated with deterioration in marital happiness. (For more detailed examples of such relationships, see the case studies described in [14]). Eleven (45.8%) of the clients displayed a parallel relationship of this type. This type of relationship was observed in clients who reported very satisfactory marriages before treatment, as well as in clients whose marital happiness ratings prior to treatment were low.

An inverse relationship between fear ratings and marital happiness was shown by only three (12.5%) of our clients. For these clients, improvement in phobic anxiety and avoidance appeared to be related to decreased marital happiness, while worsening of self-reported fear was associated with improved marital happiness. Although this relationship was relatively uncommon, it may have important implications for both response to treatment and marital relationships. It is unclear at present whether certain particular types of marital relationships are associated with a parallel relationship between fear and marital happiness ratings, and others are associated with inverse relationships. This question will require more detailed and sophisticated assessments and analyses of marital relationships and interaction patterns.

No clearcut relationship between self-reported fear ratings and marital happiness was identified in 10 (41.7%) of our clients. In these cases, the direction of the relationship between fear and marital ratings frequently varied from week to week or at different points in treatment.

The findings to date from our investigation are encouraging with regard to the influence of behavioral treatments of agoraphobia on agoraphobics' marital relationships. The majority of clients displayed either improved marital happiness or generally stable marital happiness from pretreatment to posttreatment. Relatively few clients displayed deterioration in marital happiness over the course of treatment. Marital happiness ratings were generally stable from the end of treatment to a six-month follow-up. A more fine-grained analysis of the relationship between fear ratings and marital happiness suggests that an inverse relationship between these variables may be relatively uncommon. In summary, for the majority of clients, behavioral treatment appeared to improve the marriage or at least to have no substantial effect on the marriage.

CONCLUSION

Researchers have only recently attempted to empirically evaluate the relationships between marital adjustment and the treatment of agoraphobia. At the present time, the available evidence is quite limited and, in some cases, inconsistent. However, a fair amount of evidence does suggest that some marriage relationships may interfere with treatment and that some relationships may be detrimentally affected by treatment-produced improvements in phobias. In both cases, these marriages are likely to have been maladjusted prior to the client's involvement in treatment. For these marriages, marital counseling during or immediately following phobia treatment may help the couple resolve some of their difficulties and help them adjust to the changes in their relationship brought about by reduction of anxiety, avoidance, and/or overdependency of the phobic spouse. However, no controlled studies have yet been conducted to verify this assumption. In addition, several researchers (e.g., 12, 15) have noted that many couples who seem to be in need of marital treatment refuse such treatment for various reasons.

Our current knowledge of the specific ways in which marriage patterns change following treatment and symptomatic improvement is very limited. We need to develop and employ more specific and sensitive dependent measures and analytic techniques that will provide much more information than overall measure of marital adjustment, satisfaction, happiness, etc. We need measures and techniques that will permit scientific evaluation of hypotheses derived from clinical observations, such as the hypothesis that agoraphobics sometimes are involved in "compulsory marriages," which are predictive of poor response to treatment. This type of research may be helpful in identifying variables and relationship patterns that may predict which marriages will deteriorate following clinical improvement in phobia and which marriages will improve.

One topic that has largely been neglected so far is the manner in which some marriages improve following clinical improvement in agoraphobia. What aspects of these marriages improve? Is it the couple's communication, sharing of affection, patterns of interaction, sexual relationships, or all of these? How do these couples adjust to the reduction or elimination of phobias? If we begin to answer these questions, we may be better able to prevent or treat the marital disruption that occurs in some agoraphobic couples.

REFERENCES

1. Agulnik, P.L. The spouse of the phobic patient. *Br. J. Psychiat.*, 117: 59-67, 1967.
2. Fry, W. The marital context of an anxiety syndrome. *Family Process*, 1: 245-252, 1962.
3. Goldstein, A.J. Case conference: Some aspects of agoraphobia. *J. Behav. Ther. & Exp. Psychiat.*, 1: 305-313, 1970.
4. Goldstein, A.J. and Chambless, D.L. A reanalysis of agoraphobia. *Behav. Therapy*, 9: 47-59, 1978.
5. Lazarus, A.A. Broad spectrum behavior therapy and the treatment of agoraphobia. *Behav. Res. & Therapy*, 4: 95-97, 1966.
6. Wolpe, J. Identifying the antecedents of an agoraphobic reaction: A transcript. *J. Behav. Ther. & Exp. Psychiat.*, 1: 299-304, 1970.
7. Emmelkamp, P.M.G. Self-observation versus flooding in the treatment of agoraphobia. *Behav. Res. & Therapy*, 12:29-237, 1974.

8. Hand, I., Lamontagne, Y., and Marks, I.M. Group exposure (flooding) in vivo for agoraphobics. *Br. J. Psychiat.*, 124: 588-602, 1974.
9. Hudson, B. The families of agoraphobics treated by behavior therapy. *Br. J. Social Work*, 4: 51-59, 1974.
10. Hafner, R.J. The husbands of agoraphobic women and their influence on treatment outcome. *Br. J. Psychiat.*, 131: 289-294, 1977.
11. Hafner, R.J. Agoraphobic women married to abnormally jealous men. *Br. J. Med. Psychol.*, 52: 99-104, 1979.
12. Milton, F., and Hafner, J. The outcome of behavior therapy for agoraphobia in relation to marital adjustment. *Arch. Gen. Psychiat.*, 36: 807-811, 1979.
13. Bland, K., and Hallam, R.S. Relationship between response to graded exposure and marital satisfaction in agoraphobics. *Behav. Res. & Therapy*, 19: 335-338, 1981.
14. Barlow, D.H. Mavissakalian, M., and Hay, L.R. Couples treatment of agoraphobia: Changes in marital satisfaction. *Behav. Res. & Therapy*, 19: 245-257, 1981.
15. Cobb, J.P., McDonald, R., Marks, I.M., and Stern, R.S. Marital versus exposure therapy: Psychological treatments of co-existing marital and phobic-obsessive problems. *Behav. Anal. & Modif.*, 4: 3-16, 1980.
16. Meichenbaum, D. *Cognitive-Behavior Modification: An Integrative Approach*. New York: Plenum Press, 1977.
17. Azrin, N.H., Naster, B.J., and Jones, R. Reciprocity counseling: A rapid learning-based procedure for marital counseling. *Behav. Res. & Therapy*, 11: 365-382, 1973.

16

Women's Issues in the Assessment and Treatment of Phobias

Robert Ackerman

Examining and utilizing women's issues as part of the assessment and treatment of female phobia patients can be a significant contribution to a comprehensive approach to the relief of phobic symptoms. A brief overview of the development of current successful forms of primary treatment for phobias is helpful since the use of women's issues in treatment will be discussed as a worthwhile adjunct or integrated part of a behavioral approach.

When we examine the growth of the body of knowledge and practice in the treatment of phobias, the picture is extremely encouraging. There is an observable movement towards the development of specialized primary treatment techniques which are both innovative and highly applicable. These techniques tend to recognize the failure of general psychotherapy (1) to alleviate phobic symptomatology and they integrate a behavioral approach with one or more types of adjunct therapies, such as individual therapy, group therapy, and/or medication. It was clear even to Freud that direct confrontation with the phobic situation itself was essential for recovery. He stated: "One succeeds only when one can induce them through the influence of the analysis to go about alone and struggle with the anxiety while they make the attempt" (2). Unfortunately, the emphasis in the psychoanalytic movement has remained in the analysis or analytical therapy rather than in an in vivo "struggle."

The behavioral movement supplied the very basic techniques that the psychoanalysts failed to develop. The successful work of Wolpe (3, 4) and his contemporaries utilizing desensitization techniques was the beginning of the knowledge and practice base which informed the development of the most current work in numerous phobia clinics and individual practices. Current phobia practice tends to accept the successes of the behaviorists and integrate basic knowledge of desensitization with a prescribed set of techniques which the patient uses alone and in conjunction with a therapist to examine his or her behavior in the phobic situation and support exposure to it. Some therapists such as Zane (5) and Weekes (6) have utilized tapes and records to put the techniques for being in the phobic situation into the hands of the patients.

Zane's (7) "contextual treatment" is also utilized in three phobia clinics* in the New York area which combine the learning of contextual treatment with in vivo exposure with a therapist and group therapy experience (when possible) to validate, teach, and support the patient. The bottom line is clearly the patient's entry into the phobic situation supported by knowledge and techniques that contribute to mastery.

If we accept generally the premise that in virtually all phobia cases the primary treatment of choice will be behaviorally oriented, then what other considerations are there? How can we utilize significant data on phobias to enhance this treatment? In the case of the female patient, such data exist and should be considered very seriously in both assessment and treatment.

DATA ON WOMEN AND PHOBIAS

Let us examine the data concerning women phobia sufferers. Women constitute the majority in the various phobic entity types. According to Marks (8), women constitute 75% of the agoraphobic population, 95% of the animal phobic population, 60% of social phobics and are represented equally with males in miscellaneous specific phobias. However, when we examine treatment studies we see an even larger percentage of women represented as subjects. For example, when Weekes (9) studied 528 agoraphobia patients, 91% were women. In studies conducted by Zitrin (10, 11) at Long Island Jewish-Hillside Medical Center, two-

---

*White Plains Hospital Phobia Clinic, Roosevelt Hospital Phobia Clinic, and The Phobia Resource Center.

thirds of the patients in a mixed phobia study were women and in an agoraphobia study 100% female subjects were used "since the great majority of agoraphobia patients who come to the clinic are women" (11, p. 65). The data suggest clearly that the primary recipients of phobia therapies are women.

A SOCIETAL VIEW

We need only examine the literature of the women's movement to view a cohesive picture of how the historic societal role of women has created a higher level of susceptibility to phobias. The traditional role of women as dependent, fearful, submissive, passive, and easily excitable could certainly be viewed as encouraging phobic behavior. Of course, many women are confined to the home as housewives. In England agoraphobia is called homebound housewives disease.

Women who are confined to the home to do women's work often suffer an anomic state in which their work appears to have no monetary value and is therefore unconnected to family success or personal achievement. This detachment of goals and means from the women's contribution in some traditional families eradicates feelings of self-esteem and mastery of one's world so necessary for mental health. The daughters of families with the more traditional role orientation may be bound into repeating the patterns of their mothers in the family of origin, seeing success as being dependent on a competent male provider. It is common for the practitioner to encounter multigenerational phobic behavior with the phobia as well as role expectations passed on to the next generation.

Traditional roles for women have placed them at risk generally where mental health is concerned. Women are the largest recipients of outpatient therapies both in institutions and with private practitioners (60%-70%) and they are growing as the major recipients at a much faster rate than men. While men begin life with a much greater prevalence of physical and emotional disorders, by adulthood women have surpassed them in most areas. Women have a much higher attempt rate for suicide than men. Females over 18 have a much higher rate of nervousness, anxiety-related disorders, and insomnia and are much more likely to become depressed than men. General practitioners encounter psychiatric problems as the number three presenting problem for women, while it is seventh for men (12).

Since phobias constitute a major diagnostic entity for women, it is reasonable to seriously consider societal expectations of role for women as a contributing factor in the development of their phobias.

THE PRACTITIONER'S VIEW OF WOMEN

To integrate a view of women's role oppression into our assessment of the phobic woman may be difficult. When inquiries have been made into the attitudes of mental health practitioners, the results have been quite startling.

We might expect only the most doctrinaire Freudian to interpret a woman's phobia utilizing sexist psychiatric dogma. Unfortunately, however, our sexist heritage (both cultural and theoretical) remains ingrained in the psychiatric professions. The concept of men seen as the yardstick for health and the inferiority of women was blatantly illustrated in a study conducted by Inge K. Broverman et al. (13) and published in 1970. Psychiatrists, psychologists, and social workers completed a questionnaire. Various traits were listed and the clinicians were asked to signify which roles represented healthy males, healthy females, and healthy adults. Phyllis Chesler (14) summarizes the results in *Women and Madness:*

1) There was a high agreement among clinicians as to attributes characterizing healthy adult men, healthy adult females and healthy adults, sex unspecified.
2) There were no differences among men and women clinicians.
3) Clinicians had different standards of health for men and women. Their concepts of healthy mature men did not differ significantly from concepts of healthy mature adults, but their concept of healthy mature women did differ significantly from those for men and adults. Clinicians were likely to suggest that women differ from healthy men by being more submissive, less independent, less adventurous, more easily influenced, less aggressive, less competitive, more excitable in minor crisis, more easily hurt, more emotional, more conceited about their appearances, less objective and less interested in math or science (p. 68).

Practitioners have tended to reflect the accepted views of society. Major changes for women have come about out of their own activism. We can only hope that some of the ideology of the women's movement has created changes in the mental health field.

A practitioner attempting to help a phobic woman move towards higher functioning would do well to assess the situation not just in terms of behavioral change. Diagnostic assessment should also examine how the patient's role as a woman relates to the presenting symptoms.

DIAGNOSTIC ASSESSMENT AND TREATMENT OF THE PHOBIA

Once an assessment of the behavioral limitations created by the phobia has been made and characterological issues explored, the therapist should examine the patient's female role in family and society. Some of the areas to be explored are the patient's self-image, issues of dependency, family involvement in the symptoms, work responsibilities in the home, history of work outside the home, and attitudes in general regarding mastery, competency, and helplessness. Of course, assessment must take into account the history of these expectations and attitudes. The phobic problems themselves will also have contributed to poor self-image exacerbating pre-existing social limitations.

The therapist may utilize these pieces of information to help formulate a view of the etiology of the phobia, current barriers to change, and how the patient and her significant others may be helped to accept change. Levels of intervention may include work not only with the identified patient but also with family members. The following case example illustrates these issues.

Mrs. A, a 34-year-old married mother of three children aged seven, nine and ten, had exhibited phobic symptoms for 17 years. Mr. A, also 34, married Mrs. A when her symptoms were not yet extreme but certain limitations were quite obvious. Mrs. A had trouble driving distances and crossing streets but did hold down a job as a legal secretary in the neighborhood. Beginning with her first pregnancy she stopped work and became a housewife. Over the next 11 years her symptoms increased so that she was practically homebound, crossing very few streets and driving only selected, very short distances. She became dependent on Mr. A for all other travel.

Mr. A earned an adequate salary to support the family and did not want his wife to hold down a job. When Mrs. A began phobia treatment he made, and continued to make, complaints that it was a financial burden. As Mrs. A made progress with her phobia, Mr. A refused to give any recognition of what she had accomplished. He is currently demanding that his wife accept his unilateral decision to have another child, and become pregnant. As phobic symptoms disappear, the level of family conflict grows. Not only has tension increased in the marital pair, but the children have begun acting-out behavior.

In this case we see illustrated numerous issues of sex-role stereotype. Mrs. A was already experiencing phobic symptoms and the accompanying lack of mastery and low self-esteem when she met her husband.

She felt he was extremely capable and would be a good provider. He, on the other hand, was attracted to an extremely helpless woman, already phobic. Her phobias were acceptable, even as symptoms increased, as long as she fulfilled household and mothering roles. The loss of Mrs. A's phobic symptoms is a threat to the homeostasis of this household. It has been useful to examine the issues of sex role with this family.

While both husband and wife are immersed in traditional roles, it is most typically the woman who suffers the phobic symptoms. In the case of the family cited above, bringing in the issue of sexist role expectations has been a useful adjunct to the ongoing successful behavioral treatment of Mrs. A. Hopefully, family resistance to Mrs. A's progress in working on her phobias can be diminished.

In my intervention with the A family it has been helpful to use women's issues in both individual and marital sessions. Parents and children might also be seen together, but in the A family there has been resistance to this suggestion. With Mrs. A, I have placed a heavy emphasis on the importance of time spent alone. She has begun to recognize that she has not only family responsibilities, but also a duty to herself as an individual. It has also been stressed that with improvement of the phobias she is a much better role model for her children. She has discussed the issue of a new pregnancy, which she feels would be unwise because of the phobias and current high level of family conflict. Her realization that a pregnancy would put her back into an extremely dependent and helpless state has been supported. This support has enabled her to insist that this sort of decision should reflect the wishes of both husband and wife.

Meetings with the marital pair involved the negotiation of free time for Mrs. A to work on her phobias or attend classes at a neighborhood center. During this free time Mr. A has accepted some responsibility for the children, preparing school lunches and helping with homework. It was not only difficult for Mr. A to accept these new responsibilities, but also hard for Mrs. A to give them up. Although she felt it was necessary to supervise her husband in these tasks, she was convinced to allow him autonomy.

The purpose of these negotiations is not only to free Mrs. A's time but also to develop a sense of shared responsibility for the children and confidence in the father's parenting ability, and to break down family enmeshment which calls for rigid role behavior. The introduction of this type of material need not have an ideological zeal, but should be discussed in a way which is most palatable to the identified patient and family.

We should not underestimate the value of including the children in some part of treatment. Certainly children who are aware of a parent's phobia will be less confused and frightened if the situation is discussed with them on a level they are capable of understanding. It may be the children, as well as the spouse, who resist changes in the mother's patterns of phobic behavior. Alliances in the family system to preserve the status quo are common. In addition, it is healthy for children to be aware of their mother's attempts to change because, of course, she is their role model for the adult woman, wife, and mother.

In cases of single phobic women who may or may not be living with family, it is also useful to involve significant family members in the treatment to help explore and support role change.

CONCLUSION

It is clear that the most efficacious and parsimonious treatment of phobias is a behaviorally oriented approach which works directly on symptoms. Since women constitute such a large majority of sufferers in most types of phobias, it is useful to assess both the etiology and current state of phobic behavior in terms of accepted role behavior for women. It is clear that traditional socialization of women for a helpless, passive, and fearful role is a contributing factor in the development and maintenance of phobic symptoms. Sex-role stereotypes should be viewed as a barrier to individual and family change. It is useful to include spouse and families in treatment to break down these barriers and facilitate movement in the phobia treatment. In general, helping the phobic woman to change poor self-image through altering role expectations of self and family should be considered a worthwhile adjunct to behaviorally oriented therapies.

In light of the Broverman (13) study and societal values in general, it may be useful for the practitioner to examine his or her attitudes regarding the role of women and to become sensitized to women's issues. There is a wealth of literature that has appeared, emanating from the women's movement, which outlines the effects of the historical oppression of women on mental and physical health.

It is further suggested that the practitioner utilize women's resources outside of the mental health field when appropriate. This might include referrals to women's organizations, consciousness-raising groups, day-care and nursery centers, and the use of women's literature.

The practitioner who makes a serious appraisal of the women's issues in the diagnostic assessment and treatment of phobic women is including an area of major importance into the helping plan.

REFERENCES

1. Marks, I. *Fears and Phobias.* New York: Academic Press, 1969, p. 247.
2. Freud, S. *A General Introduction to Psychoanalysis.* New York: Permabooks, 1958, p. 327.
3. Wolpe, J. *Psychotherapy by Reciprocal Inhibition.* Stanford, CA: Stanford University Press, 1958.
4. Wolpe, J., Salter, A., and Reyna, L.J. *The Conditioning Therapies.* New York: Holt, Rinehart and Winston, 1965.
5. Zane, M. I Never Stayed in the Dark Long Enough, Tape © 1977 c/o White Plains Hospital Phobia Clinic, White Plains, N.Y.
6. Weekes, C. (Cassettes and Records) Hope and Help for Your Nerves, Moving Toward Freedom, Going on Holiday, Rising in the Morning and Facing the Day. Galahad Production, PO Box 5893, Lake Charles, Louisiana 70601.
7. Zane, M. Contextual analysis and treatment of phobic behavior as it changes. *American Journal of Psychotherapy,* 32(3): 338-356, July 1978.
8. Marks, I. *Fears and Phobias.* New York: Academic Press, 1969, pp. 110-114.
9. Weekes, C. *Simple and Effective Treatment of Agoraphobia.* New York: Hawthorn Books, 1976, p. 10.
10. Zitrin, C., Klein, D., and Woerner, M. Behavior therapy, supportive psychotherapy, imiprimine, and phobias. *Archives of General Psychiatry,* 35: 307-316, March 1978.
11. Zitrin, C., Klein, D., and Woerner, M. Treatment of agoraphobia with group exposure in vivo and imiprimine. *Archives of General Psychiatry,* 37: 63-72, January 1980.
12. Levine S.V., Kamin, L. and Levine, E.L.: Sexism and psychiatry. *American Journal of Orthopsychiatry,* 44(3): 327-336, April, 1974. (Summarized)
13. Broverman, I., Broverman, D., Clarkson, F. et al. Sex role stereotypes and clinical judgements of mental health, *Journal of Consulting and Clinical Psychology,* 34: 1-7, 1970.
14. Chesler, P. *Women and Madness.* New York: Avon Books, 1973, p. 68.

17

A Behavioral/Perceptual Model: A Teaching Strategy for Phobic Symptom Reduction

Maralyn L. Teare

A teaching strategy, based upon a behavioral/perceptual model, is the focus of this chapter, which illustrates how a client at the precise moment of phobic experiencing* can effect immediate change through the rapid and consistent application of specific symptom-reduction techniques.

This behavioral/perceptual model is the outgrowth and an amalgamation of many important influences. My conceptual framework of phobic experiencing is being altered and redefined by the very nature of this constantly changing and limitless resource of human potential, and the involvement and feedback of the client-therapist relationship.

It is my hope to convey not only the important psychological interventions crucial to change (change being a reduction in phobic experiencing through the use of specific interventions that diminish perceptual distortions), but also the human aspect inherent and subtle within this

---

*Phobic experiencing, symptoms, and responding are used interchangeably throughout this article, unless defined otherwise within parentheses. This is an all inclusive definition as it relates to phobic behaving, feeling (emotion), thinking, perceiving, and physiological symptoms that develop normally and classically within the Pavlovian conditional-reflex paradigm, with the accompanying autonomic nervous system responses Pavlov induced experimentally (nausea, rapid heart rate, diarrhea, etc.). I. P. Pavlov, Conditional Reflexes (trans., G. E. Anrep, London: Oxford Univ. Press, 1927).

process/relationship. This is not a linear one-dimensional approach, but rather a holistic, multidimensional approach, with each change setting up a chain-reaction that eventually reduces and weakens the basic fear of loss of control.

So often I have found that a mere phrase, a single intervention, reframing a cognition or perception, has untangled, reversed, and ameliorated this process. This working construct that seeks to objectify a subjective process is a crystallization of these most salient phrases from many sources, as well as personal observations. Each has influenced my perceptions and been instrumental in giving form and direction to what often appears to be a nebulous and transitory process.

In Kuhn's scholarly critique of the structure of scientific revolutions, he makes reference to Galileo's concern with the "immediate experience," that is, with the perceptual and conceptual parameters as they occurred, and thereby surrendered their regularities to inspection, resulting in his well-known "laws of motion" (1).

Zane in his contextual analysis of phobic behavior states that, "Such treatment in the very setting where change is occurring greatly facilitates learning by patient and therapist of what happens in phobic situations and of what to do about it" (2). In Murphy's review of Epicurean philosophy, he notes that it is not events that upset us, but rather the way we view them (3). Freud, who was phobic since childhood, expressed pessimism as he said: "It [phobia] doesn't seem to be reducible by psychological analysis and not amenable to psychotherapy" (4).

With these thoughts as a backdrop, the following rationale for the interpretation, observation, assessment, and relearning process emerged and is presented here: 1) a rationale for treatment; 2) in vivo observations combined with client verbal report describing in vivo phobic experiencing as it occurs spontaneously within the phobic situation; and 3) specific examples of interventions taught to the client at the onset of phobic experiencing.

A RATIONALE FOR TREATMENT

A synthesis of 6,856 therapy hours with 76 male and female clients totaling 1,678 sessions over a three-year period is the basis for this study of phobic behavior as it changes within a behavioral/perceptual framework. Although there were age, sex, religious, demographic, and phobia-type (specific to an external complaint—flying, driving, hospitals, leaving home, etc.) differences, it was noted, through observing phobic behavior as it occurred spontaneously during exposure to the phobic experience and recording client verbal report, that at the apex of all phobic experiencing appeared to be a central process—a process that occurred similarly and spontaneously in all clients regardless of phobia type and individual differences.

The two most salient recurring similarities noted were that this aberrant and pejorative process appeared to center around: 1) fear of loss of control (a basic underlying fear that I believe to be at the core of all phobic experiencing), and this fear in turn being perpetuated, reinforced, and maintained by: 2) perceptual distortions (each client's unique perceptual, cognitive, emotional, and physiological misinterpretations of reality). In order to short-circuit and reverse this rapidly spiraling misinterpretation of reality that self-limits and ultimately leads to debilitating anxiety and panic reactions, the therapist attempts to intervene at the precise moment of onset of phobic experiencing, and at the same time makes the client aware of specific occurrences that increase symptoms or lessen them.

The client is taught to use the body as an instrument of biofeedback, and to focus on the onset of low-level biological cues (sweaty or cold palms, rubbery knees, stomach or muscle tension, etc.) as primary indicators that this painful process is rapidly being set into motion. This is the pivotal point for change within this behavioral/perceptual model. In vivo observations, verbal report, and an analysis of tape-recorded sessions are used to isolate and study each client's unique perceptual distortions and the various interventions effective in bringing about immediate phobic symptom reduction.

This is first achieved with the help of a therapist. Then eventually, when the client has learned how to apply these specific interventions swiftly, predictably, and confidently, phobic reacting loses its painful grasp and the individual feels in control again. At the end of these sessions together, the client may not be entirely "symptom-free," but this person is knowledgeable, in fact, an expert, at isolating the precise variables that set the stage for phobic reaction and reduction.

PHOBIC EXPERIENCING: A SYNTHESIS OF THERAPIST'S OBSERVATIONS AND CLIENT VERBAL REPORT

Phobic reactions appear to come rarely in isolation, and to be triggered the fastest through olfactory stimulation, closely followed by the auditory and visual modes. The least intensity and most latency of response lie in the cognitive realm. Recent brain/mind studies indicate that there may be a genetic predisposition to sensitivity (5). I also find, no matter what the stimulus, when the escalating panic that first starts unchecked at a low level physically (from the neck down) is not terminated quickly, the phobic experiencing becomes so debilitating in its rapid spiral upward that in order to hang on to what little control appears to be left, the client becomes physically rigid and non-communicative—blocking all sensory input at this level of anxiety. This powerful resistance that accompanies these high-level symptoms keeps the client from attending to anything external, including the therapist and any instructions. It is difficult, or almost impossible, to intervene and break through this barrier at that level.

Also, I find a direct correlation between length of gaze and symptom level. The farther the client looks into the distance and the more that is consumed visually, the higher the symptoms escalate, high being anything above the neck physically—"heady-type" symptoms described as feeling overwhelmed, light-headed, dizzy, disconnected, detached, and an observer of one's own behavior.

If these symptoms continue at such a high level, patients ultimately experience perceptual disorientation: "The walls are expanding, closing in, shifting, and the floor seems to rise and drop beneath my feet," or, as one man said, "I had to get on my hands and knees in order to regain control again." At this level the client reports being consumed with irrational and perceptual distortions, so much so that going crazy or dying appears imminent as these catastrophizing thoughts escalate.

These thoughts, along with sensory input, left unchecked bring the client into the throes of a panic attack and face to face with the basic underlying fear that maintains this incestuous process of phobic experiencing—fear of loss of control. The frightening part, too, is the client's own awareness that this irrational process serves to drive him/her even farther into this weakened, vulnerable, and highly suggestible state.

Since our bodies are self-regulating systems, homeostasis in the phobic client has been upset and reestablished time and time again through this negative feedback loop (approach-pain-avoidance behavior); therefore, a counter-conditioning process is necessary for a positive internal balance with appropriate responses to occur. An internal positive equilibrium is regained gradually and positively through this relearning process.

IMPLEMENTING CHANGE: THE RELEARNING PROCESS

This relearning process in its entirety involves a myriad of variables too numerous for the scope of this chapter. Therefore, the lack of attention given to relaxation and assertion training, adjunct relationship, family, and career counseling is only a consideration of space, not importance.

Where does the therapist begin to assess and alter phobic experiencing? By the very nature of the problem, it necessitates a highly individualized in vivo approach. Bach, author of *Jonathan Livingston Seagull,* sums this up nicely: "There is no such thing as a problem without a gift for you in its hands"(6). In reverse, the absence of the problem eliminates having the solution at hand. Watzlawick reiterates this differently in his discussion of avoidance rituals, stating that the supposed solution becomes the problem, and that therapy must be applied to the solution and not to the alleged problem (7). Since the solution is inherent in the problem, and therefore evident during phobic exposure, it only stands to reason that by the very nature of the problem it is necessary for the therapist initially to be with the client.

In order for "on the spot" change to occur, it is necessary that the client experience low-level biological cues. On a scale of 1 to 10 (10 being an anxiety attack), 3-4 would be an optimum level. At this level the client is aware, and can attend and respond to new information from the therapist. If alcohol or drugs are used, these low-level biological indicators tend to mask and slow down the relearning process. At the time of exposure, the client is constantly reassured that this is a learned and conditioned response, an attempt at self-help gone wrong, and that the body is reacting normally to the input of inappropriate erroneous life-threatening messages—this serves to keep this negative homeostasis in balance. Under the circumstances, unless perceptual distortions are altered, the client could not be expected to respond otherwise.

This relearning process moves along a continuum: initially the therapist is the primary facilitator of change, and gradually this comes solely under the client's domain. The therapist moves from being directive to nondirective, and the client from external attachment to non-attachment, dependence to independence, non-assertive to assertive. External boundaries are eliminated only to be replaced by the awareness of limitless internal potential and new perceptions. Many use the phrase: "I feel reborn, or brand new, or like a prisoner set free," as they go through these later stages of change.

ROLE OF THE THERAPIST

In the role of facilitator/teacher, the therapist initially assesses the presenting phobic problem of the client, wherever the client is most comfortable, in order to gather important baseline information useful later in implementing change. This interview also serves to establish the necessary rapport and trust crucial to any therapeutic relationship. During the initial interview, special attention is given to the client's existing repertoire of psychological strengths: appropriate and productive behaviors, special interests, and specifically what the client is doing, in the absence of phobic experiencing, that can be encouraged and utilized later. The opposite is investigated at the time of exposure. A synthesis of this information establishes the unique individual parameters for relearning, with present adaptive skills being the inroad to change.

As therapist and client set out on the first in vivo session together, the client is instructed to use a scale of 1-10 to assess the moment-by-moment "comfort level," with 1 being most comfortable (very relaxed), and 10 being least comfortable (panic attack). Since semantics are important, reframing "anxiety" into levels of comfort is helpful. Also, the therapist can ask, "Where are you?", meaning any number from 1 to 10 that reflects immediate phobic symptom level, without exposing the client to embarrassment in a public situation, and at the same time obtain an accurate and immediate indication of the client's anxiety level. Also, I find with some clients that this immediate introspection heightens symptoms. Should this occur, it is sometimes helpful to preface this inquiry with: "Before it changes—quick—what is your level?"

IN VIVO INTERVENTIONS—MOMENT-BY-MOMENT CHANGES

The following case illustration is a synopsis of a typical in vivo session and the moment-to-moment changes that occur.

For over 20 years Tony had a fear of heights that prevented him from going above ground level. As this fear generalized to other areas, he found it impossible to look across a large expanse, up at tall buildings, or down from an elevated position. Since all my sessions take us to the environment, I inquired upon leaving: "If you had to approach a flight of stairs, an open or elevated area, how would it have to be for you to be comfortable, Tony?"

As we set out to recreate the ideal or a close facsimile (on a college campus in a serene setting, with an open outside staircase and people nearby), I noticed that even as we approached any area that was elevated, recessed, or wide-open, his visual gaze was instantly drawn to the most uncomfortable aspects of the situation, causing him to freeze physically and experience immediate anxiety. His comfort level went from 3 to 7 in that moment.

During this first session we were able to pinpoint that the swiftness of onset of his anxiety was escalated visually by attending to too much too far away that was perceived and labeled as threatening. By the third session Tony was able to sit two steps from the top of the "ideal flight of stairs" comfortably if he: 1) entered the situation gradually; 2) was sitting down and moving up the stairs backwards; 3) kept constant eye contact with me, 4) stayed immersed in the moment by describing immediate sounds, smells, and the warmth of the sun (all positives—no dredging up of the past was allowed!), and 5) kept his body physically "floppy."*

The critical area for Tony centered around visual stimulation. As long as he kept his gaze close, body limp, and stayed in the moment, he had few or no symptoms. The instant he chose to glance downward he flooded himself with anticipatory thoughts, perceptual distortions, and thereby escalated his anxiety. Once the thought processes raced ahead and he got into comparative thinking, and making statements like: "I'm so high up," the anxiety spiraled. This was promptly checked by getting his attention (good eye contact) and having him describe in great detail the complicated workings of his watch. We checked in with his comfort level promptly (it had dropped from 7 to 3 instantly). We left the situation while he was still low. He understood in that moment what the distinct variables of change were. Initially the situation was manipulated by me, but ultimately he came to realize that he has all the controls within himself and will eventually know precisely how and when to exercise them as he gains more self-confidence.

Some other brief illustrations of specific interventions helpful in the immediate reduction of perceptual distortions and phobic experiencing are:

1) Reality testing and relabeling. One client's chronic complaint that prevented her from going more than a few blocks from her home was hyperventilation, and yet when she complained of this symptom it was never observable to me. After ruling out anything physical through her physician and having researched the matter beforehand, we set out to jog together (one of the pleasurable things she had missed since her phobias began). As her breathing got heavier, I asked her: "Is this how you feel when you are hyperventilating?" She said, "Yes, exactly!" I

---

*The word "relaxation" for many denotes "letting go" or giving up control, so I use "floppy," "loose," or "limp."

reassured her of my findings: that it was impossible to jog and hyperventilate at the same time. The symptom got relabeled and was never mentioned again.

2) Paradoxical intention. Another client's symptom was also in the breathing area, only he thought in a phobic situation each breath was his last. I encouraged him to take a breath, hold it as long as possible, and when he finally exhaled to describe what happened. He realized that ultimately an involuntary response occurs whether he wills it or not. Once again, another worrisome symptom was permanently put to rest.

3) Visual grounding. As a client and I drove down a lovely tree-lined street at about 45 mph, with the client at the wheel, she exclaimed: "The trees are going by me at 45 mph, and I'm standing still." The observability and irrationality of her own subjective experiencing gave way to rising panic. In that moment, I instructed her to bring her visual focus and thoughts closer to her by focusing in on and counting passing tree trunks in order to shrink her immediate environment to a manageable level. As she did this, she thereby reversed her perceptual experiencing and reduced her anxiety from 8 to 3.

COMMENT

After having spent almost 7,000 in vivo hours with these people, I find that the environment and human potential provide limitless resources to draw upon, and that the therapist is confined only to the extent of his own creativity and imagination. Personally, I find this one of the most gratifying privileges and experiences of my life. It is not necessary to wait three, six, or even 12 months to see positive changes, as these are evident moment by moment in a myriad of ways.

DISCUSSION

The challenge, purpose, and optimism of this study for me were in pinpointing and isolating each client's unique and transient misperception at the moment of occurrence within the context of the phobic experience. The focus for change is an internal one, which constantly redefines and reframes the experience in order to bring phobic symptoms under the client's control, as opposed to other modalities that define and measure change through the pursuit and achievement of external goals. To me, these external goals are only secondary; when reached, they are an outward manifestation that this internal relearning process has been mastered. Only with the awareness and understanding of the exact variables involved is this change accomplished, thereby making it possible for clients to intercede and reverse this spiraling aberrant process. They can then return previously perceived control of the external environment over their lives to the recognition that they have all the controls, but only chose to perceive that they did not.

First, this new interpretation has to come from the therapist, and then it is processed and internalized by the client. Eventually, a consistent reduction in anxiety is experienced. This becomes self-reinforcing across time as an old negative-thinking habit becomes impotent and loses power, while the body readjusts through this deconditioning process, learns new appropriate responses through the relearning process, and thereby replaces maladaptive responses with more positive and realistic ones.

Implications for the future might be to consider the fact that since such a large percentage of major illness and disease is believed to be a result of emotional stress, it stands to reason that the reduction of phobic anxiety may also reduce the client's vulnerability to coronary heart disease, cancer, and peptic ulcers, to name a few. Certainly many of the techniques used in this study would also readily adapt themselves to numerous and varied situations that require "on-the-spot" anxiety and stress management (i.e., test taking, public speaking and broadcasting, athletic performance, etc.) in order to perform at an optimum level.

CONCLUSION

A behavioral/perceptual model utilizing in vivo observations, audio and videotape recordings, and client report was used to observe, assess, and retrain adult male and female clients experiencing phobic reactions to various internal and external stimuli. Although there were age, sex, religious and demographic differences, it was noted through observing clients within the context of their phobic experience that at the apex of all phobic reactions appeared to be a similar process that occurred across all clients regardless of phobia type.

In an attempt to reduce phobic symptoms quickly, this author focused on two of the most salient and maladaptive aspects of this internal process: fear of loss of control (a basic underlying fear prevalent with all clients), and perceptual aberrations (each client's unique perceptual, cognitive, emotional, and physiological misinterpretation of reality).

Fundamental to change was a relearning process that involved a moment-by-moment awareness and assessment, through the use of biological cues (rapid heart rate, stomach tension, etc.) as immediate indicators. These cues become the focal point for teaching the client how to alter perceptual distortions that occurred rapidly and collectively in any given moment during exposure to the phobic stimuli.

For a reduction in phobic response to occur, it was necessary that the therapist accurately understand the perceptual misconception of the client in order to intervene, reinterpret, and guide the client out of an irrational experience into a more adaptive and rational interpretation of events. When this occurred the locus of control resided once again within the client as opposed to the external environment and a reduction in symptoms was experienced.

REFERENCES

1. Kuhn, T.S. *The Structure of Scientific Revolutions. International Encyclopedia of United Science.* Chicago, IL: The University of Chicago Press, 1970, p. 124-125.
2. Zane, M.D. Contextual analysis and treatment of phobic behavior as it changes. *American Journal of Psychotherapy,* 32: 347, July 1978.
3. Murphy, G. *Psychological Thought from Pythagoras to Freud.* New York: Harcourt, Brace and World, Inc., 1968, p. 32.
4. Laughlin, H.P. *The Neuroses.* Washington, D.C.: Butterworths, 1967, p. 552.
5. Fraser, A. and Wilcox, K. Differing perceptions of "escalator" visual illusion suggest genetic basis. *Brain/Mind Bulletin,* 5(11): 2, April, 1980.
6. Bach, R. *Illusions, The Adventures of a Reluctant Messiah.* New York: Dell Publishing Co., 1977, p. 71.
7. Watzlawick, P. *The Language of Change—Elements of Therapeutic Communication.* New York: Basic Books, 1978, p. 104-105.

PART IV

Specific Phobic Groups

The contribution of Slim Cummings, entitled "Up, Up and Away," is a landmark in the phobia field. Captain Cummings is not only one of the pioneers in the treatment of phobias, but has also provided more help to more phobic people than any other single person in the phobia field. He has brought the concept of treating phobias to the awareness of business as well as the general public. Phobias constitute a significant barrier to the use of the airplane, in addition to the use of other technological innovations associated with modern life, from the freeway to the elevator and the escalator, the supermarket, and even modern shopping centers. With leadership such as that provided by Capt. Cummings, it is possible that many other industries will become aware of the needs of phobic people.

The second chapter in this section is by Jonathan O. Crook and David L. Charney. They describe an effective technique for helping obsessive-compulsive people compartmentalize and then overcome their obsessive thoughts by the use of a tape recorder.

Blanche Goodwin and Eleanor Craig describe the application of supported exposure techniques to children who are phobic of school.

Finally, my chapter, "The Psychology of Phobic Fear of Nuclear Energy," is not specifically about phobias and does not report clinical experiences. It applies the modern concepts of the phobic thought process—the "what if" thinking syndrome—to help understand one of the most controversial aspects of modern life, nuclear power.

18

Up, Up, and Away

T. W. Cummings

I retired from active flying with Pan American Airways about four years ago at the age of 60, the mandatory retirement age for airline pilots. Two years before I retired I began organizing and conducting seminars for people who are fearful about flying. Most of our seminars have been sponsored by Pan Am. We work with groups of up to 100 participants. I say we, because with few exceptions I have used psychologists to assist me in the sessions and on the so-called Graduation Flight. They have been present, too, as both participants and observers, in our seminars.

My interest in psychology goes back to my college days more than 40 years ago. During the early 1970s I began to focus that interest on the plight of the fearful flyer. I read everything that I could find about phobias. Behavioral modification or systematic desensitization seemed to work well with most phobias, but the phobia which concerned the fear of flying seemed to be the most common with the least help available. Repeated surveys indicated that there were 25 million adults in the United States who were afraid of flying.

The problem of fearful flyers seemed to be the building feeling of stress, apprehension, and possible panic. It was threatening enough to keep individuals off airplanes, or, if they flew, they did so drunk, drugged or both. Some just held on for dear life and sat rigidly, looking neither right nor left, feeling conspicuous, very alone, and waiting to see who came apart first—they or the airplane.

Fearful flyers avoided flying, or tolerated it miserably, because they were afraid of losing control, being closed in, heights, the thought of dying—these things and more threatened them.

In the 1930s Dr. Edmond Jacobson (1), a pioneer in the study of tension and relaxation, pointed out that muscle tension always accompanies anxiety and fear. His many papers and books had the message that if you were relaxed you would not then be fearful, and that the ability to relax was a simple learnable skill. Dr. Herbert Benson of Harvard Medical School, in his book *The Relaxation Response* (2), said that all of us had the innate capacity to learn how to relax. He said that so doing would not only improve our physical well-being, but also give us a way to deal with tension and emotional upset.

I had a plan. Transcendental Meditation, Yoga, and Silva Mind Control all use a breathing procedure to reach a passive, relaxed state characterized by a predominance of Alpha brainwaves. I decided to combine a simple breathing procedure with repetitive suggestions for muscular relaxation. This, I reasoned, could be a tool for coping with the habitually escalating anxiety that seemed to afflict the fearful flyer with a feeling of helplessness.

An opportunity to use this method soon presented itself. One evening as I was waiting as a passenger to board a jet flight from Miami to New York, a big man in a heavy coat suddenly emerged from the plane. He was very distraught. He handed the agent his ticket declaring he was too scared to go. He said, "I know that if I go back in there, I'll start screaming." The agent then made this inane remark, "Come on, there is nothing to be afraid of." Of course, with that, the man became even more disturbed.

At that critical moment, the agent, probably seeking to unload his involvement in the predicament, motioned me over and said, "This is Captain Cummings with Pan Am, maybe he can help you." With the mention of the word "Captain" the man turned to me immediately. Yes, I thought, maybe I could help. It was an opportunity all right, but I hadn't intended to put my procedure to such a severe test.

I quickly learned that the man faced loss of his job if he had to take the two extra days required for travel by bus. The agent returned to announce that only two seats remained and that we could have them. I made my move. I told him that I had a method that would make the flight bearable for him but that I needed his pledge of full cooperation.

He hesitated, but as I gently took his arm, he turned with me and we moved through the entrance door.

Once inside the cabin, he again threatened to start screaming as the cabin door was slammed behind us. My heart was pounding as fast as his was. We crowded into our seats in mid-cabin. The man, Larry, first sat on the edge of his seat, quite uncommitted to staying. I immediately started to keep Larry busy. I told him to sit all the way back and to put his full weight down. I had him release his white-knuckled grip on the evening paper. This actually required almost prying his fingers loose. He was sweating profusely. I fastened my seat belt, and the stewardess, well aware of our delicate problem, discreetly avoided interrupting us to insist that his also be fastened.

I ignored his next threat to scream and told him that I wanted him to slowly take three deep breaths. This, I assured him, would noticeably reduce his anxiety. As we taxied and he breathed heavily, I urged him to sink deeper into the seat, to let go and to relax. Although he still indicated an urge to scream, he was following my directions and he seemed less likely to explode. As we taxied toward the runway, I asked him if he had a hobby. He said he did. He played the guitar and had written some ballads. To my surprise he volunteered to sing one. His high-pitched voice competed with the high-pitched sound of the engines as we rolled down the runway for takeoff.

If our odd behavior had not already attracted attention, his singing did. We were indeed a spectacle, huddled together holding hands. He was sweating in that big coat and singing loudly, defying his fear.

Several minutes after takeoff, he asked if we were off the ground yet. I remembered that there is a time distortion that occurs in the trance-like state of complete involvement. He slowly wound down. The threatened scream response gradually faded. He took off his overcoat. On approaching to land at La Guardia he even managed to look out of the window. The whole episode was a very moving experience for both of us.

Psychologists from the University of Houston joined me for the 1975 seminar in that city. A survey that was conducted among the participants after the Graduation Flight indicated that the relaxation exercise was the most valuable and helpful coping tool that they had acquired. Shortly after that, I combined that exercise with other procedures and put them on a cassette tape.

In further support of the credibility of the procedure, I will answer the question, What does breathing have to do with our emotional state? For the most part, the function of our heart in pumping blood and that of our lungs in furnishing oxygen to that process and the procedures of digestion and elimination of food are involuntary and autonomic. The one exception is our breathing. And the rhythm and rate of our breathing, without guidance, are directly in tune with our emotional state. Observe the deep sigh of sadness, the exhalation of relief, the quick inhalation of shock or surprise, the shallow and rapid breathing of fear, the holding of breath as in a temper tantrum and the runaway breathing of hyperventilation. All are reactive and the consequence of an emotional state.

If our emotions change our breathing patterns, can we then reverse the process? Indeed, we can. The pattern of irregular breathing caused by the anxiety and fear of the frightened flyer or non-flyer can be interrupted. With little or no explanation, you can effectively use it with your patients who are in an exaggerated emotional state. Simply direct them to change their breathing response to long, deep breaths. It will not repress the emotions; rather, it seems to divert, fragment their impact.

Besides using the deep breathing method to contend with the ravages of distress, our participants practice its use in nonthreatening settings. They listen to the cassette recording in the comfort of a lounge chair at home or while lying in bed, receptive and relaxed before sleeping. For reprogramming, I have them imagine that we are taking a flight together seated in the passenger cabin. I review all the sequential actions, with sound effects, from engine start-up to engine shut-down. Another part of the tape cautiously works on defusing or neutralizing any past trauma.

Holding on, sitting rigidly, or closing the eyes is often the fearful flyer's way of avoiding the experience of flight. We believe that, for the most part, liquor and drugs also block the experience and, consequently, intensify the threat. We instruct everyone not to deny or repress their pre-flight apprehension. We encourage crying. We hold hands a lot. Groups share much more than a common problem. They also share a certain courage and caring.

The first part of the relaxation exercise is as follows: Decide there is nothing else you need think about right now. Sit comfortably in a chair. Place your feet flat on the floor and rest your hands in your lap, not touching. I suggest you close your eyes.

It takes three seconds to count 1,000, 2,000, 3,000. After each inhalation, hold your breath that long before exhaling. This creates a little tension because it then feels so good to exhale and release that tightness.

Start now, with the first of the three deep breaths. Inhale slowly and deeply, hold that inhalation now as I count 1,000, 2,000, 3,000. Now exhale, let go, and relax. Allow a refreshing feeling of passiveness to come over you as you resume normal breathing for a few moments. Remember that this is a learning process and it may take you a few practice sessions to be able to respond easily and comfortably.

Slowly and deeply take this second breath, inhaling a little more fully and smoothly this time. Hold it for 1,000, 2,000, 3,000. Now exhale, let go. Relax. Exhale completely, sink into your chair. Breathe normally again.

To conclude this exercise, make this deep breath the deepest and fullest one yet. Inhale gently, really fill up. Good. Now hold it for 1,000, 2,000, 3,000 and now exhale and let go and relax completely. Enjoy the peacefulness that is available to you. Breathe normally again now. Relaxed, you are confident and calm and capable and unafraid.

I am going to count to five now and when I have done so, please open your eyes. One, two, three, four, five. Wide awake now, relaxed and refreshed.

I want to close with a poem contained in Wayne Dyer's book, *Your Erroneous Zones* (3). It seems to me to capture the feeling of those who aspire to free themselves from the prison of their fear. It's entitled, "New Directions":

> I want to travel as far as I can go.
> I want to reach the joy that's in my soul.
> And change the limitations that I know.
> And feel my mind in spirit grow.
>
> I want to live, exist, "to be."
> And hear the truths inside of me.

REFERENCES

1. Jacobson, E. *Progressive Relaxation.* 2nd. Ed. Chicago: University of Chicago Press, 1938.
2. Benson, H. *The Relaxation Response.* New York: Morrow, 1975.
3. Dyer, W. *Your Erroneous Zones.* New York: Avon Books, 1976, p. 16.

19

A New Technique for Treating Obsessions: Paradoxical Practice with Cassette Recorder

Jonathan O. Crook and David L. Charney

The cassette recorder is an instrument which has found extensive use in the mental health field. It has been helpful in the training of students, in the communication of information to clients, and in particular, in the education of phobic patients as to the nature and treatment of their disorder (1). The cassette recorder has yet to be exploited in its potential as an active self-help tool for clients' daily practice. This chapter will discuss one such application: the treatment of obsessions.

Clients with an obsessive disorder have an internal feared stimulus rather than an external feared stimulus. The internal stimulus is usually a recurring unwanted thought which seizes their attention. Any attempt to force the thought away increases its power. For example, confronted by the following challenge: "Don't think about an elephant for the next minute!", the mind immediately conjures up the image of an elephant. This capturing process may then spiral to the point where obsessive clients decide there must be something wrong with them, and become terrified by their apparent loss of internal self-control.

Several elements of behavioral therapy have been combined to produce an effective treatment for an obsessive disorder: daily practice, goal-setting, paradoxical intention, and imaginal desensitization.

The effectiveness of daily practice by phobic clients in the feared situation has been demonstrated by Manuel Zane. By confronting the phobic stimulus on a regular basis, phobic clients become both desensitized in vivo to the stimulus, and educated about their internal fear response (2). This therapeutic process leads to attitudinal shifts, which then reduce the spiraling of fear by controlling the phobic's thoughts and imagery. Similarly, daily practice for the obsessive was predicted to be useful.

Paradoxical intention is a useful technique with phobias. Because phobics and obsessives share a similar anxiety response (the phobic to an external stimulus, the obsessive to an internal stimulus), it was reasoned that paradoxical intention would be effective with obsessions, too.

Paradoxical intention is an approach which deals with the anxiety by recommending to clients that they try to maximize their unwanted and frightening physical symptoms rather than try to stop them. Paradoxically, the more they try, the harder it is for them to reproduce their symptomatology (3). In time, clients become reassured that their worst fears of becoming totally overwhelmed by their symptoms will not come true. Gradually, they become more and more confident.

Imaginal desensitization is another technique which has found wide use. Here clients present themselves with stimuli of the kind which they have considered fearful, but in imagination. The theory holds that in time their panicky reaction will gradually extinguish itself. Eventually, the stimulus can actually become boring. Because "flooding" exposure to the stimulus can sometimes be truly shocking, the technique of using imagery is a useful refinement. Clients are encouraged to visualize and imagine graded steps of exposure to the feared object or situation. Thus, they desensitize themselves with some degree of protective distance.

THE TECHNIQUE

Clients are instructed to set aside a specific time slot, say 30 minutes a day, when they can seek a private place at home and not be interrupted. With cassette recorder in hand, they are told to record their most agonizing obsessional thoughts in a prolonged monologue. They are encouraged to "catastrophize" ad lib. As a consequence it would be expected that as the thoughts seize their mind, they will be subject to many of the symptoms of anxiety, distress, and panic with which they are familiar, day to day. However, they are allowed to stop their train of thinking at any point when the anxiety becomes too strong. All the while, the clients are to speak into the tape recorder and describe, in addition to their obsessive thoughts, the symptoms of their associated anxiety state. They are to focus all their attention upon them. They are urged to challenge themselves by making the symptoms more pronounced.

They are instructed to approach this task in a systematic fashion whereby, as the thoughts are uttered, they are to question themselves, "What's the worst thing about that?" In time, this approach allows clients to gradually desensitize themselves to the unwanted thoughts by allowing them to be experienced fully without flight into panic. If bodily symptoms of anxiety arise, they attend to them as well. All the time recording, clients can desensitize themselves in a self-controlled manner within specific time boundaries and on a daily basis.

This method also has an added advantage of giving clients an opportunity to postpone thinking about their obsessions during the balance of the day. Towards their obsessive thoughts they can develop the attitude, "Yes, yes, I hear you, but I have a time set aside to deal with you later. Right now I have other matters to attend to." Thus, outside of their practice sessions clients can refocus upon their immediate environment and present tasks at hand. They begin to gain a measure of control over when and where their thoughts will occur, rather than feeling at the mercy of them.

Therapists can participate in this practice plan by offering to listen to the tapes at their leisure. From time to time at appropriate points in the recording they can provide helpful insights for the clients by recording over the tape with comments of their own, which the clients can later play back.

Initially, as this task is undertaken clients find that their practice sessions are distressing. They provoke the same panicky responses that they are apt to experience when a wave of obsessional thinking seizes them. However, if encouraged and challenged to continue on a daily basis, clients gradually discover that the task is manageable. In fact, over a period of several weeks it typically becomes more and more boring. Ironically, the patients now beg to be relieved of this task, not because it is frightening to them but rather because they are so dreadfully bored by it. Nevertheless, they are encouraged to continue at the task. In time, they discover that the obsessional thoughts no longer have the same power to control their mind and subject them to panicky reaction.

A CASE EXAMPLE

Mrs. S., a 35-year-old married woman and the mother of two children, entered into treatment at our center, complaining of severe obsessional thoughts regarding her health. She would imagine for hours at a time that she was on the verge of a heart attack and would be terrified by various cardiac symptoms, such as chest pains, palpitations of the heart, dizziness, and weakness. She fed these obsessions by frequent trips to her home library where she would read passages in books describing various diseases and their symptoms. This mental activity consumed so much of her energy that she found little time to devote a proper amount of attention to her dearly loved children. In fact, she was hospitalized for more than a year, treated through various approaches, including exploratory psychotherapy, and medications which resulted in little improvement.

Her self-image consisted of self-disdain, low self-esteem, a feeling of hopelessness and weirdness. A major part of our center's program for her consisted of the practical technique described above. The therapy followed a sequence of initial terror of the practice task itself, followed by reluctant participation, then gradually increasing boredom, and finally a weakening of the obsessions' hold on her mental life. As the obsessional thinking abated she was able to turn more of her attention to planning in what direction her life should now turn. For the first time in years she was able to contemplate getting a job.

CONCLUSION

Successful symptomatic treatment of obsessional thinking has been a difficult problem for the mental health professions. Psychoanalytic exploratory psychotherapy has been useful. But when obsessional thought processes are extremely powerful they sometimes seize patients with a forcefulness that makes progress difficult. A new technique is described in this chapter where, through the use of the cassette recorder and behavioral techniques, a program can be organized for obsessive patients which can result in a significant abatement of their symptoms in a relatively short period of time.

REFERENCES

1. Weekes, C. *Hope and Help for Your Nerves*. Washington, D.C. Worth Productions, 1978.
2. Zane, M.D. Contextual analysis and treatment of phobic behavior as it changes. *American J. Psychotherapy*, 32: 338-356, 1978.
3. Frankl, V.E. Paradoxical intention. *American J. Psychotherapy*, 14: 520, 1960.

20

Day Treatment: Rethinking School Phobia

Blanche Goodwin and Eleanor Craig

Day Treatment as a program allows us to move beyond the term "school phobia." We can take into account the interplay of biological, psychological, social and cultural forces in the development and functioning of these adolescents (1). We cannot view school phobia in intrapsychic terms alone. It is a multi-determined problem. We will describe our program Day Treatment, which we have designed, to meet the needs of children whose presenting problem is school refusal or school phobia. Using an "ecological approach" we will move away from diagnosis (2), and view the situation as a problem of living rather than of pathology (3). To understand this behavior we must examine the many systems which affect these children. If we view them in all the social contexts we will often find the system contributing to the behavior (4).

It is the purpose of this chapter to examine the overall design of the program, its implementation, some specific interventions and problems encountered in working with these children, their families and schools.

The research in this paper was supported by grants from: 1) The State Dept. of Children and Youth Services, Hartford, Connecticut (State Policy 17-425, Title 17 "Social and Human Services and Resources"); and 2) The Stouffer Foundation, Westport, Connecticut.

Without active intervention, the personal and emotional growth of these young people would have been thwarted by their fears. Psychological tests have revealed the severe anxiety and panic reaction they experience on trying to reenter the classroom. Unfortunately, this is often marked by what appears to be manipulative, controlling behavior and/or by withdrawal.

It is the authors' belief that parents, educators, and clinicians need to understand more clearly what school phobic children are experiencing and intervene actively in order to support them effectively.

BACKGROUND

The Mid-Fairfield Child Guidance Center typically sees clients on a one-contact-per-week basis. The clinic was aware that this format did not meet the needs of a segment of the population. For many youngsters, the alternative was residential treatment outside of the community. The Center proposed to establish a Day Treatment program, organized to serve children with emotional and maturational problems that severely inhibited their ability to function adequately within the family, community, and a normal school program.

Within our region, the Center offered its Day Treatment program, with the full range of psychiatric and psychological services of the Center. Our current population ranges from ages nine through 14. Though the program was designed to service six to eight youngsters at one time, we are serving ten children. Referrals from the school system and area professionals have been predominantly for the presenting problem of school phobia or school refusal.

PROGRAM DESCRIPTION

The Day Treatment program has three components:

1) Work with the children
   - (a) group meetings three times a week for a total of nine hours
   - (b) activity time
   - (c) mini-groups and individual work
   - (d) contracts
   - (e) ongoing contact with school personnel and tutors
   - (f) the summer camp
2) Parents' Group
   - (a) weekly meetings

(b) High School Equivalency program
3) Family and multi-family meetings
(a) regularly scheduled family meetings
(b) monthly multi-family meetings
(c) marital counseling if indicated.

1) Work with the Children

(a) The group of eight children meets three days a week from 12 to 3 P.M. Staff includes two therapists and one recreational aide. Each meeting opens and closes with an intensive group therapy session during which children share family, social, and school concerns, offer peer support, and deal with their own interaction.

(b) *Activity time* comprises an athletic, social, or creative activity planned within each meeting to enhance self-esteem and confidence. One day a week the time is spent at the YMCA pool. It is encouraging for staff to see the specific changes evident from this part of the program—to watch children who had been too frightened to separate from parents, who had refused to change clothes in the locker room, eventually learn to swim and dive!

(c) *Mini-groups and individual work* with children are planned by staff as indicated by need.

(d) *The contract* has been a significant tool in assessing the motivation of candidates for day treatment membership. All children enter the program on a probationary period during which they define the commitment they will make to specific changes in their behavior. Within a month they present their contract to the entire group and an administrator from the clinic. If it is accepted and signed, they become a member of the group.

(e) *Ongoing contact with school personnel and tutors* is a major and time-consuming part of the program because children come from different towns, each with different approaches to the problem of school refusal. Some children had received only home-bound instruction, never attending school for as long as four years. Others were threatened with court action or residential treatment. With the support of the group some children were able to return to small group situations at school almost immediately, though all attend for only one-half day.

Severely troubled children work through a hierarchy, at first receiving tutoring at Day Treatment rather than at home. Once this relationship is established the tutor begins to meet the children at school, gradually supporting them to move from individual help to the learning center or to a specific class.

Children are allowed to call Day Treatment staff every Monday to request a ride to school. After each vacation the group meets first for breakfast before the children return to school. Absences and vacations had earlier marked periods of prolonged regression. Attendance at breakfast and return to school is close to 100%.

(f) *The summer camp* is a day program utilizing the facilities of the YMCA and rooms and playground of a local school. Day Treatment children are joined by others referred by the Mid-Fairfield Child Guidance Center, exposing the Day Treatment group to greater opportunity to socialize as well as gain new competencies in sports and crafts. The therapeutic summer camp has proven an excellent opportunity for children presenting school phobia to participate in a group without the additional pressure of academic work.

Some specific interventions we use are listed below:

1) The pace at which we have been able to admit a person into our program has been a quick one. Most of the children we are working with were admitted within a week of our first intake session. Often, because we had some background material, we could admit a child within a day or two. This has cut down enormously the anxiety the children feel.
2) We offer rides to school on a regular basis each Monday morning and after a holiday weekend.
3) After each long school vacation or three-day holiday weekend, we meet the children at our program for a 7 A.M. group breakfast. Each child can then have a ride to school from the breakfast.
4) Staff are available to receive emergency calls at home. In most cases the children have not abused this privilege.
5) We have negotiated within two schools a special classroom which is self-contained for children in our program, and others. This is a small group of between three and five. From this group a child can try one new class at a time, without the pressure of being asked to participate in everything at once.
6) Staff are available to make home visits both in the early stages of our work with a child and as treatment proceeds. Often this is necessary if a child resists a scheduled ride to school.
7) We negotiate with the school for a realistic program for each child

in our group. We also ask the school to understand the behavior, which is often viewed as only manipulative.

8) We do everything the children do. We swim when they swim; we eat lunch together; we participate in all group activities, including some sharing of our feelings.
9) We have provided transportation to parents for our parent group where parents do not drive, or are ill.
10) We have negotiated with the YMCA a recreational component to our program, where children can play in a gym in a group activity, swim, dive, participate in aquatic games, and, for the newer children who are fearful of group activities when they enter, use of a track and gym equipment.
11) We participate in PPT (Pupil Placement Team) meetings and encourage children to attend conferences that make plans for them, so that they can be part of the process.
12) We team children up so that one child can walk another into school, even if it isn't the helper's school.

Case Examples

1) We reached a child and lowered the enormous anxiety about entering the program by visiting her home and taking a wounded bird to a local museum together. We followed this up with a group visit to this museum two weeks later.

2) We made a home visit where a child refused to come to our clinic and had locked himself in a bathroom, where he had spent the better part of a week. We insisted upon the entire family leaving the building, joining one of us in the car, and having the child come down to the car. We held the first session in the car.

3) We sent a parent home who had become a permanent fixture in our program. This parent had gone to school for two years with her child. After a physical explosion in which the child verbalized the fear of dying, threw a canister of pencils across the room, and called home, sobbing, "I'll die . . . I'll die," she calmed down, cried like a baby in the arms of the therapist, and a half-hour later went to school for the first time in two years without his mother.

4) In a case where we needed desensitization, our group rode in an elevator, and one extremely phobic girl, who stopped riding in elevators when she stopped going to school, was assisted and supported by the entire group. She rode the elevator that day and has been able to ride in elevators since that time. Every time we visited the YMCA, this child asked to ride the elevator rather than use the staircase!

The authors believe that the many aspects of the program might be better defined by itemizing the purpose of our interventions. We seek to strengthen ego functioning, improve self-esteem and break the cycle of helplessness and hopelessness. We try to encourage separateness and improve connectedness, encouraging positive feedback. Together with developing the ability to speak up appropriately, self-identity, and a sense of power, we hope to decrease anxiety, fears, and the need to control, and increase opportunities for peer support. In addition, we ask the school to rethink the problem, and try to improve communications among our group, the family, and the schools. Finally, we seek to extend networks in a positive way.

2) Parents' Group

(a) *Weekly meetings*—All parents are required to attend a weekly group session, a stipulation clarified before a child enters the program. In addition to attending group meetings, many parents attend High School Equivalency classes.

(b) *The High School Equivalency program*—A major intervention occurred two years ago when we were working with a group of parents and suggested that they think about some of the things they wanted for themselves, without reference to their children. It emerged that out of six families enrolled in our program at that time only two parents had graduated from high school. One woman said, "Someday, I'd like to finish school." We translated this wish into action by getting on the phone the next day to inquire about a High School Equivalency course.

At first the Board of Education thought we wanted to send people to their course. We then requested funds and a teacher and offered to sponsor a course right at our facility, where people already trusted us. The timing was right as Adult Education was being asked to expand "social service delivery systems." Within two weeks we started the course. We interviewed the teacher and explained our client population carefully. Using a small group concept, we began by sitting in a circle and sharing the feelings around the enormous risk involved in going back to school. For many it had been more than 20 years. Some parents originally told us they had graduated, though they had not—they were too embarrassed.

We spent the first three sessions in the above format. No teaching was done in the beginning; rather, only feelings and backgrounds were shared, and a rapport developed among class members and between class and teacher. This class became a cohesive force. People arrived after a long day at work, studied until 7:30 P.M. and then came to parent meeting until 9 P.M. The course lasted 14 weeks and five people received their equivalency diplomas in June of 1979. People were teamed up to take the exam.

In the spring of 1980 we started a second group, as we were working with new parents. Five new parents took the exam in June of 1980. The enthusiasm among the class members is enormous. Four more people received their Equivalencies since that first examination, with three having only one of five sections of the exam left to pass to qualify for their Equivalency degree. Another 19-year-old began with us and, through the motivation received in class, completed her exam through direct mail, as her work hours interfered with the class.

As an intervention it broke part of the cycle of hopelessness. Children were proud of their parents. Parents who were formerly so fused with their children were doing something just for themselves. In one family, a child was in our program in the daytime, a mother and a brother-in-law in our evening equivalency course. Children smilingly complained, "I can't even watch TV now because my Mom is studying." The focus is away from the child. Separateness is actually taking place. Seeing parents return to school and study encourages children to make a commitment to return to school. One parent poignantly says, "Maybe next time I won't pass up a promotion which I could not take because my self-esteem was so low."

3) Family and Multi-Family Meetings

(a) *Regularly scheduled family meetings* take place on a weekly or bimonthly basis and all adults and children living in the home are expected to attend. The therapist may also invite members of the extended family or significant others to meetings. Scheduling is flexible enough to permit meetings to be held on demand when either the therapist or family member believes a nonscheduled meeting is urgently needed.

(b) *Monthly multi-family meetings* include all parents and all children in the program and offer families an opportunity to compare methods of handling problems, to learn from one another, and to take comfort in the knowledge that their stressful situation is neither unique nor insolvable. Single parent families profit from contact with nuclear families. Multi-family meetings have been helpful with less verbal and/or more disorganized families who are less able to tolerate the depth and intensity of single family therapy.

(c) *Marital counseling* often begins with a child as "identified patient" and gradually shifts in focus to tensions and unresolved conflicts between the parents. Marital counseling may be the most appropriate and effective treatment modality after initial family meetings indicate that the child has been caught in what is really a dysfunction of the couple's marriage.

Table 1 gives some results to date.

REMAINING PROBLEMS AND A VIEW OF THE FUTURE

One major problem is our limited budget. We are only in a position now to help between eight and ten youngsters at a given time. We could triple our program tomorrow based upon the number of referrals. Our grant stipulates the age range of 9 through 13. We have received countless referrals at age 15 and 16. There is nowhere for these older children to go, and most go on homebound tutoring or drop out entirely. Some are sent to residential treatment facilities unnecessarily.

The space we have rented is inadequate. We currently function from one room for use in groups and one small office. We share space with many other programs in the school building of a church. The physical facilities are most inadequate. We recently took our group on a 24-hour sleep-out at a local camp site. The anxiety was quite a bit lowered when children could move around more freely and enjoy many varied physical activities right on the site.

The school as a system is only beginning to deal with school phobia. We are working with several different school systems, each with different rules and significantly different approaches to school phobia. We have found some school personnel frustrated by the apparent manipulative behavior of the children, others at first openly hostile to our interventions in behalf of the children. Attendance at our program is almost perfect. Children come with colds and headaches, and walk two miles on a day they didn't go to school. They are using the program and feel it is safe.

In some schools the only option to a returning school phobic is to return to a regular classroom or to be in a learning center. There is no middle ground. Tutors are not permitted to tutor within the schools. Exceptions may last only as long as three weeks. For very bright children, the learning center is often a new stigma.

Much of our energy has been sapped at times, in giving rides to school and setting up programs in schools. We would like to explore having

Table 1
Some Results to Date

Girls	Length of time out of a classroom before referral	Length of time in Day Treatment	Current Situation
A	1 year	1 year	Attends school daily
B	3 months	2 years	School half day
C	2 years	1 month	Could not come to contract. Still homebound
D	4 years	1 year	Attends school daily
E	Special Ed Class	2 months	Heavily drug-involved. Referred to residential program
F	1½ years	8 months	Attends learning center at school
G	1½ years	7 months	Tutored at school
Boys			
A	Special Ed Class	2 months	Referred to residential treatment for violent acting out
B	Special Ed Class	2 months	Referred to D.C.Y.S. for lack of supervision; "at risk" child
C	Special Ed Class	1 year	Attends school daily but has learning disability
D	Homebound for 6 years	2 years	Small group at school, some classes, half day
E	Tutored for 3 years	1½ years	Attends small class half day
F	3 months	7 months	Regular class half day
G	5 months	7 months	Attends small class half day
H	5 months	8 months	Tutored individually at Day Treatment

our own certified school where a child could be relieved temporarily of all regular school pressure. We could observe behavior more closely so that the therapy could be more relevant. We hope to have parent teams that could go into schools to explain school phobia to professionals as well as to other parents whose children are experiencing this.

The schools will have to reexamine the small group concept. Large classrooms are not settings in which children feel comfortable sharing their feelings about adolescence, economic deprivation, and the impersonality of the system. A respect for competence in oneself and others is crucial in adolescence. The search is one for self-definition. Middle school is a sharp discontinuity with the past, the role transition being enormous.

A major problem in implementation is the disinterest shown by some of the parents of our Day Treatment families. Unfortunately, although parents are told that parent meetings are obligatory, their attendance falls to about 60% overall. Some are deeply involved in the therapeutic group process, but parents of two children in our group have resisted our services as they have every other agency involved in these multiproblem family situations. Often they tell their children to take the phone off the hook or say they are not home when we call.

The need for repetition of important messages cannot be stressed enough. An example might be the need for these children to be meaningfully involved in plans for activities after school and during the summer. We are often faced with parents who overly control one moment and the next ask a child if he or she "wants to go to day camp" or "wants to go with the group on an outing."

We have worked extremely hard with all our families. In spite of this, it appears that the children often move ahead faster than their family system can move. In some cases our work is sabotaged at home. For children who are extremely motivated to get out or have coping skills which enable them to ask other people for help, things work out; for others, they do not.

We work with a population that has enormous financial burdens. Often they are single parents, working long hours to provide for their children. Many have poor job skills and find inflation more than they can cope with. Although they try, many have difficulty providing a nurturing environment for a child to develop and grow emotionally. The stresses of single parenthood plus financial problems cannot be underestimated. These are families who are not eligible for state or federal assistance. These are families who are socially isolated with few positive networks.

CONCLUSION

We have attempted to explore the term "school phobia" by viewing the various systems that affect children. Additionally, the whole stage of adolescence as being a stressful one in the life cycle needs to be addressed (5). The issues of separateness and connectedness which face all families appear to be especially painful for our Day Treatment families.

Viewing school phobic children in the many systems with which they transact allows for many creative interventions and allows us, above all, to move away from "pathology." It places a new responsibility upon the system to respond to individuals, rather than all the emphasis on individuals to respond to their environment (1).

Using an ecological approach and applying systems theory, we have described our Day Treatment program, the children and their families, and our interventions. This approach focuses on the nature of the transactions taking place between the children and the identifiable systems influencing their growth. It attempts to identify the lacks and distortions in the transactional arena.

REFERENCES

1. Mechanic, D. Social structure and personal adaptation. In: Coehlo, G.V., Hamburg, B., and Adams, J.E. (eds.), *Coping and Adaptation*. New York: Basic Books, 1974.
2. Germain, C. An ecological perspective in casework practice. *Social Casework*, 54: 323-330, June 1973.
3. Szasz, T. Repudiation of the medical model, In: W. Sahakian (ed.), *Psychopathology Today: Experimentation, Theory and Research*. Itasco, IL: Peacock Publishers, 1970, p. 47.
4. Auerswald, E.H. Interdisciplinary versus ecological approach. In: *General Systems Theory and Psychiatry*. Boston: Little, Brown & Company, 1970.
5. Hamburg, B. Early adolescence: A specific and stressful stage of the life cycle. In: Coehlo, G.V., Hamburg, B., and Adams, J.E. (eds.), *Coping and Adaptation*. New York: Basic Books, 1974.

21

The Psychology of Phobic Fear of Nuclear Energy

Robert L. DuPont

My exposure to nuclear power began a bit less than two years ago in a darkened projection studio at George Washington University in Washington, D. C. As an audience of one, I spent 13 hours at the request of the private, non-profit Media Institute, reviewing videotapes of all the network TV news of nuclear energy between 1968 and 1979. Later, my interest took me to France and Canada and to the sites of four American nuclear power plants—including Three Mile Island (TMI)—to talk with neighbors, workers in the plants, officials of the utility companies and others interested in nuclear energy, including anti-nuclear activists.

The most striking contrast I encountered was the difference between public attitudes toward nuclear power in the United States and in France. While the dominant theme in United States media coverage of nuclear power and much of the political debate is fear, the French see nuclear power as a necessity if the lights are to go on when they pull the switches in their homes at night. In fact, one issue that was not debated in the recent French election campaign was the fundamental 1974 decision to stop building fossil-fueled power plants and to increase nuclear generation of electricity to 70 percent of the total by 1990. True, François Mitterrand promised a review of that decision, and now that he has been elected, he will carry it out. But the review is based on economic, technical and political factors—not on fear.

French nuclear development has not been without accidents, but these have apparently been minor. The accidents, I was told, have not been dramatized in the media to the extent that is now commonplace in the United States. Many people in France reminded me that TMI (both the accident and the subsequent political explosion) occurred in America, not in France. I often heard in France what I seldom heard in the United States: that whatever the problems with TMI, there was no health damage as a result of the 1979 accident. This fact was confirmed by an independent Presidential Commission, even though it has been little appreciated in the United States. In fact, the blue ribbon panel found that the one negative health effect of the accident was not radiation, but what they called "mental stress" or what I call "fear."

There have, in recent years, been serious French anti-nuclear activities. A few years ago, some German anti-nuclear activists protested construction of nuclear plants near the German border, claiming that the danger from an accident threatened Germans who were downwind from the plants. More serious from the French point of view have been the anti-nuclear protests of the local citizens in Brittany. Here, anti-nuclear activism blends with separatist politics to produce more volatile and protracted struggles. There is also substantial French opposition to nuclear power along the Belgian border.

During my visit, which coincided with the build-up for the spring national election in France, there were also press reports of local opposition to the possible location of a nuclear plant on the Mediterranean coast. Here the opposition was based on two premises: first, some local elected officials felt they had not been adequately consulted and, second, they feared the plant might discourage Danish and German tourists the town was hoping to attract to its still-to-be-developed seaside resort.

All this French opposition to nuclear power had a curiously un-American tone. Little of it appeared to be based on fear. True, nuclear power in France, as in the United States, is a lightning rod which attracts diverse political conflicts. But in France the opposition to nuclear power is more like opposition to highway construction in the United States—people fight about where a highway is to be located and who is to benefit or be threatened by the construction of a highway, but few oppose all highway construction, and almost no one protests highway construction primarily because of fear of the highway.

The French experience offers lessons for that large minority of Americans who are, at the moment, dominated by their fears of nuclear power and the political (if not the health) fall-out it produces.

France has, by any reckoning, had an easier time of it. Most important, the French have no practical alternative to nuclear power. They have no oil and very little natural gas or coal. France also suffered terrible energy shortages during the Second World War and in 1956 when war in the Middle East cut the shipment of oil via the Suez Canal. That cold winter, together with the almost $4 the French pay for a gallon of gasoline, make the energy crisis real. If the French are to have any measure of energy independence—both in political and economic terms—they have no alternative, except the option to produce nuclear electricity.

Like the Americans, the French make much of solar energy and conservation. However, they seem convinced that solar energy is unlikely to make a significant contribution during the last two decades of this century. In terms of conservation, the average French citizen consumes only one-third as much energy as his American counterpart. This, however, is less reflective of any new conservation activity than it is of long-standing French conservatism about energy use and various differences in demographics and geography between France and the United States.

These basic facts about energy are remarkably well understood by the ordinary Frenchman. There is little political or media conflict about the basic facts, in contrast to the babble of conflicting voices and mistrust in the United States.

One principle I have learned in treating phobias: Necessity both prevents and cures phobias. When confronted with an option, the phobic person will almost always avoid his fear. However, when the phobic person can find no alternative, he will confront his fear and perform admirably. For example, the phobic woman who does not drive will pick up her keys and drive her car when the life of her child is at stake, just as the phobic businessman whose job depends unequivocally on his flying will usually fly despite his phobia.

In 1979, shortly after the accident at the TMI nuclear power plant, an American Airlines DC-10 crashed in Chicago, killing 275 people. The massive publicity, the confusion, and the resultant upsurge of fear of flying were in many ways similar to the reaction to the TMI accident—including doubts about air safety and trustworthiness of the manufacturer of the DC-10, of American Airlines, and of Federal regulatory agencies.

This reaction, while not entirely dissipated, has faded much faster than the fear of nuclear power plants, whose radiation has killed no one. The paradox is understandable in the same way France's relative lack of nuclear fear is understandable: Nothing conquers or prevents the development of fear as effectively as necessity. Most Americans who fly consider flying as necessary as most Frenchmen appear to consider nuclear power.

Before relating nuclear fears more directly to clinical experience with phobias, I want to emphasize that I am not saying that all opposition to nuclear power is based on irrational, or phobic, fear. There are strong arguments against nuclear power based on economic and political grounds. Examples of these arguments are that nuclear power is too expensive relative to alternative energy sources, and that nuclear power commits a nation to "big industry" when the more desirable energy future is to be found in human-scale approaches such as windmills and solar panels on the roofs of our homes. I am also not saying that anyone who fears nuclear power is mentally ill. Put simply, what I am saying is that today, in the United States, one of the streams feeding the widespread anti-nuclear sentiment is based on irrational, or phobic, fear and that sound judgments about the role of nuclear power in our lives can best be made when we identify and overcome this particular source of distortion in our personal and national decision-making.

There are several striking parallels between phobic thinking and much of the fear of nuclear power. Most of the nuclear fear I encountered in the United States was "what if" fear. People were generally not afraid of what had happened, but of what might happen. This is typical of phobic thinking—the phobic flyer knows the plane he is to take did not crash on its flight into the airport just before he is to board it; he also knows that airline safety is excellent, but he is dominated by thoughts that "it could crash." Similarly, the agoraphobic person knows he has never lost control of himself in a supermarket, and never passed out or "gone crazy," but he nevertheless fears he "could." It is hard to argue with "what if." Can you really tell this man that he won't pass out the next time he goes into a supermarket or the fearful flyer that the plane won't crash?

There is another aspect of the fear of nuclear energy which is clearly phobic; it is involuntary and specific to a particular stimulus. While some phobic people are generally fearful and timid, many are quite confident and fearless outside their specific area of fear.

These parallels were particularly clear to me from my visit to Middletown, Pennsylvania, the town closest to TMI. While many local citizens were quite unafraid of the nearby TMI plant, many were fearful. During my interviews, it was often difficult for the fearful person to put his fear into words. One man I spoke with in a store in Middletown said he was terrified and would leave the area if he could. I asked him to specify exactly what he feared. He paused and blurted out angrily, "It's nuclear, don't you understand that!" This man did not use the words, "radiation," "cancer," "birth defects," "explosion," or any of the other specific items on the nuclear fear agenda. This was not simple inarticulateness since he had no difficulty expressing himself on other issues in our discussion. This difficulty specifying the "what if" fear is also characteristic of phobic thinking.

What can we as a society do to overcome fear of nuclear power? First of all, the fact that fear rivets attention is both a big plus and a threat. Because people are fearful of nuclear power, they can be recruited to learn: They care enough to pay attention. Exposure to threatening situations can produce either an immunity or a sensitization. Much of the difference has to do with the biology of the individual, but it also has to do with what the messages are that surround the exposure. The TMI accident probably produced more immunity to fear in the public than it produced sensitization.

In coping with our mass fear of nuclear power, we need to respect the arguments and feelings of the opposition to nuclear power. We need to do what we can to end the polarization of the "we" vs. "they." We are all in this together and that means reaching out to bring in the opposition on both sides to the extent possible. The public is poorly served by either side in the debate having "enemies." Anything, it seems to me, that demeans that opposition is going to have a negative effect, especially when anyone argues that there is no risk from nuclear power, or that commercial nuclear power plants pose a threat to the entire nation or even to the entire human species. I would never, for example, work with a person who had a fear of flying by telling him the plane could not crash. Neither would I tell him a plane crash might "destroy the world." I know the plane could crash, but I fly with him on the airplane. I am making a statement, by flying, about my judgment of that risk, relative to the benefits, even as I acknowledge that flying does not involve a zero risk. That risk is, to me, an acceptable risk. I liked the recent TV ad for MacDonnell Douglas that every two minutes a DC-10 is taking off somewhere in the world. That helped me understand the risk of flying on a DC-10.

Exposure—we need to get the public involved with nuclear power in direct, personal ways. The fact that many nuclear plants now have tours, at least of the observation areas, is important. We also need to get more people exposed to the people who work in the plants—rather than to the brainy scientists who can give the sophisticated relative-risk calculations. If people can talk, as I did, to the real workers in those plants, people whom they can identify with, a lot of fear will disappear.

If people had access to easy measurement of radiation, and if they understood something about background radiation, it would help. I wish everybody who was fearful had an opportunity to wear one of those little dosimeters I wore in the nuclear plants I visited. I wish every fearful mother could put a dosimeter on her two-year-old child.

I was at TMI at the time of the krypton venting. I saw that the long delay before the krypton venting confirmed the irrational fears. When the venting actually occurred, the fears diminished. I talked to two people at a supermarket just before the venting when the controversy was most intense, and one man said to me directly, "If it is not dangerous, why are they waiting so long to do it?" The irony was that "they" were waiting to vent *because* he was afraid! The longer they waited because of his fear, the more he became fearful.

The same is true of nuclear waste management disposal: We do not need to solve that problem, as I understand it, from a technical point of view for many years or even for decades, because of the small volume of waste. We do need to solve the problem from the political point of view because the longer we wait, the worse the fear of "waste" becomes. The same issues surface with the TMI clean-up. The longer we wait to clean that up, the more it confirms that it cannot be done, that it is too dangerous. Waiting just adds fuel to the fear fire.

The nuclear industry cannot educate the whole public to the complexities of nuclear power, but it can help educate representative groups of the public. The more the nuclear industry can identify genuine citizen groups and help get them organized to insure that they have enough time to understand the arguments, including the anti-nuclear arguments, I think—on balance—the better off the industry will be. I was impressed with the mayor of Middletown, for example, who has gotten together a group of local citizens. He literally calls in the representatives of the local utility, GPU, and the opposition when any controversial subject comes up. Then, he reports to the people what his citizens group found. That is a marvelous model for understanding what is going on. I was impressed, again at Middletown, with the wisdom of the common man. One truck driver commented about converting TMI for coal generation. He thought that was a bad idea because it would require 150 railroad coal cars a day coming into the TMI plant. He said, "If you brought 150 railroad cars in here every day, how many kids would be run over, how many times would the traffic be disrupted in the town to get those cars in and out, and how would we live with the smoke?" He looked over at the TMI plant and said, "Look at it now—all that goes in and out now are the cars taking people to and from work." That simple observation is important.

We need international agencies and national agencies to show some leadership. We need leaders who are less apt to read polls to find out what people are afraid of and then cow to those fears. We need leaders who stand up and say, "Look, I understand about this; I have spent the time to understand it and this is what I know about risk; it is not a zero risk, this is not a perfect technology, but I understand something about it." We need to put the risks of nuclear technology in perspective in two ways—both legitimate. The first perspective is to compare the risks of nuclear power with the risks (and benefits) of other ways to generate electricity. The second perspective is to compare these risks (from each alternative technology) with other risks to which the public is exposed. For example, the public needs to know what the major preventable causes of cancer are and what can be done to reduce these risks. Neither of these two perspectives alone is sufficient, and both together will not eliminate fear of nuclear power. But in the absence of these perspectives, the widespread fear of nuclear power may deepen and spread.

We also need a sense of fairness when we talk about who is going to pay the health price for any technology. Let us compare health risks (and political and economic factors) for various ways to generate electricity. Who is at risk—is it the neighbors who live around the plant, or is it the miners? We should think openly about the issues of sharing the risk and think about who these people are who are at risk. Let us do the same thing with solar, coal, oil and other energy-related technologies.

It is no longer fashionable to think that information and education can change feelings and behavior. For centuries, the treatment of phobias was frustrating, if not hopeless. In recent years, a new cognitively-based approach which uses repeated, prolonged, real-life exposure to the fearful stimulus has suddenly made the treatment of phobias effective and, therefore, respectable. Is it too much to hope that straightforward information and practical exposure can help large numbers of people overcome phobic-like fears of nuclear energy? Without the benefit of current psychological knowledge, that is, of course, exactly what has happened to other once new and widely feared technologies, such as natural gas and electricity brought into homes, and the everyday use of automobiles and airplanes for transportation. Fear of nuclear power is harder to overcome because the political opposition now both feeds on and reinforces the fear, and because the location of plants far from population centers makes personal exposure more difficult. But maybe, just maybe, we will, in the future, be able to kick our nuclear fear habit.

SUGGESTIONS FOR FURTHER READING

Isaac M. Marks: *Living with Fear: Understanding and Coping with Anxiety*. New York: McGraw-Hill Book Company, 1978.

Robert L. DuPont: *Nuclear Phobia: Phobic Thinking About Nuclear Power*. The Media Institute, 3017 M Street, N.W, Washington, D.C., 20007, 1980.

Robert L. DuPont: "Fifty Million Frenchmen" Have Few Nuclear Fears. *Electric Perspectives*, Summer, 1981. Edison Electric Institute, 1111 19th Street, NW, Washington, D.C., 20036.

PART V

Descriptive Studies

The final section includes two chapters which are primarily descriptive, the first by Ronald M. Doctor which describes demographic and pre-treatment data from a large sample of agoraphobics. This paper, entitled "Major Results of a Large-scale Pretreatment Survey of Agoraphobics," forms a useful basis for understanding the patient population receiving treatment in a modern phobia clinic. My own paper, describing the follow-up results of the Washington Phobia Program, contains not only pretreatment, but also end-of-treatment and follow-up data two years after treatment of the first 100 patients seen in the Washington Phobia Program. It is designed to describe the patient population and the results expected from treatment, and to encourage other clinicians to investigate more fully the outcome both with the general patient population and with specific subsets of that population.

Also included is a journal of an agoraphobic woman, currently in our program. This detailed journal vividly describes her phobic thinking and steadfast determination to cope with her phobia. She is not a miracle-cure patient but rather a patient whose progress is slow and uneven, albeit in a positive direction. She is sufficiently perceptive to realize that her phobia protects her from having to deal with real life issues and yet, even in her ambivalence, she struggles to reduce the phobia's hold.

22

Major Results of a Large-scale Pretreatment Survey of Agoraphobics

Ronald M. Doctor

Most clinicians have had some experience with agoraphobic patients. Through this, they develop a working knowledge of etiology and methods of treatment which, in turn, they apply to the next set of patients who manifest similar self-report and behavioral topologies. It is also true that most agoraphobics have developed a working knowledge of their condition through personal experience, trial and error efforts to alleviate the problems, and from movies, dramatic productions, professional and lay books on the subject. Both sets of observers have knowledge that is valid to some extent and is often used to produce inductive formulations of generalized etiological and cognitive-affective behavior characteristics. But inductive formulations are a slow, unreliable, and inefficient scientific procedure for abstracting to a clinical population.

The great advantage of access to a large sample of agoraphobic individuals is that deductive methods can be used to abstract information and, if properly done, can prove to be efficient, reliable, and unbiased. The purpose of this chapter is to briefly summarize and describe the major results of a large sample of respondents to a comprehensive pretreatment assessment questionnaire on agoraphobia. The only other study of this magnitude was conducted by Marks and Heist (1) who surveyed members of a British self-help club for agoraphobia. Unfortunately, club membership was used as the sole criterion of whether a respondent was agoraphobic rather than an objective assessment method. Nevertheless, the interested reader will note some areas of similar results between these two projects and many new areas and findings that go beyond the Marks and Heist data.

METHOD

The dependent variables in this study were derived from responses of 404 individuals to a lengthy questionnaire. These individuals completed the questionnaire as a precondition for enrollment in the Terrap treatment program. The questionnaire responses (in some cases supplemented by personal interviews) were the primary source of information for the diagnosis of agoraphobia. Diagnoses were made by clinicians who were highly experienced in assessment, diagnosis, and treatment of agoraphobia. The questionnaire consisted of short answer and intensity scales in the areas of medical history, educational background, symptoms and internal sensations, previous attempts at cure, relationship problems, family background, fear situations, obsessive-compulsive tendencies, and a measure of intellectual level and abstract thinking abilities. For purposes of this very brief presentation, only summary or main findings within a few areas will be presented.

RESULTS AND DISCUSSION

Descriptive and/or inferential statistics are presented for each variable described below. The total sample size was 404 individuals, but in some cases sample size was smaller due to missing data or the fact that some variables were not assessed across all individuals. Where relevant to the results, sample sizes less than the 404 total will be indicated.

1) Demographic Information

Respondents were mostly Californians (92%) who were distributed fairly evenly between northern (42.7%) and southern (49.3%) California. They represented the full range of possible major occupations (as identified in the Occupational Guide) with housewife (42.3%), professional-technical (18.0%), clerical (9.3%) and sales (4.8%) constituting the four most frequent categories. There were small proportions of disabled (1.6%), retired (2.6%) and students (3.4%). Table 1 presents further demographic information on respondents.

From Table 1 it can be seen that almost 80% of the sample were

Table 1
Demographic Information on Sample with Ns, Percentages of Total and Means

	Number	*Mean*	*Standard Deviation*
a. Sex:			
Male	89 (22%)		
Female	315 (78%)		
b. Age at time questionnaire was completed:		39.3	10.9
c. Marital Status:			
married	269 (67.4%)		
single	75 (18.8%)		
separated	7 (1.8%)		
widowed	19 (4.8%)		
divorced	29 (7.3%)		
d. Number of children:		1.72	1.4
e. Age at onset		28.14	9.79

women, that most were married and had, on the average, almost two children. Taking age at onset from age at which the questionnaire was completed, it can be determined that respondents had the agoraphobic condition for an average of 11.16 years. One question for subsequent analyses is whether there is a difference between those who have had agoraphobia for a relatively short time and those who have had it longer (say more than five years).

Table 2 provides information on frequently asked questions related to the development of agoraphobia. In order to facilitate the presentation, only percentages or mean values are presented.

A large proportion of respondents indicated that they had had prior anxiety symptoms and that the agoraphobia began with a sudden panic attack. Again, in further analyses, it will be interesting to compare those who did not experience a sudden panic with those who did and to learn more about respondents who report no prior anxiety symptoms. A somewhat smaller percentage had a problem being alone than might be expected from clinical experience. It is also interesting that a substantial proportion had actually fainted. The information on changes over time confirm that the condition tends to get worse with time—something most agoraphobics do not believe when it first occurs.

Table 2
General Questions Related to Agoraphobic Symptoms

		Yes	No
a. Prior anxiety symptoms		61.6%	38.4%
b. Sudden onset with panic		61.5%	38.1%
c. O.K. to be alone		29.9%	70.1%
d. Ever fainted?		23.6%	76.4%
e. Seizures?		3.7%	96.3%
f. Changed over time?			
got better	23.0%		
got worse	61.1%		
no change over time	15.9%		
g. Hospitalized at psychiatric hospital		9.9%	90.1%

2) Kind of Help

The information presented in this section relates to efforts by respondents to seek help for their condition and the outcome of treatment obtained. It is presented in more detail because it communicates several clear and profound messages to the "helping" professions. Four basic questions were assessed: (a) What type of professional did you see before seeking the present treatment? (b) For how long a period of time did you see that professional? (c) What were the results relative to your phobias? and (d) What were the results of previous treatment on nonphobic problems? Table 3 summarizes all of these results.

The first variable involves a comparison of numbers of respondents who had seen a psychiatrist, psychologist, counselor, medical doctor, or other. "Other" included such resources as biofeedback and nutrition counseling. A greater number of respondents saw a psychiatrist than psychologists or medical doctors and these latter professions were significantly more frequently seen than counselors or other types of treatment resources. In terms of the length of time respondents were in treatment, psychiatrists exceeded all other professions and there were no significant differences among the other sources of help. Over 70% of those who went to a psychiatrist were in treatment for over one year!

Table 3
Kind of Help and Effects

		Psychiatrist	Psychologist	Counselor	Medical Doctor	Other	F	df	P
Whom did you see?		36.6% (149)	22.3% (90)	9% (28)	22% (89)	8.9% (36)	15.42	4/399	.001
How long?	1 mo. = 1	4.4%	7.3%	25.0%	20.7%	14.3%			
	1-3 mo. = 2	7.7%	32.7%	16.7%	10.3%	28.6%			
	4-6 mo. = 3	8.8%	12.7%	25.0%	3.4%	7.1%			
	7-12 mo. = 4	6.6%	9.1%	8.3%	0	14.3%			
	12+ mo. = 5	72.5%	38.2%	25.0%	65.5%	35.7%			
	$\bar{x}$ =	4.35	3.38	2.92	3.79	3.29	6.14	4/198	.01
Results on phobias									
much better	= 1	6.3%	5.6%	11.5%	2.6%	17.9%			
slightly better	= 2	18.7%	19.7%	30.8%	9.1%	21.4%			
none	= 3	64.8%	63.4%	53.8%	83.1%	60.7%			
negative	= 4	10.2%	9.9%	3.8%	5.2%	0			
	$\bar{x}$ =	2.79	2.79	2.50	2.92	2.43	4.22	4/326	.01
Results on non-phobias									
insight	= 1	19.4%	16.1%	9.5%	3.3%	19.2%			
awareness	= 2	16.3%	21.4%	33.3%	10.0%	15.4%			
skills	= 3	2.0%	5.4%	4.8%	0	7.7%			
none	= 4	53.1%	42.9%	47.6%	78.3%	53.8%			
negative	= 5	9.2%	14.3%	4.8%	8.3%	3.8%			
	$\bar{x}$ =	3.16	3.18	3.05	3.78	3.08	3.43	4/257	.01

What were the results of treatment? The first result we examined was the self-report ratings by the respondent of success in treating the phobias associated with agoraphobia. Responses were categorized on a 4-point scale from much better (#1), slightly better (#2), none (#3) to negative (#4) effect. The results across types of professional were significant ($F = 4.22$; $df = 4/326$; $p < .01$) with psychiatrists, M.D.'s and psychologists all rated as significantly *less* effective than counselors and others. Furthermore, M.D.'s were significantly less effective than psychiatrists and psychologists. (These post-ANOVA comparisons were made by Scheffé tests.) Seventy-five percent of those who saw a psychiatrist reported either no effect or a negative effect! Remember, these individuals were in treatment for *over one year* in many cases.

Psychologists fared no better but at least they averaged much shorter treatment durations. Over 88% of those who consulted a physician reported either no effect or a negative one. This result, however, might be expected since physicians do not have knowledge or experience with psychological forms of treatment. They do prescribe drugs and the lack of effectiveness certainly speaks to what might be expected from drugs alone or with minimal professional contact. Even counselors and others failed in the large majority of cases to be effective.

It could be argued that a large proportion of "treatment failures" constituted the respondent sample and therefore any profession would look bad. If this were the case, one would expect the results of ratings of treatment of non-phobic problems to be of similar intensity. They are not. The non-phobic treatment ratings were made on a 5-point scale in which positive effects were divided into three categories (gained insight, increased awareness and improved skills). The categories of none and negative effect remained the same. There were significant differences among professions again ($F = 3.43$; $df = 4/257$; $p < .01$) but the pattern changes considerably. On this variable, *only* physicians differed from the other groups in being *less* effective. In other words, the four psychologically oriented professions (psychiatrists, psychologist, counselor and other) did not differ in ratings of effects. Again, none of these professions did better than 50% positive improvement but this rate is quite a bit better than results on phobias.

In summary, we can say that while psychiatrists, physicians and psychologists were significantly less effective than counselors and other procedures, no type of profession demonstrated clear effectiveness in treating agoraphobia. This was particularly evident with physicians where their drug-oriented approach was highly unsuccessful. Psychiatrists and psychologists, who are presumably trained in treatment of such disorders, were also clearly unsuccessful. Furthermore, psychiatrists persisted with treatment for a significantly longer period of time than the other professions yet yielded inferior treatment results.

Based on these results and the presumed base-rate for spontaneous remission (2, 3, 4), traditional psychotherapies and drugs are not adequate forms of treatment for agoraphobia.

3) Life Circumstances at Onset

For each respondent, we listed or identified the life circumstance at the time the individual felt the agoraphobia began from the responses to an open-ended question. One fact became quickly obvious—that there were as many life circumstances reported as there were respondents. In other words, no one circumstance or type of circumstance was associated with onset. Through a process of progressive clustering, it was possible to reduce the list of categories eventually to five broad categories. These are presented in Table 4.

There is not time or space to describe the circumstances within categories but suffice it to say that they were all notable and stressful. The range of categories would suggest that no one stress was dominant. Relationship problems, separation and loss, and new responsiblities were the most prominent. The reader may choose to interpret these results from his or her own frame of reference. I believe that the heterogeneity of stress situations suggests that factors associated with poor

Table 4
Five Categories of Life Circumstances at Onset and Percentage of Total Sample

1. Changes in body/health		10.09%
2. Relationship conflict:		
Family/spouse	19.56%	
Parents	10.41%	
Total		29.97%
3. Separation and loss		31.23%
4. Responsibility		20.19%
5. Emotional arousal		8.52%

stress management rather than any specific stress itself are what contribute to the development of agoraphobia.

4) Where Panic Attacks Occurred

The question here is whether panic attacks tend to occur in particular types of situations. If they do, this would suggest that agoraphobia emerges from a more restricted phobia (of a particular situation). Unfortunately, situations where panic attacks occurred were even more varied than circumstances. Bridges, tunnels, boats, voting booths, theaters, freeways, trips, dentist offices, court, and so on were all reported. Some of the most common locations are listed in Table 5.

Again, heterogeneity abounds. The one common denominator to these locations is that many of them involve situations where the respondent may feel *trapped*—either physically or psychologically. Clinical experience suggests that the experience of being trapped is a common factor in fear situations. The factor trapping them is often a desire to avoid social disapproval by their actions so they try to appear "normal" to go unnoticed. More thorough behavioral analysis is needed to determine if such a common denominator is present in these panic onset locations.

5) Factor Structure of Fear Survey and Situations Scales

The result of factor analytic studies of these objective scales will be presented as a final data result.

The first scale involves an abbreviated form of the Fear Survey Scale

Table 5
Most Common Locations and Percent of Total

Auto	15%
At work	9%
Home	8%
Public places	8%
Restaurant	8%
School	7%
Away from home	7%
Store	6%
Bridge	4%
Public transportation	4%
Street	4%

(5). The 35-item scale yielded nine factors accounting for 100% of the variance. The first three factors accounted for the majority of variance and therefore are presented in more detail in Table 6.

The most common fear situations relate to social acceptance and fears of rejection or criticism. This would suggest that agoraphobia is primarily a social fear that probably emerges from a conditioning history of social punishment.

The second scale also assessed situations but the items were drawn from clinical cases seen over a number of years. The factor analysis resulted in six factors (the first two of which accounted for the majority of variance). These included: (a) presence of others/trapped; (b) alone; (c) heights; (d) elevators; (e) driving; and (f) unfamiliar situations. Note that there is tremendous overlap with factors from the Fear Survey Scale. For example, presence of others/trapped corresponds to the first factor from the fear scale (social acceptance) and the second factor here of "alone" corresponds with factor III (being alone) from the Fear Scale. Other factors seem to relate to specific situations that are tapped within each scale. The correspondence of the two first factors from these scales again supports the notion that agoraphobia is basically a social fear in which rejection or social criticism is a controlling behavioral factor. It follows that effective treatment would necessarily have to address this social fear in order to have permanent effects.

6) Factor Structure of Anxiety Symptom Scale

The third scale consisted of a list of physiological and emotional arousal associated with "anxiety" on an intensity format. Five factors were extracted. These included: (a) immobility/total body reaction; (b) alimentary tract reactions; (c) circulation; (d) tremor; and (e) lower gastrointestinal tract. As expected, each factor corresponds to a major bodily system affected by arousal of the autonomic nervous system. It is interesting that immobility is the most prominent factor. If respondents tend to feel immobile or unable to act, then any anxiety situation in which action is necessary would be highly threatening—they would tend to feel trapped.

7) Correlations with Fear Survey Scale

Several interesting correlations are present between various scales and the Fear Survey scores. While FSS scores did not correlate with situations, they were highly associated with whether respondents had had

Table 6
Factors Produced from Factor Analysis of Fear Survey Scale

Factor I—Social Acceptance (42.5%)

1. strangers (loading greater than .30)
2. people in authority
3. being criticized
4. feeling rejected by others
5. being ignored
6. making mistakes

Factor II—Sickness/Incapacity (15.9%)

1. open wounds
2. dead people
3. receiving injections
4. sick people
5. witnessing surgical operations
6. blood
7. prospect of surgical operation

Factor III—Being Alone/Territorial Apprehension (11.5%)

1. being alone
2. being in a strange place
3. strangers
4. journey by train, bus or car
5. crowds
6. large open spaces
7. premature heart beats
8. losing control
9. fainting

Factor IV—Thunder/Lightning

Factor V—Airplanes

Factor VI—Closed Places

Factor VII—Phobia/Fear

Factor VIII—Loneliness

Factor IX—Death

Table 7
Correlations of Fear Survey Scale with Other Measures

	Fear Survey Scale	
	Correlation	P
Perfectionism	.29	.004
Compulsive behaviors	.36	.001
Impulsive behaviors	.36	.002
Superstitious beliefs	.42	.002
Being alone	.17	.004
Prior anxiety	−.19	.001
Symptom Scale	.34	.001
Obsessive-Compulsive Scale	−.57	.001
Beliefs/magical	.33	.001

prior anxiety (before onset panic attack), a problem being alone, compulsive behaviors (checking locks, washing hands, orderliness, etc.), impulsive behaviors (wanting to run, jump, smash things, etc.), perfectionism (overly neat, straightening pictures, laundry folded just right, etc.) and with obsessive-compulsive scale scores (worry thinking, compulsive neatness, catastrophic thinking, etc.). The direction of results was as predicted from clinical observation and expectation and the figures are displayed in Table 7.

8) Conclusion

Even a review of major findings becomes lengthy and complicated. There is a vast amount of information available that will require a much more complete and sophisticated presentation. Certainly, a model picture of the agoraphobic begins to emerge even though we only tapped the surface. The data on kind of help and effects are very shocking and either reflect great illusions psychotherapists have about their abilities and the power of their methods with phobics or are an indictment of greed and exploitation. I prefer to think that psychotherapists will be open to effective treatment methods and that in another 10 years, when effects of therapy are again assessed by someone, the "helping professions" will live up to their title.

REFERENCES

1. Marks, I.M. and Heist, E.R. A survey of 1200 agoraphobics in Britain: features associated with treatment and ability to work. *Social Psychiatry,* 5: 16-24, 1970.
2. Eysenck, H.J. The effects of psychotherapy: An evaluation. *Journal of Counseling Psychology,* 16: 319-324, 1952.
3. Eysenck, H.J. *The Effects of Psychotherapy.* New York: Inter-Science Press, 1966.
4. Erwin, E. Psychoanalytic Therapy: The Eysenck argument. *American Psychologist,* 35: 435-443, 1980.
5. Wolpe, J. and Lang, P.J. A fear survey schedule for use in behavior therapy. *Behavior Research and Therapy,* 2: 27-30, 1964.

23

Profile of a Phobia Treatment Program: Two-year Follow-up

Robert L. DuPont

In this chapter, I hope that by describing the patients treated in the Phobia Program of Washington and the outcome of their treatment in quantitative terms, I can give a general sense of the people seeking help at a modern phobia clinic and can also give some idea about the effectiveness of the modern supported exposure treatment techniques. It is also my hope that this chapter will encourage other program administrators to conduct evaluations of their own patient population to see how they differ from the Phobia Program of Washington. This will be particularly important if the programs vary considerably in terms of patient characteristics, techniques used, and the effectiveness of outcome, not only with all patients but also with special subgroups of patients.

PROGRAM DESCRIPTION

The Phobia Program of Washington is a short-term phobia treatment program which involves once-a-week group meetings of about eight phobic people and their spouses (or other "support" people) for an hour and a half, coupled with one hour per week of practice in which the patient goes with a trained phobia therapist into the phobic situation to deal with the feelings that arise and to implement the techniques taught in the program to overcome the phobic disability. While insight and exploration of the past are not fundamental characteristics of this program, the program does use principles of dynamic psychotherapy to encourage patients to explore, understand, and function with their fearful feelings. Spouses are strongly encouraged to participate in the program, and generally do. Patients are not excluded because of other psychiatric diagnoses: The single criteria for admission is a major life activity which is being avoided because of phobic fear.

Overall, we encourage patients to stay in the program for 20 weeks. The program is essentially built in ten-week cycles. Patients commit themselves for a ten-week period of time. In this sample, we found that 16% stayed for less than ten weeks; 21% left after ten weeks; 20% left between weeks 11 and 19 weeks; 33% left at week 20, and 10% stayed for more than 20 weeks. No patient stayed for longer than 40 weeks, and in the entire sample only three patients came back for subsequent treatment after their initial discharge. In all cases this second treatment episode lasted for ten weeks. None of these first 100 patients was in treatment at the time of follow-up.

PATIENT PROFILE

All of the first 100 patients admitted to the Phobia Program of Washington were selected for follow-up study. These patients entered treatment between February 1978 and March 1979. They were followed through August of 1980, an average of two years after the initiation of treatment. We had follow-up data on 97 of the 100 patients. We were unable to contact the remaining three patients. The patients were contacted either by mail or by telephone and were asked to complete a questionnaire (see end of chapter) describing their life and attitudes at the time of follow-up. Additionally, we had data that was collected at the time the patients began treatment and at the time they left treatment, so this report covers three time points—at the start of treatment, at the completion of treatment, and at the time of follow-up, an average of two years after starting treatment in the Phobia Program. The data to be described cover these 97 patients, on whom we have both initial data and follow-up data. On some items we had incomplete data for some patients, so not all items have data on all 97 patients.

PRETREATMENT INFORMATION

Those 97 patients treated by the Phobia Program included 78 women and 19 men (80% women; 20% men). They ranged in age at the start of

Table 1
Patient Profile at Intake

	Men	Women
	(N = 19)	(N = 78)
Age at Onset of Phobia (Average in Years)	25	26
Age at Start of Phobia Program (Average in Years)	34	40
Duration of Phobic Symptoms Prior to Treatment (Average in Years)	9	14
Married (%)	58	76
Employed Full-time (%)	68	32
Employed Part-time (%)	5	12

treatment from 18 to 70 years old. The average age of the women patients at the start of treatment was 40 and the average age of men at the start of treatment was 34. I will comment further about this age differential later in the chapter. The age differential is reflected in the percent who were married. Seventy-six percent of the women were married at the start of treatment, while only 58% of the men were married. (See Table 1.)

Among the women the average age at the onset of phobic symptoms was 26, while the average age for the onset of phobic symptoms for the men was 25. The range in onset of phobic symptoms was from four to 69 years for the total sample. The women had had phobic symptoms an average of 14 years prior to seeking treatment, while the men had been phobic for an average of nine years. Within this patient population, only 24% had had no record of previous psychiatric treatment. The remaining 76% had had an average of just over two episodes of psychotherapy (range 1 to 7) with an average of just over 200 visits to a psychotherapist during their lifetimes prior to entering the Phobia Program. Only seven of the 97 patients had been hospitalized for psychiatric reasons, and one, a psychotic depressive, had been given a course of electroconvulsive treatment as part of her hospitalization. Note that this is a short-term treatment (average duration 16 weeks) for a long-term chronic illness (average duration 13 years).

With respect to diagnosis (see Table 2), using the DSM III categorization, 92 patients were classified as phobic disorders, four as Obsessive-

Table 2
Diagnosis

	Men	Women
DSM III		
Phobic Disorders	19	73
Obsessive Compulsive Disorders (300.30)	0	4
Major Depression, Recurrent (296.3x)	0	1
Marks Classification		
Agoraphobia	9	48
Simple Phobia	6	23
Social Phobia	4	2
Obsessive Compulsive	0	4
Depressive	0	1

Compulsive Disorders (''contamination phobias''), and one as a Major Depression, recurrent. We found that of the 92 phobics 57 of the patients were agoraphobic, 29 were simple phobics, and six were social phobics. Among the simple phobics, the primary fears of these 29 patients were as follows: eight had a primary fear of driving; four had a primary fear of flying; four had a primary fear of elevators; three had a primary fear of bridges; three had a primary fear of animals; two had a primary fear of heights; two had a primary fear of closed-in places; one had a fear of vomiting; one had a fear of writing in public; and one suffered primarily from a fear of being far from a toilet.

Looking at sex by diagnostic category, we find that 84% of the agoraphobics were women, 80% of the specific phobics were women, 100% of the obsessives (and the depressive patient) were also women. Among the social phobics, however, four of the six patients were men, reversing the sex ratio of all the other phobias. This reduction of female: male ratio is characteristic of other patient samples of social phobics. Because the social phobics tended to be younger and also tended to be unmarried, the average age of the men and the percent of men who were married tended to be slightly lower than the average age and percentage married of the women.

Looking more closely at this patient population, you will see from Table 1 that 50% of our patient population was employed full-time or part-time at the beginning of treatment. Sixty-eight percent of the patients reported that they were not phobic during their childhood, while 32% reported that they did suffer from childhood phobias. The phobic symptoms during childhood were interesting because only five patients reported any significant absence from school related to school phobias. The remainder suffered from phobic symptoms of one of two kinds: either a relatively early onset of phobic symptoms, often of a social phobic variety, in mid-to-late adolescence, or the onset of an animal phobia or claustrophobia in preschool or grade school years. The large majority of patients reported the onset of their phobic symptoms in young adult life. In all cases the *disability* associated with a phobia that led to their seeking treatment was a phenomenon of their adulthood.

Among this patient population, 54% reported that neither parent was phobic, while 32% reported that they did have a phobic parent. The remaining 14% were uncertain or failed to answer that item. Of the 31 patients who had a phobic parent, six (19%) reported that both their parents were phobic, while 25 (81%) reported that they had a phobic mother only. No patient reported having a phobic father unless the mother was also phobic. At the onset of treatment, 45% of the patients were taking some psychotropic medication, primarily an antianxiety drug such as Valium.

RESULTS OF TREATMENT

The results of treatment are divided into two sections. The first is basically descriptive while the second reports the results of the Isaac Marks Fear Questionnaire. At the start of treatment, 40% of the patients reported that they were employed full-time, 10% said they were employed part-time, and 25% reported that they were unemployed primarily because of their phobia. Another 25% said that even if they were free of their phobic symptoms they would not be employed outside the home. At follow-up, 53% of the patients were employed full-time and 22% were employed part-time. Only 8% reported that they were unemployed because of their phobic disability. The percentage who described themselves as unemployed by choice shrunk from 25 to 17. A total of 30 patients reported a change in their employment status. Eighteen of these (60%) indicated that the change in their employment status was the result of treatment in the phobia program. Six of this first 100-patient group became therapists in the phobia program. Four of these people were employed full-time prior to the start of treatment and two reported themselves unemployed because of their phobic disability prior to entering the program.

Fourteen of these 97 patients began school on a part-time basis after joining the Phobia Program. None was in school at the start of treatment.

At the onset of treatment 45% of the patients were using some form of psychotropic medication. At the end of treatment 35% were using medication, and at follow-up only 31% reported that they were using psychotropic medication. All but one of the 28 patients comprising this 31% were using minor tranquilizers at follow-up. Two were taking antidepressants (one along with a minor tranquilizer, and the other an antidepressant alone). Three patients reported that they took more medication as a result of their participation in the program, while 30 reported that they took less medication because of the program. Twelve people who were taking medication at the beginning of treatment reported no change as a result of their participation in the program. There were 14 patients who were using medication at the start of the program who were *not* using medication at the time of follow-up. Most of the others who continued to take medicine reported that they used less medication after participation in the program.

At follow-up we asked each patient to rate the change in his phobic symptoms from the time he entered treatment until the time of follow-up. Eighty-nine percent reported that there was a positive change, that is, a reduction in the phobic symptoms; 2% reported a negative change, that is, their phobic symptoms were worse; and 9% reported that there was no change in phobic symptoms. The 97 patients on whom we have follow-up data were asked to assess the help they received from the Phobia Program in overcoming their phobic disability. Seven percent reported that participation in the program did not help; 31% reported that it helped "some"; 40% reported that it helped "a great deal"; and 22% reported that the program "totally changed my life for the better."

We then asked the patients to describe changes in specific areas of their lives from the time they entered treatment until the time of follow-up. They were asked to rate each of five areas on a scale from minus 8 (meaning a dramatic negative change) through zero (meaning no change) to plus 8 (meaning a dramatic positive change). The results were: change in family life = average score +3.0; change in shyness = +2.7; change in self-esteem = +3.8; change in avoidance of unpleasant experiences = +4.2; and change in work performance = +3.4.

Two areas particularly interested us in this follow-up study. These were the effect of treatment on marriage as reported by the patients (we did not ask their spouses to answer any questions) and also on driving behavior. With respect to marriage, we asked the patients who were married to rate their marital satisfaction on a scale of 0 (meaning that they were totally dissatisfied with their marriage) to +8 (meaning that they were totally satisfied with their marriage), both before the program and at the time of follow-up. The mean score before treatment was +4.7 and the mean score at follow-up was +5.8. Thirty-two of the 67 patients on whom we have data on this item reported that there was no impact on their marriage as a result of their participation in the phobia program. Thirty-five patients, however, reported that there was some change; 29 reported that their marriages were better as a result of their participation; five reported that their marriage was worse as a result of their participation, and one reported that there were ways in which the marriage was better, but also ways in which the marriage was worse. Forty-four percent of those 67 who responded said that participation in the Phobia Program itself had helped to improve their marriage.

With respect to driving, 67% (or 62 people) of the 92 patients on whom we have this data reported that their phobia had influenced their driving to some extent before their participation in the Program. Thirty-two of these patients had actually stopped driving completely for a period of time prior to entering treatment. By contrast, only three had ever had an accident because of their phobia, and all of these were minor accidents. A typical accident was reported by a woman who had a contamination phobia and swerved to avoid a manhole. She was driving slowly and nicked a parked car. Although 32 patients had stopped driving, and 62 reported that the phobia had influenced their driving, the primary concern of most of these people prior to treatment was not a fear of causing an accident. In fact, this was a concern of only 12 patients. The more common fear was of "panicking and having to stop," or "getting stuck in traffic," or "being too far from home." Only one of our 92 patients on whom we have driving data reported that her phobia began as the result of an accident. She had been driving at the time the accident occurred, but was not responsible for the accident.

The average number of miles driven per year now by those patients whose phobia had influenced their driving is 7,700. Contrast this figure with 3,400 miles per year, the average number of miles driven per year when their phobia was at its worst. But also compare the 7,700 miles per year with 10,100 miles per year, the average number of miles driven per year now by phobic patients whose phobia had never influenced their driving.

We also asked patients to assess their overall success in achieving the major goal of the Phobia Program, which is to "live a full and normal life without restrictions because of the phobia." The patients rated their success in achieving this goal from 0 (no phobic avoidance) to +8 (meaning total avoidance of at least some important area in the patient's life). Thus, on this scale a low score is "better" than a high score. At the start of the treatment, the average score was +6.9; at the end of treatment, the average score was +4.0; at follow-up, the average score was +3.0.

One of the most frequently asked questions by people who are joining the program is whether the phobic symptoms will "go away" or whether patients will simply learn to live with their symptoms and live a more normal life despite them. In an effort to answer this question, we asked about phobic feelings in several ways (see Table 3). First, we asked the frequency with which the phobic symptoms occurred. We found that the percentage who reported phobic feelings, occurring once a day or more often, fell from 75% before treatment to 24% at follow-up. Similarly, the percent that reported that they "never" had phobic symptoms rose from 1% to 6% and those reporting a frequency of "less than once a month" rose from 4% before treatment to 22% at the time of follow-up.

We also asked about the intensity of the phobic symptoms. We found that the percentage who reported their symptoms were "very severe" fell from 82% at the time they started treatment to only 17% at the time of follow-up, while the percentage who reported that their phobic symptoms were "mild" or "nonexistent" increased from 1% prior to treatment to 8% at the time of follow-up and the percent reporting "mild" symptoms rose from 3% at the start of treatment to 53% at follow-up. Focusing more directly on a common concern, we asked whether the patient's

Table 3
Phobic Feelings

	Follow-Up		Before	
	%	No. of patients	%	No. of patients
Frequency				
Once a day or more often	24%	21	75%	63
Once a week to once a day	23%	20	13%	11
Once a month to once a week	25%	22	7%	6
Less than once a month	22%	19	4%	3
Never	6%	5	1%	1
		87		84
Intensity				
Very severe	17%	15	82%	74
Moderately severe	22%	20	14%	12
Mild	53%	48	3%	3
Non-existent	8%	7	1%	1
		90		90

participation in the program had primarily led to an ability to 1) cope better with the phobic feelings, or 2) reduce or even totally eliminate the phobic feelings, 3) do both or, finally, 4) do neither (see Table 4).

We found that 37% attributed their progress to their ability to cope better with their phobic feelings; 10% reported that their success was primarily related to a total elimination or dramatic reduction in their phobic symptoms, and 41% reported that both were true. Only 12% reported that they had neither had a dramatic reduction in their phobic symptoms nor learned to cope with their symptoms more effectively as a result of participation in the program. Overall, this indicates that 78% of the program participants reported that they coped better with their phobic feelings at the time of follow-up and 51% reported that their feelings were either totally eliminated or dramatically reduced, and only 12% reported that neither positive outcome occurred.

Finally, we asked the patients if they would recommend the Phobia Program to a phobic friend. Eighty-seven percent responded that yes, they would recommend the program strongly; 12% said they would recommend it but not strongly; and 1% said they would not recommend the program to a phobic friend.

Note that all indicators showed a positive change from onset of treatment through follow-up on the average for this patient population. In general, the progress was most dramatic for reductions in avoidance behavior (and to a lesser, but still significant extent, the phobic feelings themselves). This is hardly surprising since this is the primary focus of the Phobia Program. Also noteworthy, however, are the changes in other more complex areas of the patients' lives ranging from decreases in shyness and the use of psychotropic medication to increases in employment, marital satisfaction and self-esteem. These shifts suggest significant changes in the average patient's life functioning, or as some might say, "character."

Table 4
Phobic Feelings

	Number of people	%
Cope	34	37%
Reduction or elimination of feelings	9	10%
Both	37	41%
Neither	11	12%
	91	

RESULTS OF THE ISAAC MARKS FEAR QUESTIONNAIRE

The one-page Fear Questionnaire developed by Isaac Marks in London was administered to all our patients at the time they entered the program, at the time they left the program, and at the time of follow-up. Table 5 reports the results of these data in several ways. We have grouped the patients so that it is possible to separate the "agoraphobics," the "specific phobics," and "all others." Then the data are reported for a total program sample.

These data can only be interpreted by referring to the Questionnaire from which it is taken. A copy of the Questionnaire is included at the end of this chapter. Marks tabulates his data in six broad categories. The first is "Target Symptom," the phobia for which the patient sought treatment. On a scale of zero, meaning no avoidance, to 8, meaning complete avoidance, the total sample showed an improvement from 7.4 at the start of treatment, to 3.6 at completion of the program, and finally to 3.1 at the time of follow-up, an average of two years after starting the program. Note also that the agoraphobics, as a subgroup, had more dramatic results with their scores on the Target Symptom falling from 7.6 to 3.8 to 2.9.

Marks also tabulates phobic symptoms into three broad categories: "Agoraphobic Symptoms," "Blood/Injury Symptoms," and "Social Phobic Symptoms." Note that the agoraphobics had a far higher score on the agoraphobic item than the other two groups (a reassuring finding!) with the mean score on that item falling for this subgroup from 23 to 14 to 11, at the three points of time studied. Also note the scales for "Anxiety/Depression" and "Global Symptoms." They show similar trends. The overall conclusion to be reached from these data is that there is a significant reduction in symptom level from intake until termination of treatment and that the progress on the average which is achieved at the termination of treatment is actually extended during the interval to follow-up. Thus, patients tended to show further improvement over the course of time both while in the program and after they left treatment.

Using the Marks and Mathews Questionnaire data, we asked whether the patients who had suffered from phobias for shorter periods of time prior to treatment had more successful treatment outcomes. The answer, as shown in Table 6, was "yes." It is noteworthy, however, that the same trends toward improvement following treatment were seen in both the short-history and long-history patients, and that the differences in improvement between the two groups were relatively small.

The data reported in this chapter describe the demographic characteristics of one phobia treatment program. They also report in several ways the outcome of treatment. It is clear, from these data, that treatment is generally associated with significant improvement in the patients' status in all items measured. However, it should also be noted that the phobic disability is not totally eliminated for many patients. In fact, it is clear that the majority of patients continue to have some symptoms

Table 5
Phobic Symptom Level

	At Intake	After Program	At Follow-up
Target Symptom			
Agoraphobics	7.6	3.8	2.9
Specific Phobics	7.5	2.8	3.1
"Others"	6.4	4.8	4.3
Total Sample	7.4	3.6	3.1
Agoraphobic Symptoms			
Agoraphobics	23.4	13.8	10.6
Specific Phobics	6.9	1.6	1.9
"Others"	11.5	7.9	9.0
Total Sample	17.4	9.6	7.7
Blood/Injury Symptoms			
Agoraphobics	12.8	9.1	9.5
Specific Phobics	8.3	4.5	4.1
"Others"	11.0	9.6	7.9
Total Sample	11.3	7.8	7.6
Social Phobic Symptoms			
Agoraphobics	13.8	9.5	8.6
Specific Phobics	6.9	4.1	4.2
"Others"	15.4	10.7	11.1
Total Sample	12.1	8.1	7.5
Anxiety/Depression Symptoms			
Agoraphobics	23.3	14.3	11.0
Specific Phobics	13.0	5.6	5.3
"Others"	22.6	20.0	16.4
Total Sample	20.3	12.4	9.8
Global Symptoms			
Agoraphobics	6.3	3.9	2.8
Specific Phobics	6.1	2.8	2.9
"Others"	6.1	5.9	4.4
Total Sample	6.2	3.8	3.0

Table 6
Duration of Phobic Symptoms Prior to Treatment and Correlation with Outcome

24 patients with phobic histories of five years or less on whom we had target symptom ratings before, after and at follow-up.
22 patients with phobic histories of 20 years or more on whom we had target symptom ratings before, after and at follow-up.

	Target Symptom *before* Program	Target Symptom *after* Program	Target Symptom at *follow-up*	Avg. Target Symptom Reduction from *before* to *follow-up*
Mean score of patients with phobic histories of 5 yrs. or less	7.6	2.7	2.6	5.0
Mean score of patients with phobic histories of 20 yrs. or more	7.6	4.1	3.8	3.8

even after successful treatment, and that a phobia is usually a chronic, and in some cases, a disabling condition. On the other hand, it is also clear that significant improvement was achieved by the large majority of patients, and in many of these patients the improvement was dramatic.

One might question the extent to which these effects are the result of the natural history of the phobic process itself, since as had been known for many years phobic symptoms tend to ebb and flow over time. The fact that the average duration of symptoms was 14 years for women and nine years for men prior to treatment suggests that this is not likely to account for all of the improvement noted. Also, the fact that the improvement was sustained on the average and actually increased over the course of the two-year follow-up again suggests that this was not a random or short-lived fluctuation in the natural history of the phobic process. Finally, the patients themselves attributed their improvement to their participation in the program.

PHOBIA PROGRAM FOLLOW-UP QUESTIONNAIRE

1. Your name: ____________________

2. Today's date: ____________________

3. Your telephone numbers (home) ____________ office ____________

4. Medications used for phobia (give name of medicine, dosage (e.g. milligrams) and average number taken each day):
   At start of treatment: ____________________
   At end of treatment: ____________________
   Now: ____________________

   Did the Phobia Program contribute to a change in use of medication?
   Took more because of program: ____________
   Took less because of program: ____________
   No change as a result of program: ____________

5. What is the overall change in your phobic symptoms from start of treatment until today? Use the scale below and choose any whole number between minus 8 and plus 8 (such as +5 or -3, etc.). Indicate in the blank your numerical assessment: ____________

-8	0	+8
Worst Ever	No Change	Totally Cured

6. Did the Phobia Program help you to overcome your phobic disabilities?
   Did not help: ____________
   Helped some: ____________
   Helped a great deal; ____________
   Totally changed my life for the better: ____________

7. Using the scale below, evaluate numerically the effect the Phobic Program had from beginning of treatment to today on:

-8	0	+8
Much Worse	No Change	Huge Improvement

   Family life: ________
   Shyness: ________
   Self-esteem: ________
   Avoidance of unpleasant experiences: ________
   Work performance: ________

8. Changes in work status from start of Program until today.
   Check appropriate categories

	At Start of Program	At Time of Follow-up
Employed full-time:	________	________
Employed part-time:	________	________
Unemployed because of phobic disability:	________	________
Unemployed by choice:	________	________

   If employment status changed, was it the result of treatment in the Phobia Program? Yes________ No________

   School: Did you start school after joining the Phobia Program?
   Yes, full-time student (indicate level):____________
   Yes, part-time student:____________
   No: ____________
   Comment:

9. Participation of family members and friends in the Phobia Program:
How many group sessions did you attend? ______________
How many did a family member or friend attend? __________
Scale contribution of family members from minus 8 (made phobia worse) to 0 (no impact) to plus 8 (helped tremendously):

Number of Sessions	Contribution
Parent__________	__________
Child__________	__________
Spouse__________	__________
Friend__________	__________
Other__________	__________

10. Rate your overall marital satisfaction on a scale from 0 (completely dissatisfied) to plus 8 (completely satisfied):
Rating now: ______________
Rating before Program______________
Check the blanks which best describe your spouse's support of your work with the Phobia Program:
Strong support: ______________
Moderate support: ______________
Indifferent: ______________
Minimal undermining of my efforts: ______________
Moderate undermining of my efforts: ______________
Strong undermining of my efforts: ______________

Did your participation in the Phobia Program have any impact on your marriage?
No: _____ Yes: Made it better______ Made it worse________
Did you become divorced, separated or married since you joined the Phobia Program? If yes, please describe the change and how this change relates to your participation in the Phobia Program: ______________________________
____

Did either of your parents have phobias? No______ Yes______
If yes, describe phobia and rate severity (0=none, 8=disabling):
Mother: ____
Father: ____

11. Before you joined the Phobia Program, did your phobia influence your driving a car? No_______ Yes_______
If yes, did you ever stop driving because of your phobia? No_____ Yes _____
Did you reduce your driving? No______ Yes______ If yes, how?
In terms of amount of driving? ______________
In terms of distance driven from home? _________
In avoidance of bridges________or freeways_________or other__________?
If other, describe: ____

Estimate the total number of miles driven by you per year now: __________
and when your phobia was at its worst: ______________
What year did you begin driving? ______________
Since that time, which years have you not driven at all? ______________
Estimate for the years you have driven, the number of miles you have averaged yearly: ___________miles driven per year
How many accidents have you had while you were the driver? ____________
In what years did these accidents occur? ____________________________
Did you ever have an accident while you were driving because of your phobia?
No: _________ Yes (give number of accidents and describe briefly): ________
____
____
Have you avoided driving primarily because of your fear of causing an accident? No: ______ Yes: _______
Did your phobia begin as a result of an accident? No: ______ Yes: ______
Were you driving at the time? No: ______ Yes: ______

12. Contact since leaving the Phobia Program. Evaluate the following factors using this guide: A=great help, B=some help and C=no help.
Attendance at self-help meetings: ______________
Approximate number of sessions attended: ________
Sessions with Phobia Therapist: ______________
Approximate number of sessions attended: ________
Contact with other members of the Program: ______
Approximate number of contacts: ______________
Individual, couple or family sessions with Dr. DuPont: __________
Approximate number of sessions and who attended: ______________________
____
Reading of Phobia Connection Newsletter: ____________________________
Approximate total of hours spent reading issues: ______________
Attendance at Maintenance Group: ___________________________
Approximate number of sessions: ______________
Other contacts. Describe and give total number of hours:

13. The goal of the Phobia Program is to LEAD A FULL AND NORMAL LIFE WITHOUT RESTRICTION ON YOUR ACTIVITIES BECAUSE OF PHOBIAS. On a scale from 0 (no avoidance at all) to 8 (total avoidance) rate your closeness to achieving that goal now_______, at end of Program (group sessions)_________, and at beginning of Program_________.

14. Phobic feelings. How often do and did you experience phobic feelings?

	Now	Before Program
Once a day or more often	_______	_______
Once a week to once a day	_______	_______
Once a month to once a week	_______	_______
Less than once a month	_______	_______
Never	_______	_______

How severe are and were your phobic feelings?

Very severe	_______	_______
Moderately severe	_______	_______
Mild	_______	_______
Non-existent	_______	_______

Which best describes your progress in dealing with your phobia?
_______Greater ability to cope with phobic feelings, or
_______Tremendous reduction and even elimination of phobic feelings.
_______Both of the above
_______Neither

15. Would you recommend the Phobia Program to a phobic friend?
Yes, strongly_____________ Yes, but not strongly______________ No_______

16. Suggestions for improvement in Phobia Program:

17. Other comments:

18. Please complete the attached Fear Questionnaire to indicate your feelings now.

FEAR QUESTIONNAIRE

Choose a number from the scale below to show how much you would avoid each of the situations listed below because of fear or other unpleasant feelings. Then write the number you chose in the box opposite each situation.

0	1	2	3	4	5	6	7	8
Would not avoid it		Slightly avoid it		Definitely avoid it		Markedly avoid it		Always avoid it

1. Main phobia you want treated (describe in your own words)
....
2. Injections or minor surgery......................................
3. Eating or drinking with other people................................
4. Hospital..
5. Travelling alone by bus or coach..............................
6. Walking alone in busy streets.................................
7. Being watched or stared at...
8. Going into crowded shops.....................................
9. Talking to people in authority.....................................
10. Sight of blood ....
11. Being criticized..
12. Going alone far from home.....................................
13. Thought of injury or illness...................................
14. Speaking or acting to an audience..................................
15. Large open space...
16. Going to the dentist..
17. Other situations (describe)..

leave blank———

Now choose a number from the scale below to show how much you are troubled by each problem listed, and write the number in the box opposite.

0	1	2	3	4	5	6	7	8
Hardly at all		Slightly troublesome		Definitely troublesome		Markedly troublesome		Very severely troublesome

18. Feeling miserable or depressed................................
19. Feeling irritable or angry....................................
20. Feeling tense or panicky......................................
21. Upsetting thoughts coming into your mind......................
22. Feeling you or your surroundings are strange or unreal.........
23. Other feelings (describe)..

Total

How would you rate the present state of your phobic symptoms on the scale below?

0	1	2	3	4	5	6	7	8
No phobias present		Slightly disturbing/ not really disabling		Definitely disturbing/ disabling		Markedly disturbing/ disabling		Very severely disturbing/ disabling

Please circle one number between 0 and 8

24

Case Study of an Agoraphobic

Robert L. DuPont

Experts have written about phobias. In this chapter, a former phobic describes, week-by-week, her efforts to overcome her phobic disability. This woman, whom I've called "Marie," is not typical in several important ways. She has more social phobic symptoms and lives a more isolated life than most phobic people. This is seen in her being unmarried, in her withdrawn living and working relationships, and even in her symptoms (she's more uncomfortable being a passenger in a car than being a driver). Her depression, sense of emptiness, and preoccupation with choking are also relatively unusual. Her other phobic symptoms are typical. Her intelligence is both striking and fairly typical. Her introspection and self-preoccupation, reflected in her writing this diary, are also somewhat unusual.

What follows is her description of her work in and comments on the Phobia Program over the course of 19 weeks, as well as a brief commentary by her Group Leader, Jane Brashares, and her phobia therapist, Judy Barth. Jane is a former-phobic psychiatric social worker. Judy is a non-phobic registered nurse. In reading Marie's account you need to know that the Phobia Program asks patients to label their fear levels from zero to ten and to watch them go up and down observing specifically what makes them rise and fall.

Patients in the Phobia Program of Washington are asked to complete Daily Task Sheets, which are weekly one-page charts to briefly outline daily goals and methods employed to achieve them. One patient, Marie, found this form limiting and chose to expound upon her experiences in diary form. The journal which follows was excerpted from diary entries from her first ten weeks in the Phobia Program. It reveals the constant arduous up-and-down struggle to cope with her phobia. This is followed by a brief report from week 19.

Marie, an attractive, thin, red-haired woman, looking ten years younger than her 34 years, had been agoraphobic for 11 years. Her phobia began with a series of anxiety attacks at the beach and even worse panic attacks while being driven home. Once home she found herself anxious at progressively shorter distances away from home until she was unable to walk around the block. She spent one-and-a-half years confined to her home.

Family problems and past failure at two colleges compounded her difficulties. Prior to joining the Phobia Program she had received psychiatric and other outpatient therapy from five sources to no avail. Despite her tremendous anxiety, she was reluctant to use medication—taking one-half of a 2 mg Valium occasionally and only when absolutely necessary.

She was fearful of going far (relatively) from home, more scared if someone was in the car with her, and most afraid if she was a passenger in a car. Despite these overwhelming fears she had managed with great difficulty to work as a waitress for the last five years and to live self-sufficiently in an apartment by herself.

JOURNAL OF AN AGORAPHOBIC

Week One

Saturday. Hot and sticky. As I was driving to work, I felt more and more like gagging or retching, not actually throwing up. It was different from the normal rush of anxiety and I kept getting more and more afraid. (I'm very afraid of throwing up—haven't done it in about ten years.) I made U-turns several times but finally made it as far as my mom's (one mile from work). Earlier I had called the manager at work to say I was feeling sick but I would get there. I continued on and got halfway between my mom's and work and U-turned again, went to a phone booth, and called the manager and explained I had been trying to drive for 45 minutes but couldn't make it. He was mad because he really needed me and I was scared about losing my job. I went home anyway. Before I left for work I had taken one-half a 2 mg Valium.

When I got back home I called Jane, my phobia group leader; then I lay down on the floor with a pillow and cried. Level 10—depression, gloom, and disgust. She called back shortly and said to go to work—even if I went late, they would think better of me for making the effort. I said I would call her when I got there but I was scared to death; so I sat there for half-an-hour thinking, "I can't do it." Then I took another half of a 2 mg Valium and started driving. I figured since they didn't know I was coming, if I didn't make it, it wouldn't matter. I also thought—at least, I'm trying. Got to the restaurant parking lot and chickened out but went across the street and called Jane who urged me to go to work even if they sent me home. So I went to work.

Sunday. Woke up fine. Within a short time, I was feeling a steady current of anxiety for no reason—about level 2. Decided to go to drugstore for paper—only two blocks away. About two-thirds of the way there, went up to about 5 or 6 and felt very sick. Kept going. Once I was in the store I was fine. Decided to keep walking. Level 3 or 4 and sick again. Looked at everything carefully, decided to take ten steps at a time, backtracked a little to the side, and looked in an old building. Kept reminding myself that even a little step is progress.

Went out driving—even on the Beltway. Drove home. Feeling pretty good but worrying that tomorrow will again be difficult. It's very hard *not* to anticipate anxiety when it seems to be more and more difficult rather than less and less.

Tuesday. Felt sick in car on the way to work but practiced looking at cars, houses, and signs. This helped a little but when I got to work I felt still very sick.

Wednesday. Drove with National Gallery of Art as a goal. Got to Tidal Basin and got a 4-level, turned around and got an 8-level. Looked at cars and people. Got through it. Turned around and went back. At Constitution Avenue had a 4- or 5-level, turned around and drove a few blocks, turned back and drove to gallery with no anxiety. Parked right in front, went in, drove home, tired, but felt really good.

Realized that tomorrow may still be tough, but it seems less hopeless.

Week Two

Sunday. Went out again around 6 P.M. Went to drug store but came back out right away with about an 8 or 9, choking very much. Drove home quickly, still choking. Didn't park but drove around the block twice, reluctant to stop and admit defeat. Went to a drugstore nearby and bought Jujubes. Still choking and at a 5-level. Came home, had some wine, and played the radio. Cried. Felt like killing myself. After half hour, calmed down. Got in the car, drove all the way to work to show myself that I could. Of course, now I'll wonder if it was the wine that lowered my anxiety level. I hope like hell it's not going to continue like this—fair progress in the morning, ten steps back in the evening, a mile ahead the next day. I feel like nothing is solid and dependable. No progress seems to last for more than a few hours. It's so depressing.

Monday. Got on parkway feeling a little bit like throwing up. Got off at P Street but still felt good that I had gone that far. Was more anxious coming home but kept telling myself how stupid it was to be anxious since I had just done something I thought I couldn't do after choking yesterday less than one mile away. Realized that yesterday has little bearing on today.

Wednesday. Recycling day. Headed for Rockville to sell cans. Level-6. Thinking while driving, "I'm almost there, I'm doing great. I'm functioning even with this high level of fear." Turned back but ultimately made it to recycling center. Reminded myself how well I was doing. When I left I had no more anxiety.

Maybe I should set my goals a little lower so that I can have a better chance at success and self-confidence.

Week Three

Friday. I'm feeling anxious about tomorrow. Ever since I started this job (four-and-a-half years ago) I've been a little nervous about Saturdays, but especially now that this choking seems harder to predict and to deal with. I know that Valium will help but I want to make it on my own.

Saturday. As soon as I got in the car to drive to work, my stomach felt like it was floating nauseously around. Went straight to work. Felt pretty awful and asked to get out early. Once I started working I felt better, then worse, then better, etc. From one minute to the next I would feel entirely different.

Wednesday. Woke up feeling good. Today (most of it) was the first day in weeks that I haven't felt as if I were about to go to the dentist. Usually I walk around all day feeling apprehensive.

I had a small lettering job to do and did it after my drive. It came out very well on the first try—a result of my self-confidence. I'm hoping that things are on the upswing. But if they go down again, and they probably will, I'll try to remember that today was a good day and last night I was terrified to drive a block and I drove about five miles.

Week Four

Saturday. Had a level-10 that made Thursday's look like a 6. Worked OK but choking started very gradually. Choking a little more so I decided to take half a Valium to get through the afternoon. Shortly after taking it I started gagging a lot, took another half and got even worse. I had to go outside with my purse and car keys and sit in the parking lot. I was breathing very fast, trying not to vomit, and my fast breathing turned into crying. After a few minutes I came in determined not to leave.

Went for a drive. Came home for the night. Normal Saturday night depression—no date, no boyfriend, bill-paying, laundry-washing, left-over-eating Saturday night. I wonder if getting over my phobias will give me the chance to change it or if I really want to. God, I hate my life.

Sunday. Basically I feel like I'm back at square one. Depressed. Also with four choking attacks last week, I am not looking forward to tomorrow.

Tuesday. Went to Judy's (phobia therapist)—not nervous at all. She suggested riding on Metro and I could not even *imagine* doing it but we went to the station anyway. Got a level 5 or 6 just being there but after a few minutes I felt better. I bought two farecards and we went into the station and up the escalator. Looked at the trains for a long time, looked inside them and all over the platform. I still couldn't imagine getting into one. Judy said I did really well but I didn't think so, although I did keep going (slowly) when I wanted to turn around.

Week Five

Saturday. Came into work early and asked to stay late. Started choking a little during the first hour and kept choking all day, but I worked as well as usual anyway—chewed a lot of Jujubes but didn't take a Valium. It seemed as though the choking and the anxiety were separate. I gave myself an A+ for staying all day and not taking a Valium.

Then I went to the bike shop and the guys changed my antifreeze. This doesn't sound like much but I'm always afraid of being trapped with my car out of commission, even for a few minutes; and I didn't even look for an out by asking one of the guys if I could use his car just in case I got nervous. I was not even at a level 2. Boy, was I proud of myself.

Sunday. Drove on the Beltway. Level 2 but no higher. Took Glen Echo Exit which I have been afraid to take before. Anticipated a much higher level but only got to about 3. Enjoyed the beautiful scenery and how smooth it felt to drive along without the usual stopping and starting. I was surprised at being so calm about it and proud of myself. I give myself an A.

I've been noticing less and less of the constant ominous feeling I had for the first month after I decided to join the program. I'm so relieved!

Week Six

Thursday. Felt as though a tidal wave was just waiting to hit me. As I left the house took half a Valium and made it almost to the clinic before I had to turn around. Went about one half mile down the road and came back. During the last hour of the group session the choking came back but I was not anxious about it. I was pretty relaxed except when time was getting short and so many people hadn't talked yet. I give myself a B+ for the session. It would have been an A+ to get there and stay there feeling so badly but the Valium brings me to a B+.

Once again, I feel that I can accept my bad days without thinking that I've hit bottom again. It's just a setback and nowhere near as horrible as I felt all the time for the first two weeks.

Saturday. Work was a breeze. I'm not even going to grade it because it was no challenge at all. It was a rough day in some normal ways but otherwise it was no big deal. I feel like I'm getting back to normal in this area so I can work the way I used to without worrying about anything not work-related.

Wednesday. Every day has a challenge and at times the challenges are much closer to home than other times. I drove to the co-op instead of walking, even though it's only a few blocks. I felt pretty sick for an hour and then felt better. Decided to walk to the Air Rights Building only two long blocks away but I was really nervous. I set my goal for halfway there, to the railroad tracks. Then I found a shortcut and walked across the street from the building. I was more afraid of panicking than I was actually afraid. I kept saying, "I can't believe that yesterday I drove to Darnestown and today I can hardly walk two blocks." But I also tried to accept the setback and not see it as anything permanent. I think the problem now is that waiting for the anxiety is so tiring and suspenseful that I don't really know what to do.

Week Seven

Friday. Felt anxious before work and asked to get off early. At 2:00 P.M. changed my mind and decided to stay but I started choking. By 4:00 P.M. it was really bad and I thought of taking a Valium. It turned out that I didn't have to stay till 5:00 P.M. so I ate something but kept on choking. It's worse to choke so much after having a good day like yesterday than it is to choke all the time and to expect it. It's very depressing to keep having setbacks and although yesterday in my group session I talked about how I was beginning to accept the anxiety and symptoms, today I don't feel anywhere near acceptance. I feel as though I were starting all over again. And, of course, depression feeds on itself so it's extra hard to feel optimistic.

After dinner I drove to the Silver Spring Metro Station. Walking from my car to the station made my level rise to about 6, so I stopped a few times and looked around, then walked into the station. My heart was beating really fast and I was very apprehensive but I don't know why. I finally went through the entrance gates and up the escalator. I waited on the platform, trying not to look dumb, and watched a couple of trains come and go. I went into one that I knew wasn't leaving and then I left a little while later. The trains are exciting and I think I'd like to take one, but so far I'm still nervous about just stepping into one. I give myself a B for getting as far as I did with so much anxiety.

Sunday. I think I'm using my phobia as an excuse for the things that are wrong in my life. Like fat people say, "If I were thin, I'd be happy, popular, or whatever." And then when they start to get thin, they get scared or get fat again. I feel like I'm afraid to lose my phobia so I'm having some very frightened feelings. Maybe the setbacks come so soon after what looks like progress to scare me into not trying to get rid of the phobia. Why can't I be unimaginative and unafraid like so many other people?

Driving on an unfamiliar road a force-9 panic hit me, and I said,

"Wow, this is a big one." I managed to keep driving slowly and chewed Jujubes like crazy and it came down to about a 6. I drove home and a little while later called Judy. I'm starting to get that "wish I were dead" feeling again.

Judy told me that she found it odd and illogical that I felt less safe with her in the car than I feel alone. It may be illogical, but find one thing that's logical about a phobia!

Week Eight

Friday. Took a shower. With a great deal of dread and anticipation I drove to a party near Falls and River Roads—nine miles from my apartment. I was at about level-4 or less most of the way out there. When I got there I told the hostess I couldn't stay for long, which left me an out, and I talked to a few people I knew and then went into the pool (it was a pool party). The water was warm, the night was beautiful, and shortly afterward I felt my anxiety level slip down to 0 and stay there. I was very aware of feeling calm and happy. I stayed there from 10 to 11:30 and had a beer. I had to leave in order to get enough sleep, not because I was anxious. I had a good time and was very proud of myself!

Saturday. Work was awful—I felt bad and started choking but stayed till almost 5 P.M. I headed for the pool, keeping an eye on the temperature gauge of my car. It was fine until I drove up to the pool and stopped the car. Then hissing, steam, stink of antifreeze—the whole mess. I opened the hood and saw two streams of antifreeze pouring out of a hole in my heater hose. Well, I just went cold and shaky all over. I was at Landon School, all alone except for a man way down the hill in the pool. I asked him for help and told him I was phobic and this just terrified me. Boy, was he nice. He looked at the hose, went with me to try to get tape to patch it up so I could drive to a gas station, spoke Spanish to the caretaker's wife, and then tried to tape it but couldn't. So we called the AAA and then I called my sister at home to ask her to be with me as my escape route until the truck came. She agreed and the man and I went back to my car. He said (without my asking) that he would stay until she came. I was very grateful. She came and my friendly man shook my hand and said goodbye.

My sister stayed with me until the truck came. I was at a 2-, 3-, or 4-level some of the time but mostly I felt calm but stupid asking my sister to sit with me because I was afraid of being stranded. When the truck came and the guy was fixing the hose, I got a high level and felt like throwing up—maybe it was the relief. He advised me to go to a gas station to get a bigger hose. At the gas station the attendant told me the hose was the correct size. At this point I felt so unphobic I would have left the car there and hitchhiked for the rest of my life. I came home hot and tired but feeling I had learned something—I wasn't as afraid as I thought I would be. Also, strangers and relatives will do dumb things you ask for in order to be helpful. I felt so good about that I called a phobic friend and told her.

I'm still glad I didn't do what I always feared I would do—run trembling and screaming out to the main road and start frantically flagging down cars, begging for a ride to who knows where. There's no place I wanted to go. I just wanted to be *able* to go, not stranded. I feel braver now.

Week Nine

Monday. I went to Judy's feeling only a little nervous until we got to the entrance of the Beltway at River Road. We were going to go towards Virginia, actually *into* Virginia but I asked her to get right off and we drove around. We got on again and went under the Cabin John Bridge toward Canal Road. I felt like throwing up. My mouth was very dry, I was twisting my hands which were shaking and my level was around 8 or 9. We got off at MacArthur Boulevard and drove around. Each time we went over the same area I felt better, but I felt pretty bad that we didn't go into Virginia. Judy said I did well and suggested we break the goal down a little more and that I could drive the next time, which would be easier.

Wednesday. My plan was to take the Beltway to Virginia. I headed down River Road and way before I could even see the exit signs I was really nervous. I got on the ramp, went past the point where I could get back off, took the fork leading to Virginia, and said, "Well, you're committed now." Started breathing hard; my heart was pounding; I had goosebumps on the backs of my thighs; and I started choking a little. I crossed the river, congratulated myself, and thought how pretty the river was. When I saw the sign for Old Georgetown Pike, my level went from a 9 to about a 6. I got off and got back on the Beltway heading for home. I was still choking but felt a sense of accomplishment. I went to Old Angler's Inn in Maryland. As I got there, my level was dropping fast and when I started walking around and taking pictures, I was at a 0. I was aware of it and happy about it so I got back on the road to

Virginia and drove all the way to Tyson's Corner. My level stayed below a 4 the whole time. I stayed aware of my level and appreciated that it was much lower and that I seemed to be in control of it.

Week Ten

Sunday. Decided to go driving. I went straight to the second Tyson's Corner Exit, experiencing a level 3 or 4 once in a while. Every now and then I'd think, "What the hell am I doing here?" but I was basically OK. Parked the car and went into Woodies. I ventured up the escalator to the second floor, went out into the mall twice and hit some medium levels (4 or 5), mainly from thinking about where my car was, how long it would take me to get home, etc.—all those self-destructive things. When I felt like that, I tried to look carefully at the people and stores around me and to walk in a very self-confident way. At one point when I was pretty nervous, I stopped to sniff some perfumes, and at another point, I bought some barrettes.

Sometimes stopping and doing something lessens the fear more than running towards the car to get home. Running just accentuates how far you have to go and how long it will take, but if you slow down and take it in little bits, time and distance are broken down into fractions so the whole is not frightening. Does this make sense? I know that if I look at my station at work and say, "Oh, I have eight parties," I'll go nuts; but if I break each party down into the stage of the meal they're in, and then group the bits together, it's not as overwhelming. So if I'm on the second floor of Woodies in Tyson's Corner, going to the first floor is a step. Then I'll look around. Next I'll go into the parking lot slowly and look around; then I'll take one Beltway Exit at a time and enjoy the scenery; etc. I had several flashes of "Oh my God, what am I doing here in Virginia?" while I was in the store and on the road, but taking little steps helped me a lot.

Week Nineteen

Here I am in the 19th week of the program with some thinking to do about how far I have come, where I want to be, and whether I am better off than before.

Before I started the program, I was working by luck. I went out if I was lucky enough not to be feeling sick, anxious, or tired. Half of the things my boyfriend and I were going to do were put off because I was feeling "sick in my stomach" or something. Once in a while is OK, but after a while, it's hard to tolerate. Since he really wasn't very committed to a relationship with me, he left.

Now I go out, either with other people or alone (usually alone), even when I'm feeling sick or when I'm choking, because I know these feelings are phobic symptoms, and if I confront them, they'll usually fade away. I've gone to dinner when I felt too sick to eat, but stuck it out and managed to choke down something and feel better. I've gone out driving when I was gagging so much I thought I was going to have to take a Valium and lie down and pray desperately that it would go away. The point is I'm not just waiting until I feel good to do things. I hardly ever feel good anyway, except after doing something difficult; then I get ravenous and feel that I'm cured.

During the first several weeks of the program, I lost ten pounds because I was nervous and sick in my stomach just about all the time and couldn't eat, but after successful practicing, I'd go home and practically clean out the refrigerator. My poor stomach! Now, I don't live in the same constant dread of the first seven or eight weeks (I hope to God I never have to face anything like that again) but I am depressed a lot. I have a dead-end waitress job with no future, and I'm closer to my ten-week goal than I was, but since I'm in my 19th week, that's kind of a drag. But I'm trying to accept everything. My progress has been slow, but my practicing has been grueling. I'm afraid to face the high levels, but I'm pushing a little more each time. I may not make it to the beach (ten-week goal) in 20 weeks, or 30, or 40, but I'm learning how to make it through the panics so they aren't as powerful as they can be. Now I have to go farther from home to have a level, and that extra distance is hard to face, but when I go farther than I thought I could, I can really pat myself on the back.

One thing I wish I had understood weeks ago, which would have helped me not to waste so much time, is this: You have to go into a situation you *think* will give you a level 10. Whether it does or not is not important. If you face a possible 10 with acceptance, that's the best practicing you can do. I was angry with myself for not getting 10s even after being out driving for hours or for miles away from home. I felt dissatisfied when I got home and felt like I should practice more because I hadn't hit a 10 that day. I also felt that I was getting mixed messages from the people in the clinic: hit a 10, be glad if you don't hit a 10 and then go headfirst into it. Be glad if you don't get a level, but if you do, it's a good opportunity to practice. Also, don't beat yourself to death practicing. Once in a while, you need to stop being such a perfectionist and just relax. I've wasted more time this summer lying by the pool with my fists clenched, thinking of the practicing I should be doing, instead of just enjoying myself.

Here's what I think is good about the program—being in a group of people who have experienced the hell of panic just like me. When I get horribly depressed, I think about people whose phobias are worse than mine, or people who have gotten over worse phobias and are making it in the world, and it gives me a shot of hope. Another good thing about the program is having group leaders and therapists who are former phobics. Having living proof that it can be done is more reassuring than all the textbook case histories in the world.

I wish there were more of an emphasis on assertiveness, which we talked about a few times in the group, but there's no session devoted to it, and there should be. Phobics are so anxious to make no waves that they lie down on the ground or fade into the scenery. One of the most important things about a phobia is that it is not a mental illness—most phobics are intelligent, over-imaginative people with one segment of their life gone haywire. Otherwise, they're "normal." I'm unassertive because my phobia makes me feel worthless. I can work fairly well within my limits and I'm a good person, but I put down all my accomplishments because of some "abnormal" things about me. I think if there had been an emphasis on assertiveness and self-esteem right from the beginning of the program, I might feel better about myself, and I might have associated successful practicing with rising self-value. I want to feel better about myself more often than I do.

I think the techniques used in distracting yourself from the panic feelings, like spelling backwards, are good for two reasons: They are simple enough that they can hold your wobbly attention when you are scared, and they are silly enough that you can start laughing at yourself. I find that if I'm laughing or angry or crying, I forget about being scared.

Looking back on the program, I would make these suggestions: I wish my therapist had been a former phobic, although she was really terrific. I wish that assertiveness had been emphasized right from the beginning of the program. I wish that it had been made clearer to me that seeking the high levels, not necessarily hitting them, was the important thing. Maybe I just wasn't thinking clearly. I know that for several weeks I was really groping around, trying to understand, and disappointing myself needlessly.

On the good side, I think that having people to call, no matter how stupid, sad, or depressed I felt, was great. I think that having to put something on paper every day, like homework, was good because phobics are masters at putting things off, speaking as one who knows how to procrastinate. Most of all, the people in the group helped each other with their stories of their struggles and successes, and their obvious caring about each other.

REPORT OF GROUP LEADER, JANE BRASHARES

Marie was an attractive 34-year old who joined the Phobia Program as an agoraphobic patient. She had become increasingly dysfunctional the year before joining the program. One of her concerns was that she might lose her job as a waitress because more and more frequently she had to leave early, finding her symptoms unbearable. She lived alone in an apartment and could drive her car only a short distance—basically from home to work and back. During a panic attack, Marie would have the classic symptoms of heart palpitations, dry mouth, trembling body, and sweaty palms. The most disturbing symptom for Marie was a choking sensation that made her feel that she was going to vomit. Marie never did vomit however, and constantly sucked on hard candies to "keep herself swallowing."

Marie was the most visibly panicked member at the group's first meeting. She sat next to the door, looking very pale and trembling slightly. Her panic extended to her ability to communicate. As group leader, I asked if she would tell us why she had joined the program. She was only able to shake her head indicating she was unable to speak. She continued to sit by the door and needed to leave the group.

During groups two and three, Marie spoke some only when called upon. She needed to leave the group for about ten minutes out of each one-and-a-half hour session. Gradually during the first ten-week cycle of the program, Marie appeared more at ease with the group and joined in group discussions.

During the first ten weeks, Marie began staying at work during the panic attacks; driving a greater distance from her home each week; and acknowledging that driving alone, working alone, and living alone were easier for her than being with another person. When she was alone, she explained, she could quickly and unobtrusively head for home when the symptoms felt overwhelming. Even with her supportive contextual therapist, Marie *felt* she was criticized and considered a failure if she did not meet her weekly goals. So she always wanted to go alone.

It was difficult financially for Marie to sign up for the next ten weeks but her commitment to getting better was strong. She began plodding toward goals, but was very discouraged at week 14. Other group members seemed to be advancing more quickly. The team working with

Marie decided to suggest antidepressants as a way of reducing her very powerful symptoms. The suggestion to use an antidepressant met with her strong objections. She felt that must mean she couldn't do it on her own; she felt set apart from members of her group. She came to group 15 in a furor. For the first time, she did not appear afraid. This anger was Marie's turning point. She was going to show us all that she could do it and do it without medication. She willingly began to put herself into circumstances that she knew would bring on panic and she remained there. We learned that in past weeks she had been "almost" getting to panic but had left the situations before her symptoms had become acute.

Marie completed the 20-week program much improved, but not free of anxiety. One of the most striking changes over the 20 weeks was her increased ability to relate actively to other group members. She became more attractive and assertive over the course of the program. At the end she was outspoken and well liked by other group members. At the last meeting when she discussed that she had not fully met her goals, she began to cry saying, "Oh, don't worry about me. These are just tears to get sympathy. I'm going to do just fine." The group members and therapists agreed with this assessment.

In the one year since she terminated therapy Marie has had no further formal treatment but she has continued to make remarkable progress. Three months after treatment she reported, for example, that she had practiced riding the subway several times—which she had been unable to do before joining the program. She also reported a choking feeling when she had to go to a party at her mother's house. When it was pointed out to her that she "could always leave," she felt more comfortable and lost the choking sensation. Her goals at that point were to be able to go to the beach, to sail in a boat (which was hard because she felt trapped on the boat once it set sail), and to get a job in the area of her greatest interest, photography, rather than continuing to work as a waitress.

Six months after leaving the program she reported that she felt even better and that she had gone to several job interviews—which she had not been able to do before. She also reported that she had ridden as a passenger "with other people driving their cars" which had been her most difficult problem before treatment. Her principal goal at that point was to find a job in photography.

Nine months after terminating treatment, she reported she had broken up with her boyfriend and, for the first time, did not feel in despair over the loss. Rather, she said, "Now I see he was immature and it was not my fault that we broke up." She also reported driving alone to relatively distant suburbs and even going to a double feature movie, both of which had previously been impossible for her. She also said she had observed that she could not "talk back" to her mother while her two younger siblings were quite outspoken in their anger towards their mother from time to time. She made the connection between her inability to be openly angry with her own phobias, while her siblings were free of this problem. She said she knew she needed to be able to be openly angry with her mother, but she doubted she could.

In the nearly one year since leaving the program, Marie was in telephone contact with an outreach worker three times on a regularly scheduled basis. The calls are initiated by the outreach worker as part of a routine follow-up of all program graduates. In addition, Marie came to half-a-dozen self-help meetings for former program participants. At these meetings she was consistently open and active in her participation, continuing the attractive appearance and active engagement which characterized her participation toward the end of the program. She said the biggest change for her during the year was her feeling that she was "OK" and that she could tackle her problems and solve them, rather than feeling helpless and overwhelmed. She felt her biggest areas of continuing need involved working out relationships with her mother and with boyfriends.

REPORT OF PHOBIA THERAPIST, JUDY BARTH

Marie and I began working together approximately 18 weeks ago when she entered the Phobia Program. We met once a week, usually in the evenings, and our sessions were approximately one hour and 15 minutes in duration. Our primary goal was to expand the physical limitations imposed on Marie by her agoraphobia. In order to do this she had to learn to deal with the physical and emotional manifestations of acute anxiety and panic. Several extraneous issues complicated the desensitization process and contributed to making it a slow one. Her inability to trust people and lack of meaningful relationships are issues that eventually will have to be dealt with.

We began by driving short distances from her home. A hierarchy of difficulty was quickly established. It was easiest for Marie to drive alone in her car, harder for her to take me with her and most difficult for her to be a passenger in my car. In the latter situation, I agreed to turn around immediately at her request (eventually this was replaced by pulling over, waiting a few minutes, and then trying to go on) and even to allow her to drive my car if necessary. We used the first four or five sessions testing and experimenting with our system. Marie also carried a bottle of water, Valium, and her favorite candies at all times. At the sixth session I suggested that she purchase a map and systematically plot a radius of five miles. Once she mastered her goal within this distance, we gradually increased the radius to approximately 20 miles.

We would decide on an objective at the end of each session and Marie would work toward it during the week. Each objective or goal was broken down into steps with no time limit. She practiced daily and diligently. Success was achieved by working toward the goal or by expanding the circle in any direction or both. Having this flexibility was important for three reasons. First, she could always succeed and feel good about her progress. Second, she learned that by breaking down a goal and approaching it at different times and in different ways she would also succeed. Third, it gave her the control that she needed. This system worked well and Marie made progress.

One of the major issues Marie and I had to deal with was her difficulty in working through even low levels of anxiety. Her overwhelming desire to turn and run often got the best of her. At about the tenth session I suggested that she consider an antidepressant. Her reaction was negative. She felt hurt and angry. We talked about her inability to confront the higher levels and the importance of doing so. She became determined to deal with the situation "without drugs." Her positive attitude helped and she did indeed challenge higher levels of anxiety for the first time.

Index

Page numbers for material in tables and figures appear in italic.

Abandonment fears, archaic, 50
Abstract thinking, 204
Ackerman, R., 92, 153-59
Acrophobia, 57
Adolescence, separation from parents in, 141. *See also* Children
Age:
  and behavioral treatment, 162, 169
  and drug treatment, *61*
  in pretreatment survey, *205*, 205
Agoraphobia, xi, xvi, xvii, 25, 36, 41, 57-76, *62*, *65-68*, *70*, 75, 107, *218*, *See also* Phonophobia
  case study of, 231-46
    journal record, 232-43
  and cognition, 93-98, 108
  complex, 141
  and depression, 92, 126-32
  and discrimination, 121-25, *124*
  integrative approach to in contextual therapy, 44-53
  and marital status-patterns, 140-52, *148*
  nonutility of diagnosis of, 78
  and panic, 57-58, 205
  pretreatment survey of, 203-14, *205*, *206*, *207*, *209*, *210*, *212*, *213*
Agras, W.S., 12, 26*n.*
Air travel, phobia of, xii, 58, 171, 173-77, 218
Alcoholics Anonymous (AA), xiv
Alexithymia, 108
Allen, R.G., 3-7
Alpha brainwaves, 174
Amphetamines, 61
Animals, phobias of, xi, xii, xvii, 218
Annihilation fears, archaic, 50
Antianxiety drugs, xiii
Antidepressant drugs, xiii, xix, 55, 59-69, 76, 127, 220, 244, 246
Anxiety, 32, 36, 37, 39, 78, 100, 108, 140, 150, 154, *225*, 232, 233, 237, 240
  anticipatory, 45-48, 58, 129
  and cortisol levels, 118
  described as comfort levels, 166
  and drug treatment, *66*
  and future thinking, 112
  inevitable presence of, 111
  management of, 102

neurosis, 107-108
and obsessive-compulsives, 179, 180
and panic, 81
in pretreatment survey, *206, 213*
primary, 107
prior to treatment, xviii
and school phobia, 189
secondary, 108
and sensory input, 164
separation, 48, 59, 78, 103, 141
adult, xvi
and panic, 127
signal, 108
Assertiveness training, 60, 78, 79, 85-86, 165, 242
Assimilation in treatment, 99, 100
Audiotapes, 13, 15-24, *16*, 46-47
Automatic orientation reflex, 79
Avoidance:
and cognition in agoraphobia, 93-94
and heart rate, 118
and panic, 128
Azrin, 149

Bach, R., 165, 170*n*.
Barlow, D.H., 92, 140-51, 143, 152*n*.
Barth, J., 231, 235, 245-46
Behavioral treatment, 134
and age, 162, 169
behavior modification, 173
and changes in phobic behavior, 25
classical conditioning, 161*n*.
and drug treatment, 59-69, *65, 67*
and feedback, 129
and gender, 162, 169
paradoxical practice, 178-81
and religion, 162, 169
strategy for, 161-70
Benson, H., 174, 177*n*.
Bergman, A., 103, 106*n*.
Birds, phobia of, xii, xvii
Bland, K., 142, 143, 152*n*.
Branford Counseling Center, 77-89, *80*
Brashares, J., 231, 243-45
Bridges, phobia of, xii, 218
Broverman, I.K., 156, 159, 160*n*.

Cameron, O., 117-19
Cannon, 117
Castration fears, xiii
Cats, phobia of, xii, xvii
Centrum Phobia Clinic, 44-53
Chambless, D. L., 141, 151*n*.
Changes in phobic behavior, 11-26
audiotapes on, 13, 15-24, *16*, 46-47
conceptualization of causes of, 14-15
conclusion on, 25
discussion of, 24-25
and group treatment, 51-52
method of study of, 12-14
clinical studies, 13-14
systematic studies, 13
as problem, 11-12
and relearning process, 164-65
Charney, D.L., 92, 126-32, 171, 178-81
Chesler, P., 156, 160*n*.
Chicken Little Syndrome, 112
Children:
developmental phases of, 48
explanation of phobias to, 42
model child position, 51
and school phobias, 171, 182-92
Classical conditioning model, 161*n*. *See also* Behavioral treatment
Claustrophobia, xvi-xvii, 57
Clinical Global Impression (CGI), *72, 74, 75*
Cobb, J.P., 143, 145, 146, 152*n*.
Cognition and agoraphobia, 93-98, 108
and avoidance, 93-94
and discrimination, 97
and maturity/immaturity, 97-98
and security-predictability, 96
and subjective truth/objective truth, 96-97
Cognitive restructuring, 46
Cohen, M.R., 10, 44-53
Compensation for inferiority feelings, 51
Compulsory marriage pattern, 144-45. *See also* Marital status
Concept of Dread, The (Kierkegaard), 107
Conceptualization in treatment, 99
Connolly, J., 118, 120*n*.
Contextual therapy, 9-43, 107-15, 130, 132
and changes in phobic behavior, 11-26
and family members, 35-43
and initial contact, 27-34
and integrative approach to agoraphobia, 44-53
and maternal bond, 104
Correlational thinking, 113-14
Cortisol levels, 118
Craig, E., 171, 182-92
Crook, J.O., 171, 178-81
Cummings, T.W., 171, 173-77
Curtis, G., 91, 117-19
Cybernetic approach to mood disorders, 127

Dark, phobia of, 15-22, *16*

Day Treatment program, 182-92
 background on, 183
 conclusion on, 192
 description of, 183-89, *190*
Death, depression and phobias, 134-39
Dependency, 48-52
 and guilt, 40
 and pregnancy, 158
Depression, 81, 95, 155, *225*, 231
 and agoraphobia, 92, 126-32
  and behavioral techniques, 129
  biological approach to, 130
  conclusion on, 132
  types of, 131
 death and phobias, 134-39
 and drug treatment, *75*, *76*
 major, 218, *218*
 and panic, 134-39
 psychotic, 217
Depressive Compulsive Disorders, *218*
Desensitization process, xiii, xix, 45, 48, 60, 78, 129, 154, 173. *See also* In vivo exposure technique; Supportive exposure therapy
Desynchrony, 117-18
Dewey, J., 108
Dexedride, 61
Diagnostic and Statistical Manual (DSM-III), 217, *218*
Diazepam. *See* Valium
Dickinson, E., 107
Diet, xix
Differentiation in separation-individuation, 104
Discrimination:
 and agoraphobia, 121-25, *124*
 and cognition in agoraphobia, 97
Displacement of fear, xiii
Dizziness, 58, 112
Doctor, R.M., 201, 203-13
Dogs, phobia of, xii, xvii
Donohue, P., 6
Driving, phobia of, 38-39, 42, 218
Drugs. *See* Medication *and individual drugs and drug types*
DuPont, R.L., xi-xix, 3, 6, 7, 111, 116*n.*, 193-200, 215-46
Dyer, W., 177, 177*n.*

Education and drug treatment, *61*
Ego:
 auxiliary, and autonomy, 51
 integrity of, 50
 strengthening of boundaries of, 52, 53
Electroconvulsive treatment, 217
Elevators, phobia of, xii, 42, 218
Emmelkamp, P.M.G., 142, 151*n.*
Emotional refueling, 105
Escalators, phobia of, xii
Exploratory behavior, 48
Extremist thinking, 94-95

Fainting, 118-19
Faith and fear, 3-7
Family members:
 aid from, 32, 35-43
 and school phobia, 188-89, 191
 and supportive exposure therapy, 35-43
Fear and faith, 3-7
Fear and Avoidance Hierarchy, 147, 149
Fear Survey Schedule, (FSS), 211, *212*, 213, *213*
Feedback:
 and behavioral techniques, 129
 pathological positive/therapeutic negative, 110
Fight-flight reflex, 117-18
Flaxman, N.J., 91, 121-25
Flying. *See* Air travel, phobia of
France, nuclear power in, 193-96
Freud, S., xii, xiii, xix, 107-10, 113, 115*n.*, 153, 162
Friends, aid from, 32
Fry, W., 144, 145, 151*n.*

Gelder, M.G., 134, 139*n.*
Gender:
 and behavioral treatment, 162, 169
 and drug treatment, *61*
 and incidence of phobia types, xvii, 218
 in pretreatment survey, 205, *205*
George Washington University, 193
Goals, 178
 in group treatment, 79
 in supportive exposure therapy, 39
Goldstein, A.J., 141, 151*n.*
Goodwin, B., 171, 182-92
Graduation Flight, 173, 175
Group treatment, 44-53, 105, 153
 and changes in phobic behavior, 51-52
 conclusion on, 52-53
 effectiveness of, 80
 and ego integrity, 50
 goals in, 79
 validation in, 50
Guilt, 36, 81
 and dependency, 40

Hafner, R.J., 142-45, 152*n.*
Hallam, R.S., 142, 143, 152*n.*

Hand, I., 142, 152*n.*
Hardy, A.B., xiv, 6, 7, 9, 36, 91, 93-98, 134, 137, 139*n.*
Hartmann, H., 49, 53*n.*
Harvard Medical School, 174
Hay, L.R., 143, 152*n.*
Heart rate and avoidance, 118
Heights, phobia of, 58, 218
Heist, E.R., 203, 204, 214*n.*
High School Equivalency Program, 184, 187-88
Homework assignments, 60, 112
Horses, phobia of, xii-xiii
Hudson, B., 142, 143, 152*n.*
Hyperthyroidism, 59
Hyperventilation, 21, 33, 167-68, 176
Hypnotism, xix

Imaginal desensitization, 178, 179
Imipramine, xiii, 59-69, *62, 65-68, 71,* 71, *72, 73,* 73, *74, 75,* 130, 132
Initial contact, 27-34
Insects, phobia of, xi, xvii
Insomnia, 155
Intake interview, 28, 29
Intelligence:
  defined, 108
  and phobia, xviii
Internal environment, 103
Introjection in treatment, 99-103
Introspection in treatment, 12, 99-100
In vivo exposure technique, xiv, 9-43, 130, 166-68; *See also* Desensitization process; Supportive exposure therapy
  and marital problems, 142, 143-51, *148*
  psychobiology of, 117-20
    and drugs, 119
Isaac Marks Fear Questionnaire, 219, 224-30, *225-29*

Jacobson, E., 174, 177*n.*
James, W., 108, 115*n.*
Jealousy in marriage, 145
Jencks, C., 109, 115*n.*
Jonathan Livingston Seagull (Bach), 165

Kazdin, A.E., 12, 26*n.*
Kernberg, O.F., 109, 115*n.*
Kierkegaard, S., 105, 106, 106*n.*, 107, 115*n.*
Klein, D.F., 60, 76*n.*
Kohut, H., 105, 106*n.*
Kuhn, T.S., 162, 170*n.*

Lamontagne, Y., 142, 152*n.*
Last, C.G., 92, 140-51
Lazarus, A.A., 140, 151*n.*
Leopard phobia of, xi, xii
Liepman, M., 117-19
Little Hans case, xii-xiii
Long Island Jewish-Hillside Medical Center, 154-55

Magical thinking, 92
Mahler, M.S., 48, 51, 103, 104, 106*n.*
Major Depression, 218, *218*
Marital counseling, 189
Marital Happiness Scale, 147, 148, *148,* 149
Marital status-patterns, 80, 92, 220-21
  of agoraphobics as result of treatment, 140-52, *148*
  and drug treatment, *61,* 136-37
  in pretreatment survey, 205, *205*
Marks, I., xiv, xx, 119, 120*n.*, 134, 139*n.*, 142, 152*n.*, 154, 160*n.*, 203, 204, 214*n.*
Mavissakalian, M., 143, 152*n.*
Media and nuclear power, 195
Media Institute, 193
Medication, 79, 153
  with psychological treatment, 57-76, 131
  experimental study designs on, 59-76, *61-68, 70-75*
Mice, phobia of, xi
Midbrain and mood disorders, 127
Mid-Fairfield Child Guidance Center. *See* Day Treatment Program
Miller, J., 55, 77-86
Milton, F., 142-45, 152*n.*
Mirroring experiences in treatment, 50
Mitral valve prolapse, 59
Mitterand, F., 193
Mixed phobias, 57-69, *62, 65-68, 70*
Modeling, 48
Monoamine oxidase (MAO) inhibitors, 59, 71, 73, 75
Mourning process, 137
Multiple arousal stimulation, 46
Murphy, G., 162, 170*n.*

Nausea, 58
Nemiah, J.C., 108, 115*n.*
Nesse, R., 117-19
Neurosis, 36
  anxiety, 107-108
  neurotic style, 78
Nuclear energy, phobia of, 171-72, 193-200

Object constancy, 49

Objective truth and subjective truth, 96-97
O'Brien, G.T., 92, 140-51
Obsessive-compulsives, xviii, 143, 146, 171, 204, 217-18, *218*
  and anxiety, 179, 180
  paradoxical practice treatment of, 178-81
    conclusion on, 181
  and psychoanalysis, 181
Oedipal complex, xiii
Outreach Program, 27

Palpitations, heart, 33, 58, 59, 112, 243
Pan American Airways, 173, 174
Panic, 16, 21, 32, 40, 44
  in agoraphobia, 57-58, 205
  and anxiety, 81
  and avoidance, 128
  and depression, 134-39
  and drug therapy, 57-58, 60, 64, *67*, *72*, *73*, *74*, 75, 76
  and fear monitoring, 46
  and obsession, 180
  and pretreatment survey, 210
  and self-object separation, 49
  and separation anxiety, 127
  spontaneous, 57-59, 75, *75*
Panophobia. *See* Phobophobia
Paradoxical intention, 168, 178-81
Pavlov, I.P., 161*n*.
Perfectionism, xviii, 95-96, *213*
Personality:
  microcosmic model of development of, 102-103
  and phobia, xviii, 48
Phenelzine, 71, 73
Phobia Program of Washington, xv-xvii, 6, 201, 215-30, 232
  description of, 215-16
  patient profile at, 216, *217*
  pretreatment information at, 216-19, *218*
  results of, 219-30, *222*, *223*
Phobia Society of America, xv
Phobic Anxiety Questionnaire, 79, *87-89*
Phobic-depersonalization syndrome, 49
Phobophobia, 91, 107-15
  and correlational thinking, 113-14
  summary/conclusion on, 114-15
Pine F., 103, 106*n*.
Placebo treatment, 59-69, *65*, *68*, 71, *72*, *73*, *74*, 75, *75*. *See also* Medication
Powell, D., 9, 27-33
Pregnancy and dependency, 158
Pretreatment survey of agoraphobia, 203-14, *205*, *206*, *207*, *209*, *210*, *212*, *213*. *See also* Phobia Program of Washington, pretreatmment information at
  method of, 204
  results-discussion of, 204-13, *205*, *206*, *207*, *209*, *210*, *212*, *213*
Prolactin, 118
Psychoanalysis, 109. *See also* Psychotherapy
  and changes in phobic behavior, 25
  and obsessions, 181
  therapeutic ineffectiveness of, xiii, 134
  and women's issues, 154
Psychosomatic patients, 108
Psychotherapy, xix, 108-109, 136-37, 217. *See also* Psychoanalysis
  and drug therapy, 59, 60-69
  and future-anticipation, 108
Public speaking, phobia of, xvii, 3, 6-7
Pupil Placement Team (PPT), 186

Rachman, S., 133, 138*n*.
Rapprochement phase of development, 48, 49, 105
Reality testing, 39, 52, 167-68
Regression, 32
Relabeling, 167-68
Relapse, after treatment, *70*
Relaxation Response, The (Benson), 174
Relaxation techniques, 79, 84
Religion and behavioral treatment, 162, 169
Respiration and emotional state, 176
Restructuring, cognitive, 46
Roosevelt, F.D., 37
Roosevelt, T., 7
Roosevelt Hospital Phobia Clinic Phobia Resource Center, 99
Ross, J., xix, 6, 7, 9, 35-43

School, phobia of, 171, 182-92
  and family members, 188-89, 191
Schor, N., 91, 107-14
Schweder, R.A., 113, 116*n*.
Secondary gains, 78, 83
Sedative-hypnotic drugs, 119
Seif, M.N., 91, 99-106
Selan, B.H., 92, 133-38
Self-esteem, 50, 155, 157, 181, 184, 187, 242
Self-help groups, xiv, 31, 132
Self-observation, 110-12, 115
Seligman, M., 133, 135, 138*n*.
Separation-individuation:
  conflicts over, 50-52
  and differentiation, 104

and internalization of maternal image, 104
as phase of development, 48, 49, 53
subphases, 104
Sexuality, dysfunction in marriage, 145
Shands, H.C., 83, 91, 107-15, 115*n*.
Sheehan, D.V., 71, 76*n*.
Sherrington, C., 14, 26*n*.
Shopping, phobia of, 40-41
Sifneos, P.E., 108, 109, 115*n*.
Silva Mind Control, 174
Simple phobias, 58-69, *62, 65-68, 70,* 75, 76
Skinner, B.F., 109, 110, 116*n*.
Smith, M.J., 79, 86*n*.
Snakes, phobia of, xi, xii, xvii, 12
Spatial ability, 48
Spiders, phobia of, xii
Stage fright, xvii
Stereotypes, sex-role, 159
Stern, R., 134, 139*n*.
Strupp, H.H., 78, 86*n*.
Subjective truth and objective truth, 96-97
Subjective Units of Discomfort (SUDS), 79, 86
Suicide attempts, 19
Super highways, phobia of, xii, xviii
Supportive exposure treatment, xiv, 9-43, 91
and changes in phobic behavior, 11-26
and family members, 35-43
and changing roles, 40-42
conclusion on, 43
effectiveness of, 36-38
in practice session, 38-40
and initial contact, 27-34
and integrative approach to agoraphobia, 44-53
Support systems, 78
Symptom Severity and Phobic Avoidance Scale, 73
Systematic desensitization. *See* Desensitization process

Teaching strategy for phobic symptom reduction, 161-70
conclusion on, 169-70
discussion of, 168-69
and in vivo interventions, 166-68
rationale for, 162-63
and relearning process, 164-65
and synthesis of observations-client reports, 163-64
and therapist role, 165-66
Teare, M.L., 92, 161-70
TERRAP Program, xiv, 9
Therapeutic alliance and individualized treatment, 78
Three Mile Island (TMI), 193-96
Thunderstorms, phobia of, 42
Thyer, B., 117-19
Thyroid stimulating hormone, 118
Transcendental Meditation, 174

Unconscious and contradictory dilemmas, 51-52
University of Houston, 175

Valium, xiv, 55, 94, 119, 219, 233-37, 246
Vanggaard, T., 107, 115*n*.
Vomitting, phobia of, 218

Washington Phobia Program. *See* Phobia Program of Washington
Watzlawick, P., 165, 170*n*.
Weekes, C., xiv, xx, 133, 139*n*., 154, 160*n*.
Weight loss, 81
White Plains Hospital, New York, xiv, xv, 9, 18, 25, 27, 28
Wilson, G.T., 12, 26*n*.
Winnicott, D.S., 103, 106*n*.
Wolpe, J., xiii, xix, 123, 125*n*., 133, 138*n*., 154
Wolpe-Lange Fear Inventory, 60
Woman's Assertiveness Group, 81
Women:
data on, 154-55
and diagnostic assessment, 157-59
socialization of, 159
societal view of, 155
Work and Social Disability Scale, 73

Yoga, 174
Your Erroneous Zones (Dyer), 177

Zane, M.D., xiv, 9, 11-25, 21, 30, 46, 109, 114, 116*n*., 133, 136, 139*n*., 154, 160*n*., 162, 170*n*., 179
Zitrin, C.M., 55, 57-76, 154, 160*n*.